5/15

From Germany to Germany

ALSO BY GÜNTER GRASS

The Tin Drum
Cat and Mouse
Dog Years
The Plebeians Rehearse the Uprising
Four Plays
Speak Out!
Local Anaesthetic
Max: A Play
From the Diary of a Snail
Inmarypraise
In the Egg and Other Poems
The Flounder
The Meeting at Telgte
Headbirths
Drawings and Words, 1954–1977
On Writing and Politics, 1967–1983
Etchings and Words, 1972–1982
The Rat
Show Your Tongue
Two States — One Nation?
The Call of the Toad
Novemberland
My Century
Too Far Afield
Crabwalk
Peeling the Onion
The Box

From Germany to Germany

JOURNAL OF THE YEAR 1990

Günter Grass

Translated from the German by Krishna Winston

Houghton Mifflin Harcourt
BOSTON • NEW YORK
2012

Copyright © 2009 by Steidl Verlag, Göttingen
English translation copyright © 2012 by Krishna Winston

For information about permission to reproduce selections from this book,
write to Permissions, Houghton Mifflin Harcourt Publishing Company,
215 Park Avenue South, New York, New York 10003.

www.hmhbooks.com

Library of Congress Cataloging-in-Publication Data is available.
ISBN 978-0-547-36460-5

Printed in the United States of America
DOC 10 9 8 7 6 5 4 3 2 1

From Germany to Germany

Explanatory notes on the text can be found on page 241.

Vale das Eiras, 1 January 1990
While I was planting a sapling this morning on the east side of the house — Leonore Suhl gave it to us on New Year's Eve, promising that in six or seven years it will have grown into a stately tree with blue blossoms — the new year started off with a bang. And when we went to look for mushrooms in the cork forest above Casais in early afternoon, a full-grown bolete would have fulfilled all my expectations for New Year's Day, but our favorite spots offered slim pickings: after an unusually long rainy season — we heard it had poured for nine weeks straight in these parts — the few water-logged chanterelles offered a good subject for a drawing, but not much else.

The drawing, however, gives me an excuse for inaugurating this journal with mushrooms rather than with the major political events that were competing for attention during the past few months, concluding with the bloody revolution in Romania and the equally bloody demonstration of military might in Panama, as if the Communist and the capitalist systems were determined to show their true colors one last time.

I am not one of those people who love keeping a journal. Something unusual must be happening to inflict this ritual on me. I felt a similar compulsion in 1969 when a democratic change in government became possible in the German Federal Republic, and I abandoned my writing desk to devote myself to campaigning for the Social Democrats. Their narrow victory soon provided the material for a book. Or our half year in Calcutta. (Without a journal the city would hardly have been bearable.) This time I will keep trying to vault over the border that separates the two German states, and will also stick my nose into both election campaigns, in May and December. Now that my work on *Dead Wood* is done, I would have liked to start on a regular manuscript, one that might have turned out to be quite long: the story of two widows, Frau Piątkowska and Frau Reschke, who meet in Gdańsk on All Saints' Day and craft a plan, which is soon implemented because the time for it happens to be ripe: the establishment of a Polish-German cemetery association, ltd. But this journal is more pressing.

This evening, the toad in our inner courtyard. As big as a full-grown guinea pig, it assumes for me the identity of one of those toads that last autumn could be heard calling from far and near as soon as darkness fell: the call of the toad. I grasped it behind its front legs and held it up for Ute to photograph. Its sacklike body dangled. Everything motionless, including its blank green eyes with orange horizontal stripes. The only sign of life a pulsing in its throat. What is this creature doing in my journal, I wondered, except that it is unfamiliar, incomprehensible, and at best suggests a title — for something, I don't know what: "The Call of the Toad"?

Vale das Eiras, 2 January 1990

As if trying to fortify myself by doing something positive, I planted another tree, this time a carob, on the west side of the house, a tree that grows slowly, which brought the following comment from Ute, who objected to the spot I had chosen: "Well, I won't be around to see it get tall."

It began to rain again. The gas heater lit upstairs, I sat down to work on "Writing after Auschwitz." I think I picked this subject, which is bound to defeat me, to force myself to take a position; a suspicious number of my fellow writers who used to be able to rattle off their newfound antifascist credo as fluently as Schiller's poem "The Bell" are now brimming with nationalist sentiment to the point of idiocy. To me, however, robbed of many prized German possessions over the years — with the exception of the language — Auschwitz seems to offer one last chance to think about Germany. (In the Frankfurt speech I want to try to demonstrate how the alleged right to German unity, in the form of a reunited state, is refuted by Auschwitz.) Write slowly!

It would work better to have the widow Piątkowska meet a widower by the name of Alexander Reschke in Gdańsk while both are buying flowers in the Dominican Market hall on All Saints' Day. In the year the Wall came down, of course. Or is it All Souls' Day? At any rate, in November. Flowers for cemeteries. But her mother is buried in Wilna, where the daughter was born, and his mother in the Rhineland, although she, like him, was born in Danzig. That's what they talk about: where they would like to be buried. This conversation and others, in the course of which a relationship develops, give rise to the idea of a German-Polish cemetery association. He says, "It must be possible, now that so much else has become possible, to choose one's final resting place." She wants to be laid to rest in Wilna, which she had to leave as a sixteen-year-old, while he wants to be buried in Danzig/Gdańsk, which he left as a seventeen-year-old soldier. Others want the same. Thousands of them. One need only make it possible. Hence a legally incorporated association.

Vale das Eiras, 3 January 1990
The first fish of the year in the oven, with vegetables — tomatoes, zucchini, peppers, onions, and sweet potatoes. Went shopping in Lagos. No German papers except *Bild-Zeitung,* with a screaming New Year's headline, "*Madness!*" A word that since the opening of the German-German border has become increasingly inflated. Or does it now foretell and invoke actual madness? — "The Call of the Toad."

Working on the Frankfurt speech forces me to recall my time as a Hitler Youth. Granted, I was not totally fanatical, but I was hardly plagued by doubts either. A completely different person now? Definitely, as far as the evolution of my political thinking and actions is concerned; yet my youthful obsession with ambitious projects, almost epic in scope, such as creating tables of historical and cultural developments (anticipating Stein's *Timetables of History*), strikes me as familiar. This aspect of my personality may have undergone correction, polishing, professional development in the meantime, but fundamentally it has not changed.

Last night a conversation with Ute, till long after midnight, about my plan for the new year: from February to September I intend to be in the GDR every month, for longer or shorter periods, crisscrossing the country from Rügen to the Vogtland, to keep my eye on the changes taking place after this enormous political and revolutionary transformation. The plan also calls for a stay in the soft-coal mining region around Spremberg. That is where I was wounded in the spring of '45, on 20 April. I want to capture the devastated landscape in drawings. Ute will join me only occasionally. That means buying a sleeping bag just for myself.

It may be too early at this point to form an image of Professor Alexander Reschke. At any rate, he teaches something, not yet specified, at the University of Essen. Probably history. An old leftist intellectual in whom the recent developments in Germany have awakened a kind of sentimental nationalism, but tempered with irony. She, the widow Halina Piątkowska, is a pediatrician. Between the end of November '89 and May '90 a lively correspondence develops between the widower and the widow, increasingly focused on their shared project, which gradually takes shape, resulting in a first purchase of land: a rolling three-and-a-half-hectare plot south of Brentau that includes a patch of forest and could eventually be extended in the direction of Ramkau. There is also a sum of money in dollars, deposited in a savings account, large enough to make possible a similar land purchase on the outskirts of Wilna (Vilnius). Neither of them, the widow nor the widower, would have credited themselves with so much business acumen.

I have started another drawing for *Dead Wood* after all. To escalate the positive to the point of madness, a third tree found its way into a hole on the south slope: what the Portuguese call a *nespereira,* a loquat, which promises juicy, somewhat sour fruit. We continue to have downpours; I hope the ground is not too soggy.

Vale das Eiras, 4 January 1990
From year's end until the day before yesterday I was reading Philip Roth's *The Counterlife,* a book that invites contradiction and is constantly undercutting itself, belaboring Jewishness and anti-Semitism to come up with an answer to a fairly banal question: Is it permissible for a writer to exploit himself and his family as mate-

rial? The answer Roth clearly had in mind all along is yes. Perhaps I find the book off-putting because I don't really care for writers who constantly make themselves the subjects of their books. Even when the author invests his fictitious narrator with dazzlingly telling arguments, it seems hardly worth the effort; no wonder "Judea," the chapter on Israel, is colorless compared to Amos Oz's collected interviews, *In the Land of Israel*. I wonder why Jurek Becker recommended this book to me the evening before the SPD party convention in Berlin. I'll have to ask him.

The sky is still overcast, with more rain likely. Today all I managed to plant were five rosemaries and three lavenders.

An increasing source of pleasure: the absence of television and telephone. An outline from last year that now could be titled "The Call of the Toad" has the working title "Crabwalk." Whatever title I settle on, no matter how badly this German-Polish escapade ends, the story should turn out to be fiendishly funny: widow and widower are the ideal subjects, with their fatuously humane attitudes. The subplots, such as the piecemeal acquisition of the Lenin Shipyard, need to be worked in sparingly. Both protagonists are in splendid health, even if Reschke is a hypochondriac.

Last night, after waking up several times, I dreamed I was looking for a place to stay in Leipzig (with my sleeping bag), a dream that also pitted several members of my extended family against each other. At the end, if the dream had an end, Nele's mother pulled Ute's car out of the ditch with her own car, after I was gone, on my way.

Vale das Eiras, 6 January 1990
Yesterday I cooked a four-pound tilapia for Mieke and Jules Heindels and Leonore and Jacob Suhl. Before I stuffed it with sage and shoved it in the oven, I drew this sketch:

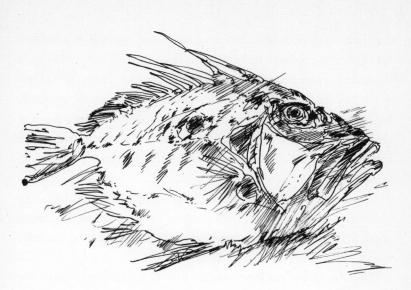

A happy evening: Jacob — Jankele — a Trotskyite passionately preoccupied with stock trading. Jules, who has quit smoking and no longer drinks, will soon convert entirely to vegetarianism, like Mieke.

Yesterday morning I planted a palm on the east side of the house, refusing to halt my defiant tree-planting. Today it was cactus shoots from Leonore that I planted in little colonies. Then I sat down to work on the Frankfurt speech again.

In their letters, widow and widower try to trump each other with the number of newly registered members of their German-Polish Cemetery Association. Reschke gives lectures on Kant's essay "Perpetual Peace," calling the graveyard "the last opportunity for international reconciliation." Frau Piątkowska has set up a friends' organization to which several Catholic priests and a prelate from Oliva belong. Polish emigrants to America, born in Wilna, express an interest in financing free plots for those of modest means. In one of his letters, Reschke says he hopes he can get

the fairly steep membership fees ruled tax-deductible. His suggestion that the cemetery be nonsectarian marks his first run-in with
the board of directors and encounters opposition from the Catho-
lics. After the two German states move closer together — adopting the concept of *Vertragsgemeinschaft,* or union by treaty — old
Danzigers from Pomerania and Mecklenburg raise their voices: at
first there is a currency problem, which Reschke tries to ease with
West German funds — burden-sharing.

Perhaps Reschke wrote his dissertation on patricians' tombs in
Danzig's churches. He is also an expert on the Hanseatic League
and a firm opponent of nationalism, of both the German and the
Polish variety.

The idea of building a retirement home on the grounds of the
wooded cemetery came to Halina Piątkowska when more and
more elderly people started arriving from the Federal Republic and
the German Democratic Republic to have a look for themselves,
and displayed great enthusiasm for the beautiful, well-tended
setting.

The waxing moon promises clear weather for the next few days.
We may be able to go mushroom-picking after all.

Vale das Eiras, 7 January 1990
The cactuses and agaves I planted a year ago in front of the old
house have been thriving without any special attention, putting
out new branches and now looking as though they have always
been there. Standing among them, I begin to have doubts: maybe
she should not be called Piątkowska, maybe Reschke is not the
right name for him. Does she have to be a pediatrician, he a history
professor? Maybe all we need to know about their place in society
is that they are a widow and widower. I can also picture how things

will end for them: they will die in an automobile accident while traveling together, and when no relatives turn up, they will be buried in a village cemetery (in Italy). The "idea" they share should be commented on as it becomes a reality, let us say in letters, telegrams, newspaper articles, and the like. Letters, for instance, from a Hong Kong Chinese man whose family graves near Beijing are off limits to him; from an Israeli, born in Danzig, who asks for a Jewish section — "very small" — in the German cemetery in Gdańsk; from a Polish writer from Wilna who lives in New York and who, despite being thoroughly Americanized, wants to be laid to rest "at home."

Professor Reschke — I am going to continue calling him that — speaks in a voice soft but emphatic, as if muted by sorrow. He dresses with old-fashioned elegance, berates himself for his political errors, still views himself as a leftist despite his conservative leanings, and has a tendency to spout sentimental platitudes, which consistently give way to cynical remarks.

Yesterday Ute helped me transplant the nine-branched cactus we rescued (stole) as an amputated skeleton a year ago from the neglected garden at our old house. She wanted it moved from the bed in the inner courtyard to the south side of the house. We had to place a board under it to make sure none of the branches broke off, though you can stick any broken branch into the ground, with the broken-off end in the soil, and let it take root. In the process, I found myself thinking of the German-Polish Cemetery Association, which will eventually engage in similar transplantations to Gdańsk, to Wilna. No wonder transplanting the cactus seemed so meaningful.

Reading *Der Spiegel,* I could see Rudolf Augstein, for decades a confirmed cynic, unraveling into a nationalist.

Am getting around only now to reading Salman Rushdie's *Satanic Verses*. A fabulous novel, in the true sense of the word. The writing is clever, naïve, masterly. Despite its apparent impudence, a book remarkably pious; by contrast Rushdie's enemies appear godless. It will be a source of continuing gratification that I resigned from the Academy for this writer's sake.

Vale das Eiras, 8 January 1990

Yesterday I collected almost three quarters of a liter of *sepia natural* from four medium-sized *chocos,* or squid, and with it drew today a "Dance of the Praying Mantises," using a specimen from last fall, nicely preserved in alcohol. When this ink is fresh, its blackness is unreliable, but with time it sometimes becomes a consistent blackish brown. The process of harvesting the ink — today we had the *chocos* cooked with vegetables — is a pleasure. (I first used this ink in the late sixties in Brittany, then resumed using it in the mid-eighties, especially after my return from Calcutta, at the beginning of February '87.) Now that I am close to the source in

Portugal, I use it as an alternative to the charcoal of the *Dead Wood* series.

Back to Augstein. His editorials in *Der Spiegel* are dangerous because, like a gifted adolescent, he bases them not on reasoned arguments but on a prevailing mood, partly already present, partly whipped up by him. There is an unfortunate constellation consisting of Schönhuber, Waigel, and Augstein, though for the present only Schönhuber has the guts to cite his brothers in the Germanic spirit. I plan to develop this point into a whole paragraph for Tutzing, citing as a counterexample Brandt's address to the SPD convention.

In my speech for Frankfurt I've got as far (on page 18) as *Dog Years;* the last third will have to be more compressed, and at the end German unity (unification) must be held up to the distorting mirror of Auschwitz.

A fine study upstairs, tucked away.

Down by the shore today. Waves. Shells. On the path to the water, which leads through uncultivated stretches and modest plots of farmland, with pseudo-Moorish villas, I scooped up creepers, agaves, shoots of spoon plants, which I transplanted in the afternoon. An easy life here, from hand to mouth, as it were. The world exists only in old newspapers. Full moon tomorrow.

After promising, then increasingly rigid, and finally inescapable plot lines, "Crabwalk" or "The Call of the Toad" must leave room for contrasting reflections, counterplots, even a happy ending, with the Bengalis and other Asians arriving; yet I still hope it can remain a longish story. Before corpses are transplanted, the cemetery should be half full, at which point a shortage of new occupants should set in, making the reburials important for keeping business brisk. The retirement home will attract visitors: the children of refugees, grandchildren, for whom a hotel will be built on land purchased in Kashubia.

I want to remember my praying mantises through drawings: beautiful from all angles with their grasping arms.

Vale das Eiras, 11 January 1990

Tomorrow this "lightness of being," a pleasant interlude, will be half over. The playful transition from breakfast outdoors (now that the weather has turned springlike) to pottering about with the hoe or going into Lagos to buy fish. In the afternoon I go back to working on the Frankfurt speech, unless a drawing has to be completed before I start to write: "What was left of the tilapia." Or today, above the bay, when I again sketched wintry fig trees, leafless: the exotic tangle of branches, each tree displaying a different form of ecstasy.

Actually I wanted to anchor this lightness of my everyday existence with the chaotic phenomenon known as the extended family, the source of my occasional happiness but also of many medium-sized annoyances, which heighten the sparse feelings of happiness. Yet I have a hard time being intimate. What is it that compels me to keep the most private things under wraps? Maybe the fear that naming them would disrupt this tolerable and (if I play my cards right) livable precarious equilibrium. In essence, this extended family of mine consists of eight children (six of them biological) and four mothers, to whom I am devoted and whom I greatly enjoy gathering around me in patriarchal fashion: the children can all fit under one umbrella, but not the mothers. "The Mothers": that could be the title of a book, which I shall not write, unless in my seventies I achieve the kind of serenity that has no need to keep score.

My dream last night: I was looking for a place to be buried in Berlin with lots of room, so that anyone who wants to lie there next to me can do so.

My German-Polish Cemetery Association takes a different approach. It adopts regulations consistent with German guidelines: no black Swedish granite, polished to a high sheen, may be used for grave markers.

By the way, the grandchildren in the cemetery's hotel and the older folks in the retirement home (Johannistal Forest Lodge, also known as the "Death Home") soon meet and develop a fondness for one another. The first weddings take place in Gdańsk. The idea of building a maternity clinic is broached, and then, four years after the cemetery became operational and two years after the foundation was laid for the retirement home, a granddaughter married to a grandson experiences a premature birth, at which time the decision to move ahead is made immediately, because Polish hospital conditions cannot measure up to West German standards. Frau Doktor Piątkowska is excited about the symbiosis between the retirement home and the maternity clinic. Before long one can see young German mothers taking walks with their infants on the cemetery paths in lovely weather. In the novel all this would have to be reported by an elderly man from Danzig, of Kashubian ancestry, who has never left Danzig and now finds a job as a cemetery watchman. He can tell the story from a Kashubian perspective, at an equal distance from the Poles and Germans.

Shortly before Christmas I managed to gather part of the family in Berlin-Friedenau for a meal; I served ratatouille with a smoked pork roast. Franz, who had come from his farm with Gianna for the occasion, got up to offer a toast in Swiss German. Ingrid Krüger and Veronika Schröter sat across the table from each other, seething a bit, as did Helene and Nele for a while. Even Malte judged the party a success. Maria, whom I had made a point of inviting, since for better or worse she belongs to the family, snapped pictures and no doubt had thoughts she kept to herself. Veronika had brought dessert. Her daughters (born before Helene), Jette and Katharina, were adorable, and Stefano, Tinka's young husband, also offered a toast, in Italian, to please the patriarch.

Caught a large grasshopper today in the old house and preserved it in schnapps.

Vale das Eiras, 12 January 1990
This is the grasshopper preserved in alcohol. Once it dries out, I plan to draw it in graphite, in the foreground of landscapes or towering over them. Now, with the manuscript almost completed, this Frankfurt speech is wearing me down. Twenty years, even ten years ago, I could not have taken on the topic of "Writing after Auschwitz." Why now?

I fear my planned trip to the GDR is going to take place dur-

ing the letdown after the first successful revolutionary rush. But the old power structures are proving durable, as might have been expected. The mass exodus continues. The opposition is weighed down with organizational problems. Maybe in June and August I'll be sitting on Rügen or in the Elbe Sandstone Mountains writing about the progress of the German-Polish Cemetery Association: in Wilna final approval has been granted for the construction of a mortuary chapel, while in Gdańsk the German cemetery is supposed to be expanded or have a seaside cemetery added to it, at the mouth of the Vistula near Nickelswalde.

Vale das Eiras, 15 January 1990
In the afternoon I wrote the last page of the Frankfurt speech. Almost too neat a conclusion. A sense of dissatisfaction remains, as predicted. Maybe I can work in some irritants.

After a good two weeks of consistently fine weather, our stay here is starting to have something preternatural about it. The two-month rainy period is already nothing but a legend, and only when I hack into the ground to plant more and more cactuses does the damp layer of loam and clay offer a reminder of the floods of yesteryear.

Herr Gysi's rapid transformations are reminiscent of a character from the French Revolution: from now on, he has only two choices — he can either fail spectacularly or turn into a telegenic stage villain.

Of the four mothers with whom I have lived and live — all of whom have next to nothing in common with my own mother — three come from the GDR and all four come from three-daughter families: Anna and Veronika were middle daughters, Ute the eldest, Ingrid the youngest. This phenomenon yields no theory, however, let alone any complex.

At what point will the organization of the German-Polish Cemetery Association expand to Breslau, Stettin, Glogau, Bunzlau, Hirschberg, Landsberg, Küstrin, Posen? After the recognition of the Oder-Neisse Line, might a positive parliamentary resolution in Warsaw become possible? Also voices (calls of the toad) warning against this first "land seizure"? And at what point does Reschke realize that his and Piątkowska's idea is being misused?

I plan to be in Leipzig when the Social Democrats in the GDR hold their party convention at the end of February. Tomorrow I want to get back to picking captions for the *Dead Wood* images, then write my short speech for Tutzing.

Vale das Eiras, 17 January 1990
A day of cooking: prepared tripe in advance for tomorrow. For supper we had crayfish sautéed in oil with garlic and two large codfish that I dredged in flour and fried in the skillet. I sliced up the rest of the cod and set it to marinate in vinegar with fresh coriander and onion rings. I cooked the tripe Neapolitan style, with large tomatoes, garlic, potatoes, and marjoram. Even cooking is a delight here. And Ute made a stock with the crayfish shells that will serve as the base for a fish stew. Today the covered market in Lagos was again overflowing with possibilities.

Because Ute had mistakenly parked right in front of the market hall, we had a run-in with a Portuguese policeman. His sense of his own power was in no way inferior to that of a GDR policeman. That rocking on the toes. Talking without pausing to listen.

Apparently not much has changed in police circles here, in spite of the revolution. Not until we had paid our 2,000 escudos at the police station did he display some semblance of courtesy. What would it be like to have a fellow like that, ready to strike at the slightest provocation, as a father, a husband? Or is he easygoing at home, jovial?

On the way back we stopped in to see a couple from Hannover who spend several months of every year in Portugal, yet cannot put down roots here. She has severely impaired vision, and says, "Of course I see everything wrong, distorted, including on television, but since I used to see properly, I know what trees and people and everything else look like, so in my head I can correct what I'm seeing." That, too, would make an interesting narrative perspective.

I planted more trees, this time three pomegranates, on the east side. By now, hacking holes in this clayey, rocky soil has become an obsession.

Gradually the title "The Call of the Toad" is growing on me. Through writing, prefigure disaster. Knowing, with calm confidence, that it will end badly. The mournful nocturnal calls from one Kashubian lake to another. Reschke and Madame Piątkowska could take an excursion to Karthaus/Kartuzy because some land has been offered to the association, and toward evening they might hear toads calling.

Started on the speech for Tutzing. Possible title: "On Rootless Cosmopolitans."

Vale das Eiras, 20 January 1990
Yesterday, while I was hacking holes for planting, I put down my glasses, which I usually take off only when I go to bed, on a pile of

rocks, which created this image. How matter-of-fact, how representative of me, that fragile object looked amid round and pointed rocks.

In the meantime, the pile of topsoil is visibly shrinking. Our days here are coming to an end. Yesterday the short speech of a rootless cosmopolitan was also finished. I wonder whether in the last four days I will be able to concentrate on *Dead Wood,* the afterword to the book?

The Satanic Verses is giving me more and more trouble, even though the basic idea is still valid.

All the news from the GDR confirms how harsh daily life is, now that the great surge that came with the revolution has subsided. I fear the only thing that will carry the day is the hard West German mark.

Bad, tormenting dreams last night, their frenetic quality in sharp contrast to the monotony of our days here.

Doubts as to whether I can still motivate myself to undertake a book like "The Call of the Toad." (The texts of the two speeches are not conducive to further writing.)

Vale das Eiras, 21 January 1990

Today in blazing sun: the rabbit and I. Nothing is more lifeless, more naked than a skinned rabbit. The more I draw it, the more naked it becomes: muscles, sinews, streaks of fat are exposed and form a touchingly beautiful composition of an animal cadaver on its side, despite the hacked-off fore- and hind paws — perhaps because the skinned rabbit, with its rounded back and foreshortened front and hind legs close together, resembles a human embryo.

I drew it with a landscape in the background, and then, with soft graphite, in vertical format, a cod that I later stuffed with sage and steamed in butter for supper, with the flame in the oven on low.

Later in the day I managed to get started on the afterword to *Dead Wood*. I want to keep it short, with the link to the picture captions unmistakable.

No newspapers in Portimão: the airline pilots are on strike. No chance to stay informed on events in the GDR.

"The Call of the Toad" thus far has been proceeding in a straight line, too logically. My protagonists, the widow and the widower, are not sufficiently lifelike. She should have something tough and persistent about her, because she promised her husband, who did not want to be laid to rest in foreign soil, that she would bury him in Wilna, whatever it took; he, on the other hand, is motivated more by an idea than by personal inclination.

In the neighborhood, a quarter of an hour's walk away, live a couple from England with two small children. Until three years ago he was in Hong Kong: a businessman. One of the many drop-outs here, like Volker Huber, Jules Heindels, Jacob Suhl. We visited them yesterday afternoon for drinks in their unfinished refuge. He's planting vegetables, but the constant rain in November and December rotted the seeds. She teaches at the international school. The pretext he presents for leaving: in the past few years the Chinese in Hong Kong have become unbearably arrogant. This from an Englishman, who also considers his fellow countrymen arrogant, by the way.

Halfway to the neighbor's we dug up young mimosas and planted them on our property. The unusual, gratifying feature of this place is that every evening I find myself looking forward to the next day; this anticipatory pleasure is something with which Ute does not identify. Only on Møn does she feel anything similar.

Vale das Eiras, 25 January 1990
Ute is packing. I have carted the garden tools to the garage, tidied my study upstairs, and finished writing my "Obituary" for *Dead Wood*. The first draft is all of a piece — that's how it reads, anyway.

It was exciting to work on three different texts in quick succession, because their subjects — Auschwitz, the German question, and the dying forests — have a good deal in common. I did nine drawings to keep in reserve. It is so relaxing to turn to Portuguese motifs after the Calcutta images and the drawings for *Dead Wood* — for example, fish before and after the evening meal.

No matter how much I look forward to seeing the children, especially Nele and Helene this time, I would not have minded one or two more weeks here.

In "The Call of the Toad," once the cemeteries are established, and the retirement home, the hotel, the maternity clinic, and the church (also for weddings) are built, and the first vacation houses on the Kashubian lakes for which West Germans received building permits are occupied, all this resulting in more and more Germans coming to Gdańsk, a formal request could be submitted for new, bilingual road signs. A "mixed" panel discussion takes place in the city hall. Professor Reschke, despite being in favor of the signs, eventually opposes them, out of consideration for the feelings of the Poles. The request is authorized, but limited to the names of streets in the rebuilt Old Town. Frau Piątkowska comes back from Wilna railing against the nationalistic Lithuanians, to whom the Russians are giving too much freedom. After an argument about nations, Reschke declares his love to Piątkowska.

Despite the skillful plotting, unfortunately *The Satanic Verses* runs out of suspense: after the fantastic beginning, with its wickedly witty, ironic evocation of the time of Mohammed, we get all too obvious criticism of contemporary English society. Toward the end, the book gives in to sensationalism.

Our English neighbor, who still maintains business relationships with Hong Kong and Taiwan, talks about plunging prices on the New York Stock Exchange. Reports of such developments are coming ever more frequently.

Even today, I helped Ute with some final planting. Yesterday, when Rémy Bongard and his girlfriend came by — we had the rest of the rabbit, stewed in red wine — he brought us a piri piri pepper, which has now been planted between the rosemary and the marjoram.

Dresden's mayor, Berghofer, has resigned from the Socialist Unity Party and is said to be planning to join the Social Democrats, which could mean not only a gain — a prominent, seasoned politician — but also a burden for that young party.

Tomorrow morning Germano, our neighbor, is driving us in our Jeep to the airport very early: six-thirty!

On the plane from Faro to Hamburg, 26 January 1990
Goodbye to my cactuses! The newspapers (bought in the Faro airport) trigger the familiar German-German stomach cramps. *Die Zeit* has a conversation with Brandt under the heading "Confederation Is Also a Form of Unity." So why all the vague allusions to a German federation? It is certainly phenomenal the way the Old Man — which is his role now, since Wehner's death — invokes the history of the Social Democratic Party as the basis of his commitment to the GDR's Social Democrats.

"The Call of the Toad" is traveling with us. At the very beginning of the story, a Bengali busybody in Gdańsk, actually a Marwari from Calcutta, will make an appearance. Before long he has set up a bicycle rickshaw service: inexpensive, environmentally friendly, with Polish rickshaw drivers. He is also the one who recognizes the symptoms of worldwide climate change and predicts that someday rice will be grown in the Vistula Delta. He mocks the German-Polish Cemetery Association's "wasteful use of space." He then serves as the intermediary for wealthy Marwaris to buy into the former Lenin Shipyard, previously the Schichau Shipyard, soon after which Bengalis begin to emigrate from Calcutta and Bangladesh. But this ever-increasing byproduct ought to be kept in the background, saved for the end of the story. My Bengali (Marwari) could be a mixture of Daud Haider (our guide in Calcutta) and Salman Rushdie: at once crazed and concrete, intellectual and naïve, enlightened and superstitious. According to his faith, which draws on all major world religions, toads' croaking does not mean bad luck but rather announces welcome changes in the offing.

The bicycle rickshaws operated by Polish coolies are a great favorite of German tourists and senior citizens from the "Death Home" for sightseeing tours of the city.

My Bengali (Marwari) might deliver lectures filled with speculation about sacred matters, the subjects ranging from the goddess Kali to the Black Madonna of Częstochowa.

Important to maintain the momentum, stay active during the few days in Behlendorf before I have to leave for Tutzing.

My cactus plantation, I now realize, is laid out like a novel: covering a lot of ground, with all sorts of gaps that will be filled in as the plants grow. I probably cannot stop myself. A few days ago, when I told Ute how many plants I had put in front of the old house — eighty-seven! — she laughed at me and said that in the GDR in the fifties I would have been a true Hennecke.

Behlendorf, 26 January 1990
Hänschen is there to meet us at Hamburg airport. Standing on the other side of the glass partition between the waiting area and the baggage pickup, he holds a copy of the *Morgenpost* with the headline "Hurricane!" (Later the evening news provides more detail: more than ninety deaths in England, France, and Belgium.) I wonder whether the increasing violence of these storms, predicted by scientists, is already a sign of climate change.

Back in Behlendorf, and the house is fine. In my studio I immediately spread out the manuscripts. On my drawing board are the last drawings from before we left for Portugal: the pike Herr Lübcke gave us, a meter and three centimeters in length. Drawn in pencil. A sketch in brush and reed pen, using ink I made from walnut shells, which blackened in the fall; the ink produces a sienna shade that apparently holds its color.

On the telephone, Ute is telling her sister in Freiburg about the grotesque dreams she had in Portugal. In the first dream she wants to get married — it is not clear to whom — but she puts everything on hold because her mother is missing, but later she finds her, dead drunk. In the second dream her mother, seventy-eight and shaky though she is, is pregnant — unclear or irrelevant by whom — but Ute comforts herself with the thought that her mother might give up alcohol because she has to nurse the baby; also, in the "home for the aged" the situation is viewed not as tragic but rather as something that will liven up the place. There is no need to analyze dreams like that, I think.

The three-quarter-liter bottle of squid ink made it home safely in our hand luggage.

Tomorrow I want to see how our old orchard fared in the hurricane.

While we were on our way from the airport to Hamburg's main station, Ute's mother was arriving by train from Freiburg, somewhat late but cheerful and relaxed — and not the least bit pregnant.

Behlendorf, 28 January 1990
Today the lineup for the Bundestag election will probably be decided in the Saarland. Will Lafontaine be able to hang on to an absolute majority of parliamentary seats? And will he or will he not be the SPD's candidate for chancellor? It is not looking good

for him, because according to the radio the turnout is down from four years ago (the weather is stormy), which will give the small parties a better chance to get over the 5 percent hurdle, and that includes the Republicans.

Here, too, a gusty northwester is sweeping across the country-side. The nearby forest is groaning. I have retreated to the cocoon of my studio. Rewrote the short speech for Tutzing again. Brandt was on television last night, attending the convention in Gotha for the founding of the Thuringian SPD. It makes me uneasy to see him promoting unification. His reservations expressed too ca-sually and vaguely: unification from below, no unified state but a federal state based on the individual provinces' sovereignty. But also increasingly frequent preemptive rejection of foreign criti-cism of the "German people's desire for unity." Could it be his young wife who has made him so nationalistic? Or is he trying to put the finishing touches on a lifetime of political involvement? Or might he feel he has to wash away the stain of the "rootless cosmopolitan"? Or is it just his political instinct telling him to lay claim to the topic? Or all those things together?

In my studio I started working on a new and final image for *Dead Wood,* maybe for the jacket. Ute has gone to her sister's to fetch the dog. Am cooking pork in *Schwarzsauer* sauce, and put some Portuguese figs in the stock.

Talked on the phone with Franz. How pragmatically he assesses the political situation, our onetime cloud-pusher. He is building a bigger cow barn.

I am no good at predicting election results. Oskar won a sur-prisingly big majority. As a candidate for chancellor, he will be played off against Brandt's national vision for the sake of German unity — unless the two of them modify their positions.

While I was glued to the election coverage, the sauce cooked down too much. Kohl's priceless comment: "The results are related to the campaign."

Behlendorf, 30 January 1990
Back from Portugal only a few days, and I am stuffed to the gills with information, overwhelmed with details, all trying to convince me that reunification is the only game in town, that the train has long since left the station. With this baggage (and with diarrhea that set in during yet another sleepless night), it is off to Tutzing. Will it be possible to challenge the alleged will of the people? The politicians, at least, if they have any integrity, must realize that although a hasty reunification can be pushed through, the price to pay would be distrust and lasting internal discord.

Behlendorf, 2 February 1990
Back from Tutzing: the conference Antje Vollmer and I conceived and organized apparently took place at the right moment, and could have a lasting effect. My brief speech, not delivered until the final day, focused the discussion again, the more so because on the previous day the politicians had been unable to come up with any "new answers to the German question." It was not easy for me to take a position fundamentally counter to Willy Brandt's; but if anything caused him to reconsider, it was probably the rather softly spoken but firm points made by the young conference participants from the GDR, people like Konrad Weiss.

It was amusing to see how angry the German president became because he could not express his reservations about the unification process with journalists present. Antje Vollmer, who despite being in a chronic state of excitement and prone to emotional breakdowns and outbursts, always kept to the subject. Ibrahim Böhme, as chairman of the SPD-East, has too heavy a burden to carry, and that with too little sleep and too much expected of him. I signed up for the party convention in Leipzig on 22 February and for several political events.

Tutzing Castle is located directly on Lake Starnberg. Large, old trees on the grounds. In clear weather you can see the Alps. A landscape that is almost too beautiful, as in the regional films popular in the fifties. The director of the Protestant Academy is incapable of uttering a single sentence without having to suppress a smile. Even Heinrich Albertz made a point of being there; he arrived on the night train. It is pathetic to see the Greens constantly chafing against the Social Democrats, even when there is no perceptible difference of opinion between them and Norbert Gansel (the case in Tutzing).

The nights too short, the days too long and stressful, too many demands in general, which makes me feel my age. When we got back to Behlendorf yesterday, the important news from 1 February was waiting: Modrow's plan for Germany, with a neutral country its ultimate goal; and the American president's decision to reduce U.S. troop numbers considerably. Yet another new situation. But it is becoming clear that all the plans call for a confederation, something that could last for several years. That would give the GDR and its citizens a chance to have a say in how unity is configured, once they are able to stand on their own feet and have improved their economic situation. If the Social Democrats gain a majority in both states, a new German self-image might emerge after all.

If I start the action involving the widow and widower's plan in Gdańsk on All Saints' Day '89 — in November, that is — the German-German process currently under way would have to play a significant part. For example, Poland will take a back seat as far as the widower is concerned. The German-Polish Cemetery Association will not come into being overnight, including the finances. In letters the widow will express her impatience, while the widower in his replies will ask her to be patient. Poland must wait. The German corpses will arrive later than originally planned.

While I was in Tutzing, the drawing for the cover of *Dead Wood* was on hold. This is how it might look:

Tomorrow Steidl is arriving with Erich Loest and Loest's son and daughter-in-law. I may participate, including financially, in his plan for a publishing house that straddles both German states. For instance, *Dead Wood* could be published with Steidl and also with Loest's Linden Verlag.

Behlendorf, 4 February 1990

He came, with his son and daughter-in-law: three Saxons. He says, "Saxony has been brought to its knees several times — after the Thirty Years' War, after the Seven Years' War, and now once again, with the Wandlitz Gang done for, and each time the region has bounced back." Apparently that is how they are, these Saxons.

Because Loest is still a GDR citizen, he has been eligible to register his Linden Verlag in Leipzig. Now he is looking for a vacant building to restore. In September he wants to present his own book, *Durch die Erde ein Riss* ("The Earth Split Open"), at the Leipzig Book Fair, along with a book by Klaus Staeck and my *Dead Wood,* the latter both Steidl books. I am thinking of asking Faber (of Aufbau Verlag) in the next few weeks to bring out *The Plebeians* without delay. If Faber does not agree, I shall give the rights to Loest/Leipzig, so Steidl can print right away. Loest also wants to attend the SPD party convention in Leipzig and announce there that he is joining, which will be gratifying for him after seven and a half years in Bautzen penitentiary and all the grief he endured afterward. I drew a jacket illustration for his autobiographical *Durch die Erde ein Riss.*

And behind all this Poland is obscured, yet painfully obvious. Poland's terminally depressed prime minister could play a shadowy role in "The Call of the Toad." The protagonists want to talk him into attending the dedication of the German cemetery. I don't know at this point whether he will.

At any rate, pressure on Poland from West Germany and, after the elections in March, from the GDR will increase. Resettled Poles who consider themselves Germans and Polish emigrants are being pushed out. The terminally depressed prime minister looks to France for help, but all he gets is words. In desperation he turns for support to the Soviet Union, which is preoccupied with troubles of its own. Only the German-Polish Cemetery Association is bringing in hard currency.

The Frankfurt speech is finished at long last. Yesterday another hurricane ripped through France and West Germany. More than twenty deaths. It is not inconceivable that the violence of the storms can be ascribed to the early stages of climate change.

Ute's mother has an irresistible way of bringing every conversation around to Hiddensee or Rügen. Here is what was left of the carp after Loest and his family were here:

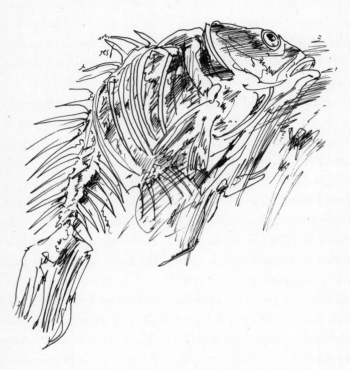

On the train from Molln to Berlin, 5 February 1990
Springlike weather. In my compartment a woman from East Berlin who predicts the Social Democrats will win 50 percent of the vote, while I am hoping for 30 percent. The new travel experience: at the border all I have to present is my identity card. Brandt's interview with *Der Spiegel* makes for strange reading: he refers alternately to federation and confederation, names Switzerland as a model, and

at the end accepts a confederation as unification. Apparently he was listening in Tutzing after all.

I find myself wishing I could be in Leipzig and Gdańsk at the same time. How is my German-Polish Cemetery Association faring? The land has been purchased. A permanent staff of landscape gardeners is planting weeping willows, birches, and boxwood hedges, taking advantage of the mild weather. Even material for building the cemetery walls can be procured for hard currency. In April the first corpses could be flown in. The airport is nearby.

Berlin, 6 February 1990

Back on Niedstrasse since yesterday: a huge stack of mail. No longer the endless drudgery of polite letters of refusal, however, but instead the pleasure of being able to say yes: yes to an event sponsored by the East German Social Democratic Party in Prenzlauer Berg, where I am to give my first reading in the GDR from *The Plebeians* — a pleasure late in coming. And for 10 March a reading in the State Theater in Schwerin, and after that perhaps in Stralsund. Today, after a telephone conversation with Tomáš Kosta, preliminary arrangements for a week in Prague at the end of May, including the possibility of finally accepting the open invitation, issued in 1968, to Group 47 — what is left of it: President Václav Havel can take off his yoke and participate as an ordinary writer.

This evening Beatrice did the cooking: rabbit with polenta. My daughter-in-law from Switzerland is a good cook. Afterward she and her friend, who is also pregnant, launched into a conversation about baby gear the friend had brought along, among them items inherited from her grandmother. Such breathless enthusiasm leaves me speechless.

Beatrice gave me a potted cactus this morning for the bedroom, a kind that grows outdoors in Portugal.

For the first time in years I am here in Berlin without daughters: Laura is in Aachen, Helene in England during the so-called skiing holidays, and Nele is in Switzerland with her mother, actually skiing. So I have a few hours to myself.

At the moment I am leaning toward an epistolary novel, the correspondence between the widow and the widower. Letters from the German and Polish sides, as well as newspaper reports, minutes of meetings, parliamentary speeches, and advertisements for the cemetery association, could enrich the epistolary novel.

Maria put on my desk a good two hundred engravings for me to sign.

Berlin, 8 February 1990
Back from Spandau, where the European members of the Socialist International wrapped up their congress with a farewell din-

ner in the Citadel by the Julius Tower. I sat with three Polish Social Democrats, who were of course eyeing one another suspiciously. Among the guests were some I had met three months ago in Gdańsk with Lipski — and Tadeusz Fiszbach, who recently founded a social-democratic party after the dissolution of the Communist Party; at least during the martial law period Fiszbach declared his support for Solidarność, whereupon he was removed from office.

I suggested to the warring Polish factions that they come to Niedstrasse for two days as my guests to work things out and reach a meeting of minds.

Today my Tutzing speech was printed in *Die Zeit,* and the *Frankfurter Rundschau* carried Christa Wolf's speech in Hildesheim: resigned and with sorrowful undertones, a moving piece.

Berlin, 10 February 1990

Addenda: Prenzlauer Berg last night. The only publicity the Social Democrats had done was to distribute flyers. The school auditorium half empty. Nonetheless a memorable evening. I even had a slight attack of stage fright (for the first time in years) because I was reading from a play: scenes from the first and second acts, then the entire fourth act, of *The Plebeians.* An attentive though young audience listened breathlessly. The seventeenth of June is ancient history to them, but the reading, in conjunction with the events of the past few months, made it come alive for them. During the discussion after the reading and the bar conversation later with comrades in the Oderkahn, the depressed mood, the profound pessimism, was unmistakable. The core of the opposition is crumbling even in situations, such as that of the Social Democrats, where it is beginning to get organized, with help from the West and constant mentoring. People told me to expect violent disagreements to break out at the party convention in Leipzig.

During the drive to Prenzlauer Berg in Fritze Margull's new car: an eclipse of the moon. East Berlin very dark around Leipziger Strasse. The startlingly casual check at the border.

Late at night, a conversation back at the house with Raoul, who wants to persuade me to write a film script "just for a change." As I give him a brief summary of the German-Polish Cemetery Association, it occurs to me that "The Call of the Toad" could actually be a film as well, but the commotion involved in filmmaking scares me off. I would much rather spend a nice long time alone, concentrating on the manuscript. This constant temptation: to be by myself, listening to my own babbling.

Yesterday afternoon, the conversation with Roehler about the Writers' Election Office in 1965. In the meantime we have reached the point of memorializing our own history. Roehler, weakened by his accident, keeps trying to prove that his memory is unimpaired: he thinks he can remember what the weather was like on certain days. Eva Hönisch digs out old letters: from Karl Schiller, from Willy Brandt, Brandt's handwritten letter composed right after a performance of *The Plebeians* at the Schillertheater.

A growing sense of being hemmed in. Germany's unity is being talked into existence, as if under compulsion; all that is missing is the head-over-heels implementation. It is gradually becoming dangerous to speak out against this most recent insanity. If I keep saying no, it is not out of defiance; rather — aside from and in spite of all the arguments in favor — I have a powerful premonition of disaster.

In the *Frankfurter Allgemeine* I read a speech by Rushdie, delivered for him by Pinter, with the title "Is Nothing Sacred?" A defense of *The Satanic Verses.* Once again very close to my own position, though he draws on postmodern theoreticians (why?). I try to picture my fellow writer, now so cruelly isolated, moving from hiding place to hiding place with his entourage of bodyguards.

Let us assume the German unification process gathers steam, helped along by the self-fulfilling chaos, to the point where in a year's time the greater German republic has taken on firm contours and borders directly on Poland: wouldn't the German-Polish Cemetery Association find itself under pressure, under nervous Polish pressure and increasing German demands?

Helene is back from England. This evening with her, Fritze, and Raoul to the premiere of Volker Schlöndorff's film version of a Canadian novel.

From Berlin to Büchen, 11 February 1990
Volker's film, *The Handmaid's Tale,* based on a novel by the Canadian Atwood, has a slickness to it that keeps the unremittingly terrible goings-on in a totalitarian police state (following an ecological catastrophe) at arm's length. Pinter's screenplay hardly gave the characters any latitude for development. Only with the help of good actors and Volker's skill as a director is any tension created.

After the film, to the old Paris Bar with Helene, Raoul, and Fritze. I hope Volker, who is aware of the film's shortcomings and called it a "forceps birth," soon breaks free of America; the new situation in Germany is luring him back. Helene had two glasses of liqueur and talked about her weeks in England, without falling into her usual bubbliness. Apparently she was at a private school for children of the upper class. The pupils' parents pay a good 24,000 marks a year.

Around noon, Walter Höllerer, Christian Delius, and Peter

Schneider came over. We discussed the plan of having Group 47 gather in Prague with Czech writers. The meeting had originally been scheduled to take place there in 1968, but the occupation got in the way; that and the fallout from the '67 meeting at the Pulvermühle, which led to the breakup of Group 47. I hope Hans Werner Richter, who is ill, can come.

A good meeting; Höllerer's laughter is still infectious.

And today I went (with Eike) to pick up Ingrid and Nele at Zoo Station. Later the three of them saw me onto the train to Hamburg. How affectionate Nele is, how jolly! Ingrid more relaxed than usual, but weighed down by professional concerns again: she wants to leave Luchterhand and move to Rowohlt or Kiepenheuer. In Behlendorf a letter from Nele is waiting for me.

In "The Call of the Toad" a West German or West Berlin burial society — called Grieneisen, for instance — could join the German-Polish Cemetery Association. In Poland there is a shortage of caskets and linings.

Behlendorf, 12 February 1990
Back from Hamburg. The debate with Augstein for *Panorama* became heated. He: a lovable fool who feels compelled to grope secretaries, fights corruption all over the world with *Der Spiegel* but tolerates corruption in his own house — "Karasek is clever and corrupt" — and enjoys assuming the role of a dyed-in-the-wool German nationalist: "The unification train has left the station."

From Hamburg to Frankfurt am Main, 13 February 1990
Yesterday I was able to concentrate and dashed off two pages to send to Augstein, who said he would make sure they got printed: the enlightened despot. I used his recurrent, often parroted, re-

frain, "The train has left the station," as my title. Back to the debate. Wagner, the moderator, reads his introduction from the Teleprompter, creating the illusion for TV viewers that he has the whole thing flawlessly memorized. A deception that has become standard practice. As for the idea of a confederation, I should have gone into greater detail, at the expense of the debate, once it got stuck on Augstein's hobbyhorse — Bismarck and the consequences.

Today in the *Frankfurter Rundschau* the draft of a constitution, worked out by two human rights experts from Leipzig and West Berlin. The draft calls for a first stage that entails a conjoining of states, similar to a confederation. A federal parliament would be elected from among members of the Bundestag and the Volkskammer. Furthermore, there is a federal executive council and a court for the conjoined states. In Article 26 of the proposed treaty, provision is made for voiding the treaty if a referendum shows that a majority favors the creation of a German federation. To me, this draft would be an acceptable compromise. It provides a solid context for Willy Brandt's all too vague notions.

Last night I hardly slept. Thought through the structure of "The Call of the Toad" again. On the one hand, a simple story, almost a fairy tale, punctuated by letters between the widower and the widow, as well as other letters. The correspondence between the widower and the widow could mirror a late love affair, its development at first hesitant, then passionate, finally head-over-heels. There is something to be said for this intimate genre, which allows current political happenings to be filtered through the personal story. Must clarify how many children and grandchildren the widower and widow have, if any. Should they write letters, too? (The widow's radical son.)

Yesterday on Second German Television, the unspeakable *Literary Quartet*. I simply do not understand why Jurek Becker allows himself to get mixed up with that crew. When Reich-Ranicki started to defame Christa Wolf and Stephan Hermlin again — Karasek wanted to drag me through the mud, too — Jurek did not protest nearly as firmly as he should have. Whose feelings is he sparing? Reich-Ranicki's attack on Luchterhand. Apparently the protest after the previous broadcast got under his skin.

From Frankfurt to Göttingen, 14 February 1990

So that was it: the speech in Frankfurt, "Writing after Auschwitz," delivered to an audience of over a thousand, mostly students, in Adorno's overflowing lecture hall; I was told that more than five hundred people followed the whole thing on a video screen in a lecture hall one floor below. Not until I finished did the tension get to me, and I was startled when, after sitting for an hour in silence, the audience responded with a storm of applause. As I spoke, I realized that, spurred on by the topic, I was revealing myself in this text as never before.

The reception given by Luchterhand (in the overly expensive villa) proved quite relaxing. Before that, the exhibition at the university library. In some of the early photos I see myself as if for the first time: in the early sixties, wearing a Panama hat, with Uwe Johnson, Hans Magnus Enzensberger, and Wolfgang Neuss. A pleasure to see Anna giving ballet lessons. Next to that the Friedenau print, "The Ballerina." An intelligently curated exhibition.

Today: the Authors' Council. The two lady publishers are in over their heads. We have demanded that from now on Elisabeth Raabe be in the office four or five days a week, not two. Frielinghaus is wonderful, but not firm enough. It is still not certain that Elisabeth Raabe can pull it off, because the other employees — of whom there are about twenty-five — are, with a few exceptions, an inarticulate, unenthusiastic bunch, the editors literary bureaucrats. This at a time when the house faces real challenges and its authors in both Germanys must endure attacks and libelous accusations.

Bichsel's hilarious story of being so drunk that after a reading in Kiel he thinks he overslept and missed a reading on television, but he is assured afterward that he read very well.

Now I am going to do two lithos on stone in Steidl's workshop, one in vertical and one in horizontal format.

Behlendorf, 16 February 1990

I managed to do two more lithos than I had planned, so now I have more than enough images in the portfolio, for which I had already done almost thirty, fifteen of them unusable (the Russian printer ruined them). Among them the owl as a cloud above the forest.

Shortly before midnight the debate with Rudolf Augstein. On television he made an even worse impression. I heard today that many viewers assumed he was drunk. Perhaps the influence of this potentate, short in stature but large in self-regard, was somewhat diminished. Tomorrow the debate will be rebroadcast on Channel 3.

Lunch with Franz at the Italian restaurant. His new cow barn is getting bigger and more costly. What a handsome, canny, naïve, sturdy, anxious fellow my eldest son is, always worried about money. I like spending time with him.

During the ride home on the train I was too exhausted to write in my journal. Also no thoughts about "The Call of the Toad." The term *kuronski,* for soup-kitchen vouchers, coined by the Polish minister Kuroń, keeps going through my head. Maybe the German-Polish Cemetery Association should establish a soup kitchen in the retirement home, for elderly Poles (using *kuronskis*). The rickshaw business started by Daud Chaudry, the Bengali, proves so successful because taxis are too expensive: former taxi drivers as rickshaw coolies.

And today, following telephone conversations with *Kennzeichen D*'s Dirk Sager, a quiet day. I typed up the captions for *Dead Wood* and composed a large charcoal drawing: tree stumps on a rolling hill. I cannot seem to let go of the subject.

Sent the final corrections for "Writing after Auschwitz" to *Die Zeit.* So now all the manuscripts written in Portugal, as well as the "Obituary" for *Dead Wood,* are in press. What a pleasure to work on large-scale drawings!

I am wondering if we should go on to Poland after two weeks of vacation on Rügen: pace off the cemetery grounds in Gdańsk and gather material, such as food prices, etc. Around the house crocuses and other flowers are in bloom. Meanwhile, stormy weather, with flooding in France, Switzerland, and southern Germany. Climate change is only starting to be discussed, crowded out by the topic of Germany plus Germany.

Behlendorf, 17 February 1990

Watched my debate with Augstein again on Channel 3. First the clip from 1960. Jaspers, with his gentle, reedy, professorial voice. Augstein: a Welfish-Prussian first lieutenant. His officer's bark. He labels Zahrnt a village preacher. Kogon compares Jaspers to Socrates, who used his walking stick to make people stumble so they would reflect on stumbling. Zahrnt says, "Jaspers made us smarter."

Today I started another large drawing in vertical format, more tree stumps. The tranquility in Behlendorf makes it possible to get a perspective on assorted worries. Will it still be "my Germany"? The Czechs and Poles are asking the Soviet Union not to withdraw its troops too quickly. The peremptory tones issuing from Bonn offer a preview of what we can expect from those gentlemen. The dismissive way Modrow was treated in Bonn, as were the ministers from the round table group, is shameful, and also a manifestation of what Augstein characterizes as Realpolitik; his own tone (in the television debate) was indistinguishable from the unpleasant noises emanating from Messrs. Kohl, Waigel, Dregger, Rühe, et al. And the Social Democrats say nothing. If Oskar Lafontaine does not come back and make a decision in the next few days as to whether he is running for chancellor, and with what policy on Germany's future, the SPD will never be able to seize the initiative. Stoltenberg speaks of putting the Bundeswehr and the National People's Army under one command — and no one says boo.

Yesterday on television: Mazowiecki and Modrow together, melancholy times two: humane, full of insight, sensitive, almost touching, in contrast to our loudmouth political leaders: revolting.

Behlendorf, 18 February 1990
Preparations for the trip to Leipzig. A telephone conversation with Antje Vollmer: she points out that the Bundestag cannot legitimately act on unification because when the elections took place the subject was not on the ballot — an objection worth bringing up for discussion, though it would lead only to more fruitless wrangling.

More important to insist on the Bundesrat's right to participate in the decision. Strange that I go on hoping — no, am certain — that objections and reservations may yet have some effect, at the latest at the meeting of the six, then again at the Conference on Security and Cooperation in Europe, in September.

Postscript: Unseld's pompous air in Frankfurt when, as sponsor of the event at the university, he handed me the check himself. In a similar vein: Haussmann, the economics minister, at the opening of the Ambiente trade fair, standing on the ever-so-tasteful podium and scolding the GDR government for not understanding and appreciating the gift of the "currency union," and pointing out that Hungary would happily accept such a gift. The idol worship directed toward the deutschmark. Crass materialism as the basis for national identity. "Why won't you Zonies dance around the Golden Calf when we tell you to, damn it?"

In "The Call of the Toad" the Poles might put an end to the cemetery mumbo-jumbo, or try to, by sealing off the cemetery, even leveling it, or maybe after they have sealed it off they are forced by economic pressure from the Germans to reopen the cemetery, along with the auxiliary operations. The latter is the more likely scenario, and could be reflected in letters as a dramatic episode. The reburial program then runs without a hitch, especially once the widow and widower — not quite two thirds of the way through the book — are outvoted on the board and forced to resign. Only now do they plan their trip to Italy. See Naples and . . . Exactly what they wish for.

Did I already make a note of this? At any rate, the widow's son is a radical (Trotskyite), the widower has four grown children and several grandchildren. Reports on the children feature in the correspondence: their divergent attitudes toward the cemetery project. Biographical details, very freely rendered.

A brief meeting with Manthey at Steidl's. A leftist conservative. His refined speaking style always sounds slightly aggrieved.

Plan to take a sketchbook along when I go to Leipzig. Ute is sad she cannot come with me, on account of her mother.

Berlin, 19 February 1990

During the train ride from Büchen to Berlin, a conversation with a couple from Oranienburg, in their mid- to late forties: "Some people don't know that the concentration camp in our town was in use till '49." Then a conversation about everything under the sun, because when the subject of the elections comes up, she, a hairdresser (he's a painter), suddenly turns out to be a Bible expert: "God's already picked the winner, so I'm not going to vote." He wants to vote for something: to get rid of the Socialist Unity Party. Great fears, small hopes. Both of them are ashamed because so many antisocial elements — "Supposedly we didn't have any" — are crossing into the West. Whenever she speaks as a Bible expert, her voice and her facial expression wax prophetic. Their son (one of three children) got out by way of Budapest to Kiel, and they were visiting him there over the weekend. Now they are hoping he will return, when things get better in the East. She says, "What the Bible foretells, the Thousand-Year Reich, you know what I mean, it's coming. What Hitler promised was just a little offshoot." Both work for a cooperative and have no savings because three years ago they sank everything they had into a house. Requests for autographs.

Here the telephone is ringing off the hook. Of course *Der Spiegel* did not print my "Letter to Augstein: The Train Has Left the Station, but Where To?" Those indefatigable opponents of censorship are themselves practicing it — repulsive! I am going to offer the text to the *Tages-Anzeiger*.

A sketch for the last image in *Dead Wood* before the trip to Leipzig:

From Berlin to Leipzig, 20 February 1990

Passing, in Jüterbog, a large military training area. The ground chewed up by tanks, with sparse stands of birch and pines. Passing a railroad station with the town's name painted over in white: a freight train on a siding, loaded with tanks and various tracked vehicles, large-caliber artillery. (Soviet units about to be shipped out?)

Fritze Margull took me to Lichtenberg Station. A lively part of town. On Weitlingstrasse a tobacconist's where I bought (for fifty Eastern marks) Cuban cigars and cigarillos. The woman behind the counter said, "As long as we still have 'em." Then she asked me to sign her copy of the *Tagesspiegel*. (Must read Weitling.)

On track C, the train to Malmö, by way of Greifswald and

Sassnitz, pulls in late: groups of children, pale little city mice setting out for holidays. In my compartment an elderly couple and a chubby young man. All silent.

Snap up a bargain. This expression, which Steidl uses when he has bought auxiliary rights or dusted off some artists' proofs or sketches, could be applied to the GDR whenever West German businessmen talk about possible investments or politicians speak more and more openly of "annexation." Colonial masters practiced at seizing the spoils. What is about to be done to these disempowered, cowed people is shameful.

For "The Call of the Toad," the plan includes sections for urns in the German cemetery in Gdańsk. Read yesterday that West German casket manufacturers are delivering caskets to the GDR at a 1:5 exchange rate, because customers are rejecting the GDR cardboard caskets for cremations, their handles being too flimsy or missing altogether. Should a modern crematorium be built or planned for possible use by the Poles?

Walked from the imposing main station in Leipzig up Nikolaistrasse to the church. In the rectory, the first surprise: the pastor, Christian Führer, has not found me a room in a private house, which I intended to pay for, but instead has put me up in his son's room, where I am now recording this fact, sitting at the boy's desk.

A walk through the Old Town from St. Nicholas's to the Naschmarkt, past the town hall, then around St. Thomas's to the Bach statue. After six P.M. few people are out and about, for the most part young. In front of Auerbach's Cellar, which is closed, I rendezvous with Führer. We go to the Thüringischer Hof to eat, where I have sauerbraten, but without dumplings, alas. Führer is still obsessed with the days leading up to 9 November 1989, when his church was providing sanctuary for the opposition. The young people who came out every Monday and let themselves be rounded up by the police, taking immense risks, have been pushed aside now, whereas someone like Pastor Ebeling, who refused to open St. Thomas's to the protesters — not until the congregation's leadership council passed a resolution was it opened — is grandstanding as the spokesman for the DSU (a branch of the Christian Social Union).

On television a report claiming that subsidies for food and other necessities are about to be discontinued and that people have begun hoarding; Modrow's warnings will have no effect, of course. *Report from Munich* tries to portray Modrow in a dubious light, likewise leading Social Democrats, who did not always believe in reunification. The West German version of *The Black Channel.*

Führer, who has his first funeral of the day tomorrow morning at eight, tells of conditions in the cemeteries. Mass burials of urns "in the meadow," anonymously. Flowers are resold after the burial. Gold teeth are extracted from the deceased. He confirms the flimsiness of the cardboard coffins.

The old city center is quiet, far removed from traffic. The bittersweet smell of soft-coal fumes. Nicely decorated shop windows. Election posters on the long side of the town hall. SPD posters defaced: "Vote for Schorlemmer, not Böhme." Twice I ask for directions: this unselfconscious Saxon dialect.

Phone conversation with Baby Sommer. The tour is all arranged. Dresden, Bautzen, Karl-Marx-Stadt are in the bag, also Neubrandenburg. Telephone conversation with Schorlemmer in Wittenberg. I shall probably drop in to see him on 14 March, on my way from Leipzig to Stralsund. He has decided not to run, wants to remain a pastor.

Leipzig, 21 February 1990
This elongated sketch of the view from the son's window gave me some quiet moments today. So too did the visit to the Bach Museum next to St. Thomas's. I was the only visitor, bending over documents whose meticulous handwriting offers a glimpse of Bach as a responsible head of household. In the church, boards on easels showing all the famous people christened there. Bebel was married at St. Thomas's. Masur is on tour with the orchestra. In

the Karl Marx University building, I take the elevator to the eleventh floor because people tell me it will not stop on the twelfth. Then a conversation with the German literature faculty, joined later by students. Everyone suffering from a guilty conscience: "We did nothing. The ivory tower remained a tower, cut off from the people, who took to the streets." I tried to talk them out of their latent resignation. Pezold invited me to lunch. He was Hans Mayer's assistant when I visited the university for the first and last time, in 1961, to read from *The Tin Drum,* and brought greetings to the students from Uwe Johnson, who had been stripped of his GDR citizenship. Before lunch, arrangements were made for a reading from *The Plebeians* on the afternoon of 26 February (Shrove Monday). Over lunch Pezold told me hesitantly of his growing disenchantment with the Socialist Unity Party. Not until the party refused to dissolve itself did he resign.

Then, outside the concert hall, the interview with Channel 4. Fat Doctor Schumann with a woman (his wife) putting up posters for themselves. An indefatigable, muddle-headed enthusiast.

When I got back, I found in my room (the room of the son I have not yet met) an invitation from Magirius, the district superintendent for St. Nicholas's, to the Leipzig round table. Frau Führer walked me to the new town hall, a gloomy structure from the turn of the century. Magirius guided the much too large gathering with patience, authority, and humor. This round table is continuing until 6 May, with twenty-four commissions, the work of the council that resigned because of election fraud. Three additional groups and parties — the citizens' initiative group known as Hope Principle, the Peasants' Party, and the Forum Party — wanted to join, belatedly, but were rejected. Magirius: "I included myself among those signing up to speak."

Discussion topic: Where does recreation belong? With tourism or with sports? Then, at last, point 3: elections, the district elections commission, training on election procedures. There are not enough voting booths. The representative of the Initiative for Peace and Human Rights refused to participate in any votes. A pamphlet attacking the SPD, launched by the DSU, was unanimously condemned, with the DSU and CDU also voting. How cumbersome democracy is. Should campaign events be allowed in the center of town (Marxplatz) during the Leipzig Fair — for instance, the advertised appearance by Kohl? The round table declares itself opposed for reasons of traffic congestion. At the Führers', guests till late. I am too tired to sit there all evening listening to his religious outpourings.

Leipzig, 23 February 1990
This unsettling springlike weather persists. The SPD convention here bears no resemblance to similar events in West Germany. The need to improvise still sets the tone. The speeches by Hilsberg and Böhme don't yet sound mechanical, despite all they have learned in the meantime. Everything feels like a time warp: the agricultural exhibition hall like something from the early sixties. Discussions with old GDR Social Democrats: their long-delayed gratification. How confidently, by contrast, the young Social Democrats reject the smears directed at them by the DSU.

Today Oskar is to speak. No thoughts of "The Call of the Toad," only the certainty that my original conception is hot on the heels of reality. Up late chatting with Scharping and his wife, Steidl, and Staeck at the Hotel Merkur.

Leipzig, 24 February 1990
Yesterday, early in the morning — I was trying to catch some sleep — the pastor's youngest son was singing out in the hall:

"High atop the mountain, a pylon in the mist. That's where the girls get electrically kissed." This song, rehearsed in his nursery school for Carnival, stirred memories in me.

After the party convention, the exhausting procedural back-and-forth, which impresses me because there is no substitute, and it reveals the drawn-out and often boring procedures by which public opinion is formed. Here we have almost a textbook example, because democracy takes practice.

In the midst of it all the bomb threat. The crowd milling around outside in the spring sunshine. Suspicion points not to right-wing radicals but to Stasi groups that are still active. Ibrahim Böhme, an emaciated little fellow with a rather old-fashioned theatrical air, is gaining in stature from one appearance to the next. He is elected party chairman with a decisive majority. Late in the day I am invited up to the lectern, partly to cheer up the weary delegates a bit.

And today, after a long wait, painful because the discussion of the party platform was interrupted for a precious three quarters of an hour, Willy Brandt arrived, was elected by standing ovation to the post of honorary chairman, and again delivered a grand speech, grand because it acknowledged the delegates, then the city of Leipzig, and finally the citizens of the GDR, yet also sent a message beyond the borders of Germany. I would certainly have liked him to be more explicit, for example by invoking the historical antecedents of a German federation, St. Paul's in Frankfurt, and establishing a connection to a future German federated state, but he likes to keep things vague, and it works for him. All in all, this turned out to be a historic party convention.

Soon after Willy's speech, Loest's son took me to St. Nicholas's Church, by which time the delegates were caught up in a series of votes again. And outdoors this unsettling spring weather holds. In the evening, before my departure for Berlin, there is supposed to be a "cultural encounter" in the vestibule of the exhibition hall. Erich Loest, who turns sixty-four today, will join the SPD. I am supposed to speak again, but will limit myself to a birthday tribute.

And "The Call of the Toad"? My refuge during the breaks in the action. My bottled-up longing to return to pacing without interruption in front of my desk, muttering to myself, chewing on sentences until they taste just right, whether my pipe is cold or warm.

Berlin, 25 February 1990

My birthday tribute to Loest never happened, because the wrap-up party was going to take place too late, so I left for Berlin around six. Grüning, who came to pick me up, told me about himself during the drive to the station and later offered a sort of confession (as Pezold had done in Leipzig), saying that although he had not been a member of the Party, he had received favorable treatment because he was a friend of Sindermann's son. He also justified his duplex apartment, very large by GDR standards: because he often had important visitors from the West, Minister of Culture Hoffmann gave him this large apartment with a guest room, which I am now occupying. At last a shower. Later Christoph Hein and his wife came by. We stayed up late.

Leipzig, 26 February 1990

So much to add about the last few days. But I am too tired. Maybe the whole trip, with three events in two days, the reading of "Writing after Auschwitz" in Berlin, the appearance in Neubrandenburg with Baby Sommer, and the reading today (*The Plebeians* in Leipzig), was too much for my sixty-two years after all. I hope I shall find time and energy tomorrow, before I head for Dresden, to do some catching up. Just one thing before I turn in: today, unmistakable during the drive from Neubrandenburg to Leipzig, the fifth storm in this month of February. Apparently there were more than thirty deaths again; and even the Shrove Monday parade in Cologne, which usually nothing can disrupt, was affected. With the German-German bickering continuing unabated, I doubt that any attention will be paid to this radical change in the climate, which is now undeniable.

Leipzig, 27 February 1990

Among all the smaller happenings, back to the morning in Berlin: the gathering on Sunday in the State Opera's Apollo Hall. Hein's fine introduction. The audience looking so bourgeois. Veronika with Helene, Fritze with Chana, Maria Sommer, all present. I don't see Ingrid Krüger and Nele. Apparently my speech strikes a chord. It is to be broadcast, published. An interview with the East German program *Aktuelle Kamera*. A dinner, the government picking up the tab, as in the privileged old days. In addition to my lady publishers and Helmut Frielinghaus, the publishers Faber, Gruner, and Marquardt are there. And Minister of Culture Keller, who seems exhausted and depressed, while I am apparently the only one convinced that we will not have reunification in the form of annexation to the Federal Republic. When I respond to Keller's mournful after-dinner speech and try to cheer up Christoph Hein and Christa Wolf, I am apparently violating the general mood of resignation. Next to me, my little Helene sits in silence, the exotic vegetarian. (As I am writing this, Führer is whistling in the hall, the unshakably joyful Christian, who again served up biblical quotations at breakfast.)

The drive from Berlin to Neubrandenburg through economically devastated villages and towns: Fürstenberg, Neustrelitz. In

Oranienburg, signs pointing to the former Sachsenhausen concentration camp. Tumbledown Red Army barracks. Here and there a Soviet soldier, apparently left behind. The driver, a young, wisecracking Berliner, was a member of the SED, recently left the Party, but is voting for the PDS, a constructive measure, he explains, the idea being to strengthen the anticipated SPD government by providing a strong opposition. The pleasant, rolling landscape, full of lakes, around Neubrandenburg, which we reach around five P.M.

Baby Sommer has set up his instruments in the teacher-training college, in a new building recently dedicated by Margot Honecker. Before that, to the SPD office, a rundown apartment in an older building, formerly used by the National Front. After several phone calls, the National People's Army agrees to provide spotlights for our performance.

It is fun to be rehearsing and performing again with Baby Sommer. Afterward a discussion with the SPD candidate (a pastor) and the audience. A big success in a modest setting.

At the end of the war, Neubrandenburg was completely destroyed. Only the city wall was left standing, punctuated by pretty little half-timbered houses that would be pleasant to live in.

A comrade who looks like a Hungarian Pandur puts me up for the night. He lives in a new building with a view of allotment gardens and, in the distance, an industrial complex. Close to midnight, the speech I gave in the morning is broadcast over the radio. I listen because I seldom have the chance to hear myself. I am sleeping in the daughter's room. His wife is a doctor, and he is a traffic planner. The marriage suffers because he is so involved with the Party.

I get an earful about that when we set out at eleven in the morning for Leipzig, by way of Berlin. Another confession. This time a youthful-seeming fifty-year-old who was not a member of the SED and paid the price. His constant fear of spies, extending all the way to the Party leadership. Anxiety about productivity pressure in a future society dominated by the deutschmark.

During the five-hour drive under stormy conditions he clutches the steering wheel. The tin-can car visibly bending under the buffeting. From north to south. This wounded, mournful, gray country.

Then, at four-fifteen, my reading at Karl Marx University. The hall not completely filled due to inadequate publicity. I read scenes from *The Plebeians*. The discussion afterward drags on, moderated too diffidently by Pezold.

Today, after lunch, departure by local train for Dresden with an hour's delay; waiting in Leipzig's cavernous, bare main station, like a relic from the past. The reading I did yesterday will have to be edited down for my appearance at the Leipzig Book Fair on 13 March. It is inconceivable that this GDR, a country retarded in every sense, can simply be annexed without social tensions and explosions. Besides, there seems to be no will on the part of West Germany to undertake far-reaching investments. We must make use of the predictable delay. Since yesterday it has cooled down, and, fool that I am, I left my winter coat in Berlin with Veronika.

Dresden, 28 February 1990
Yesterday when I got off the train in Dresden-Neustadt, no one was there to meet me.

The drafty main concourse. In the cold, damp weather the drab sameness of the clothing bespoke poverty. Here and there children in garish Carnival costumes, their faces streaked with color. An

Ensor-like atmosphere. Because the costumes lacked the store-bought slickness you would see in the West, they looked authentic and scary.

Finally I called Baby Sommer. He was on his way from the main station, where he had expected me to get off, and it was a good while before he arrived to take me, by then frozen through, to the Dresden radio station, located in the Museum of Hygiene. A half-hour discussion that was broadcast in the evening. I warned once more against annexation in the guise of unification, and pointed to Auschwitz as an inescapable imperative.

The train trip alone, in a first-class compartment. The windows dirty, the gray countryside godforsaken, its factories ripe for the wrecking ball, the cowering villages looking as though they had been spared only by chance. Suddenly snow flurries. All at once a searing wish to be back in Portugal with my cactuses, to which I feel closer than to this cold, alien land.

Late in the evening, a conversation with Baby and his wife, she a paragon of strength, competence, and Protestant-socialist sternness. He: evasive, anxious, always on the lookout for ways to duck out. Yet the two of them cling to each other like burrs, also chained to their house, this two-story Biedermeier-ish doll's house, a testament to their marital obsession with collecting. Later friends come by for coq au vin, a sculptor and his wife. They all see themselves in desperate straits, fear the grasping hand of the West at the same time as they long for it, though it will certainly bring a new form of paternalism. They bemoan the fact that the SED is still lurking everywhere, more likely to sell dilapidated houses to Westerners than to GDR citizens. Soon, all too soon, a colonial ruling class will have its tentacles everywhere.

After a restless, stormy night, a late breakfast. Now we are about to drive to Bautzen, where Veronika and Helene will meet us. I was there at New Year's in 1973–74, when Veronika was pregnant with Helene and there was no end to the quarreling.

Dresden-Radebeul, 1 March 1990
Back in Bautzen, the path along the old city wall, St. Nicholas Cemetery in ruins, the Sorbian Museum and the Sorb woman, thoroughly Kashubian in manner, who gives us a guided tour: there are still about seventy thousand Sorbs here. Many villages swallowed up by the soft-coal mining. The eerily fixed expressions of the cloth dolls in traditional Sorbian dress. The public dislikes these dolls. Sorbian translations of the Bible. The Old Town still there, if in total disrepair, a hodgepodge of houses. How will it look once Western money arrives, ten years from now, let us say?

Visiting friends of Veronika's who live along the wall, then a

56

rendezvous with Veronika, Helene, Katharina, and Stefano. The Hentschke daughters are debating whether they should take over their father's construction company.

The event in a cinema. A full house. First Stefano conducts an interview for *Espresso*. Baby and I are in a good mood and focused. The panel discussion with two representatives of the local Social Democratic Party and with audience participation: well received. All the questions reveal uncertainty, anxiety. Apparently the DSU, along with the CSU, is attracting support at the expense of the Social Democrats. The smears — identifying the SPD with the former SED — are working.

The grumpy waitress at the White Horse. Then talking with friends until after midnight. Helene cornering Baby. Veronika enjoys having me there in her hometown. Driving back late to Radebeul. (On the drive to Bautzen, the diseased forests.)

After a long sleep, reports on the radio this morning of the fifth, or is it already the sixth, hurricane, wreaking particular havoc in Swabia and Bavaria: paths of destruction through the Black Forest. Afterward I drive with Heidrun Sommer to Dresden. We visit Eberhard Göschel. In an emptied-out apartment he paints delicate pictures with a palette knife, not that different from works by Westerners. He reports on the situation from his chronic oppositional perspective. Everywhere he sees old conformists in new roles, including Hubertus Giebe.

Later with Heidrun to the state puppet theater, a charming historic building that in the West would have been shut down because of its dilapidation. Some artists, Göschel among them, are considering taking over the theater, along with the restaurant and adjacent spaces. This is where our performance will be today.

Strange: the likelihood that I will write "The Call of the Toad" is increasing, along with the growing danger that the right wing, with the DSU in the lead, will win the election. Once again, is literature possible only from the perspective of losers?

In the center of Dresden the destruction from the war still much in evidence. By contrast, the backward and poverty-stricken but unscathed world at the foot of the vineyards in Radebeul. Middle-class villas, wineries . . .

Dresden-Radebeul, 2 March 1990

Yesterday's event with Baby Sommer in the Dresden puppet theater went well. Because it was his hometown, Sommer even had stage fright. From the discussion that followed, as well as the conversations before and after, I could see that in the GDR the right-wing mentality that used to be buried but is now bubbling to the surface is even more raw and powerful than I had feared: nationalistic, xenophobic, anti-Semitic, crassly materialistic, and altogether intolerant. The predicted majority for the SPD is seriously in jeopardy. An additional factor is that all the groups that for so long kept their heads down in silent opposition and finally pushed the change through are now exhausted, drained of initiative, full of suspicion toward outsiders and each other.

Amid all these new impressions the news that in Nicaragua the Sandinistas have lost the election had less impact. Now, with the Soviet Union severely weakened, this small, unfortunate country will be completely under the sway of the USA.

The last station on this trip, Karl-Marx-Stadt, soon to be Chemnitz once more, is next.

Karl-Marx-Stadt, 2 March 1990

The huge head of Marx in front of the district council building. It is to be sold, the proceeds going to finance the restoration of the city's name. The event in the museum, with a snack beforehand in one of the exhibition halls. The museum director is a former SED member. He speaks of it openly, but with some embarrassment. Recently Kohl was here and asked the masses, in the style of Goebbels at the Berlin Sports Palace, "Do you want German unity? Do you want our prosperity?" It does not get any more vulgar than that.

Behlendorf, 4 March 1990

Yesterday, back to Berlin from Dresden, initially through snow flurries. Heidrun Sommer drove me in her West German car because she had documents to deliver to a printer on Stuttgarter Platz. In the house on Niedstrasse Beatrice was sitting, knitting baby clothes. She is going to deliver soon. The *Kennzeichen D* TV recordings were canceled because I've had too much exposure on television recently, and so forth.

With Nele and Ingrid Krüger I played a round of Ludo. Nele won. Ingrid has resigned from Luchterhand; she had reasons enough. During the train trip from Berlin to Büchen I began reading the proofs for the paperback Steidl will be bringing out, *Streit ums einig Vaterland* ("Contested German Fatherland"). Augstein has made only minor changes. Ute met me in Büchen. She made note of an expression for GDR coffins that I could use in "The Call of the Toad": "earth furniture."

And today back in my studio. I finished and put fixative on the two drawings that were almost done when I left. Spread drawings out to look over. How quickly I feel at home again.

In the afternoon Channel 3 carried Stephan Lohr's coverage of the conference in Tutzing. Lohr thinks the ideas on confederation I presented are gaining in importance because the challenges of and resistance to unity through simple annexation are becoming increasingly apparent. That may be true. What I am more afraid of is a bad outcome for the elections, which have been moved up to 18 March.

Nele wants a dog for her birthday. I am going to write her a letter to head that off, because a dog is a four-legged companion that is not only devoted but also dependent, as witness our bundle of fur, Kara.

Behlendorf, 5 March 1990

On *Aktuelle Kamera* I saw a feature on the election, in which the Greens and the Women's League are participating. The round table has adopted a social platform and called for a ministry for women's affairs. Two weeks before the election certain facts are being established that the new government can use as points of departure: a right to housing, tenants' protections, free schooling, a right to free school meals, nursery schools, etc. Respect for political entities that, despite the whipped-up chaos, quietly and calmly set about passing resolutions. One of the participants was folding an origami crane.

In the afternoon my sister came by with a friend, bringing enough pastries for twelve and the list of people she wants invited to her sixtieth birthday. Hans brought me a litho stone and picked up the corrected proofs of the debate with Augstein. I mounted two sheets of paper but have not yet found the energy to start drawing.

Behlendorf, 6 March 1990

I am writing to the druggist Voigt in Leipzig to ask whether he can put us up on the eighteenth; for the Leipzig round table he invited us to stay in his guesthouse. We drove to Lübeck to buy a dark blue linen suit for me. The stormy weather continues. Also a new low-pressure system is supposed to be making its way here from the northern Atlantic. The damage to the forests from six major storms is incalculable; I could add a whole "live wood" project. But I am still working on dead wood — for instance, an image in vertical format. I also got started on a small litho for the limited edition of *Dead Wood*.

Behlendorf, 8 March 1990

Yesterday in Hamburg visited F. J. Raddatz with Gerd and the Fechners. A depressing evening: painful to watch a friend feeding his newfound nationalism with CDU accusations directed against Brandt and Bahr. Is it his own brief time in the GDR that he is trying to compensate for with a convert's zeal? It is this attitude that turned parts of his interview with Minister of Culture Keller into an interrogation. What makes him comment, in reference to me, that the "German question" drives wedges between friends or even destroys friendships?

Steidl brought proofs of *Dead Wood*. Today I made decisions on the order and the captions. I continue with the large-format drawings. The suspicion that Schnur, the chairman of DA, was a Stasi spy will probably affect the rest of the campaign, despite his denials.

Behlendorf, 10 March 1990

Shortly before we set out for Schwerin. The day before yesterday, Oswald Nell-Breuning said at the party for his hundredth birthday, "So much to be grateful for! But the egotists are spoiling everything again." The relationship between the GDR and the BRD since the revolution could not be summed up more succinctly.

Yesterday the Bissingers and Müllers came over for pheasant

and wild duck, served with potato dumplings and sauerkraut simmered with white wine and pineapple. The dreadful prospect is gradually dawning on us that the DSU (and with it the CDU bloc, which only yesterday was still conformist) could emerge as the strongest party, ahead of the SPD, on 18 March. Spoke on the phone with Hans Werner Richter, who by the end of the conversation had forgotten what I had said at the beginning. He wants to be the one to issue the invitations to Prague.

Must keep my eye on what is happening in Lithuania, in Wilna, for "The Call of the Toad." The increasingly nationalistic mentality is making the Polish cemetery in Wilna problematic. I am setting out with mixed emotions.

Did a sketch right after the border crossing near Mustin: a dead birch forest.

Schwerin, 11 March 1990

> *After little sleep:*
> *Loudspeakers all through the land,*
> *Unity their command.*
> *Keep silent: the watchword now,*
> *Lest we fail to hear*
> *Each other, and also*
> *The next storm warning.*

Schwerin, 12 March 1990

My reading in the lovely theater, followed by a lively discussion. By now I have the entire text of *The Plebeians* at my fingertips.

In the evening, a noisy SPD youth event with a fat talkmaster from North German Broadcasting. Afterward to the theater: an astonishing production with Free German Youth songs and folksongs: nostalgic and ambivalent. The macabre reversal of the rosy-cheeked optimism of those Free German Youth songs — "Build up, build up!" — or of the folksongs: "Now adieu, beloved home-land" or "Where can my dearest Christian be, in Hamburg or in Bremen." The older actors sang the FGY songs against a backdrop of blown-up photos of youths. Our hosts, Herr and Frau Ürkwitz — she is a secretary at the theater — have a dry, naïve sense of humor; he is a good-natured, incessant talker: "That was back in Adolf-Nazi-days . . ."

From Schwerin to Leipzig, 13 March 1990

Just beyond Schwerin, cranes in a field. Yesterday went on a tour of the city after our visit to the museum: seventeenth- and eigh-teenth-century Dutch painters, then, in the prints section, wood-cuts, lithos, and etchings by Kollwitz's *Weavers' Revolt*. A lovely image: *The Consultation*.

In the part of town known as the Schelfstadt, morbid old half-timbered houses that could certainly be restored. The Pastor's Pond, around which the protest march with candles took place in '89. A row of neoclassical façades. In the center of town, a depart-ment store from the twenties. Walking around the monstrosity of a castle. The romantic boat landing in natural stone. The mish-mash of styles anticipates postmodernism.

Then a discussion in the Cultural Union building: "Quo vadis culture?" Concepts and plans that refuse to recognize the real po-litical situation. Wiek, the dramaturge, urges me to make a few re-marks. I point out the need to ban motorboats if they really want to attract "gentle tourism." Guidelines for historic preservation that impose appropriate costs on new developers. The gathering's obvious fear of recognizing the political realities.

After a nap, an evening event in the parish hall. I read from *The Rat,* with discussion following. The aggressive cantor. No mercy for Honecker from older "Christians."

Leipzig, 14 March 1990

The *Plebeian* reading in Leipzig — definitely the best thus far — in the Gewandhaus's chamber music hall was not followed by a discussion because no one spoke up. My lady publishers, both present, cannot stand up to Faber, the head of Aufbau Verlag. Spent time with Kurt Masur, whose optimism is full of purpose. (Shortly before my reading, Helmut Schmidt held an election rally here.) The small savings accounts are to be revalued at 1:1 — Kohl's contribution to the campaign. Grotesque that at the book fair here I am associated with three publishing houses: in addition to Luchterhand and Aufbau, there is now Linden plus Steidl. The debate with Augstein is selling well. That is how fast things happen when small publishers swing into action.

Book fair commotion in the morning. With Erich Loest in the booth behind the Linden display: two tough old cart horses.

Yesterday, during the trip from Schwerin to Leipzig: the trees that fell after the last storm, named Wiebke. Now on to Wittenberg.

From Wittenberg to Stralsund, 15 March 1990

By car from Leipzig to Wittenberg, past battered forests and villages, with DSU (or CSU) posters everywhere. The water level in the Elbe is way up. At the seminary Friedrich Schorlemmer is waiting for me, an activist full of enthusiasm about everything, including himself: clever, articulate, brave to the point of folly. He shows me the handsome inner courtyard, then the Luther House and Museum. Impressive: the room in which Luther entertained friends and family with his "table talk" and speeches, "promptly recorded." A smaller room in the museum is allotted to Luther's failure in the face of the Peasants' Revolt.

Later, word comes that Schnur has admitted his role as a Stasi collaborator and, at the urging of the CDU, has resigned from his position as chairman of the DA. A repetition of the Barschel affair? Maybe a slight weakening of the Alliance and stabilization of the SPD.

The performance with Baby Sommer before an audience of about two hundred turned out well, as did the subsequent discussion. The caretaker, crusty at first, then obsequious, complains about the food served at the House of Culture, catered by the state-run cafeteria and usually cold. Like all buildings in the GDR, this one is overheated.

Afterward to Schorlemmer's. He has been leading a bachelor existence since his wife left him. (He says the Stasi wanted to recruit her, and later she came under the influence of Western feminists, which led to their breakup.) Here, too, complaints about the loss of the initial momentum toward democracy. The young man from the Black Pump collective who simply turned up at Schorlemmer's, touchingly helpless in his wire-rimmed glasses.

I sleep soundly, and when the alarm clock wakes me, I don't know where I am. Buy an Eastern edition of the *tageszeitung* at the railroad station. A mocking, even insulting tone toward the Social Democrats, but no indication of whom the paper might be backing. Solidarity on the left? Because the weather outside is so springlike, I venture to predict the election outcome:

SPD, 33%; Alliance 90, 5%; Greens + Women, 4%
DSU, 3%; DA, 5%; CDU, 37%
PDS, 12%; Liberals, 4%; Peasants' Party, 3%

Stralsund, at the Cultural Union House

First a walk to the dock where the White Fleet ties up, across from Rügen, then through the crumbling town. Here, too, the SPD has been pushed aside by the Alliance and the PDS. Conversations on the street reveal the uncertainty prevailing among younger people as well.

The view from my window of the Stralsund Bodden, the open sea, and Rügen. Across the way a tumbledown warehouse.

Ute is not here yet. Before they call me to supper, I want to lie down for an hour and — to put it nicely — think my own thoughts.

Stralsund, 16 March 1990

Last night we had dinner at the home of Dr. Müller, a physician. Ute joined us. He, too — a former SED member — immediately begins to talk about himself, reproaching himself, explaining his actions.

The path along the eastern shore to Schillstrasse, Fährstrasse. I'd forgotten to take the house key. A young woman opens the door. Ute and I both have trouble falling asleep. I wonder whether the

Schnur scandal plus the little Ebeling scandal will slow the rush to join the Alliance.

Today in town: St. Nicholas's restored in garish colors. Figures atop columns painted with vivid faces. Then to the archives and library of the St. John Monastery. The beautiful ruins of the church forming an open space for concerts and theater performances. The smokehouse, at one time an old-age home, the cloister, the Franciscan monks' refectory splendidly restored. The two courtyards ringed with half-timbered houses and cottages, some inhabited, some falling down. A young man named Links, with a wife and two children, a goldsmith by trade, his brother a publisher of children's books, has just purchased three uninhabited houses for only 2,000 marks. Now he is looking for bank loans to fix them up. I make him an offer — for Ute's sake as well.

Leipzig, 18 March 1990
In five and a half hours Ute drives us from Stralsund to Leipzig, where we are staying with Armin Voigt and his family, who live in Wiederitzsch. A house like something Wagner might have dreamed up, but the creation of a druggist! The swimming pool, for example. From April on, it is supposed to be heated by solar panels. Around the pool, to the left and right of a larger-than-life Christ figure, stand six saints, among them the Evangelists. The roof is supported by slender Doric stuccoed columns. As Voigt puts it, the Hellenistic element is supposed to be fused with the Christian. The sandstone sculptures (late nineteenth century) come from St. Mark's, destroyed by SED bigwigs (as were other churches). In the garden next to the pond a bronze head of Goethe, one and a half meters high, which was slated to be melted down. But Voigt swapped it for copper. A candelabra, also in the garden,

was to be sold along with other candelabras to a buyer in Holland, but Voigt persuaded the shipper to let part of it fall into a pond, from which Voigt later rescued it. Two labradorite columns from the cemetery, a porphyry basin (Rochlitz), etc. In the house an assortment of carpet tiles as floor covering. Everything has a history, as Voigt says. And the stories he tells sound like Udo Steinke tales. The failure of his joint-venture schemes. His good-natured wife, who puts up with his restlessness, smiling indulgently. Everywhere he constructs places to sit, yet never sits down himself.

Later we meet the Suhls at the Hotel Merkur and have an expensive meal (book fair prices) at the Milano. The taxi driver who brings us back to the Voigts' has made up his mind to vote for the CDU. "Money is what we need, money. It doesn't matter how we get it, the main thing is, we get it."

We await the election results with a sinking feeling.

Leipzig, 19 March 1990

And it turned out worse than expected. The Social Democrats' defeat and the victory of the Alliance with the CDU bloc are so lopsided as to be grotesque. We were in Democracy House on Bernhard-Göring-Strasse. First with the Greens, then with Alliance 90. The young people's disappointment was subdued; apparently they are used to being marginalized.

Behlendorf, 21 March 1990

Only now have I pulled myself together. After the long trip back from Leipzig, driving past the vineyards on the banks of the Unstrut, through the unwooded part of Thuringia, past Mühlhausen and the border, then first to Nienhagen, where we stopped to see Franz on his farm and had bread and cheese with malt coffee and showed the Suhls the cheese room, we finally reached Behlendorf late at night. Nice to find drawings almost finished and (today) start on two new ones: still dead wood.

Back to Election Sunday in Leipzig. By St. Nicholas's side door, pasted to a corrugated-tin construction fence, is a sticker with a blue border and blue lettering, in the style of a street sign: "Suckers Square. The children of October send greetings. Yes, we are still here." Am thinking of writing a polemical piece with the title "The View from Suckers Square" and dedicating it to the children of October. First, a discussion of the bloc parties' victory and their legacy; next, a definition of "fear voters" (our taxi driver); third, a send-up of Kohl's notions of destiny and the hour of destiny; fourth, a definition of the good old German stench as an omen of misfortune; fifth, dismay at the Social Democrats' pusillanimousness and criticism of the hasty whitewashing of the SED/PDS; sixth, a description of the children of October during election night; and seventh, an attempt at suggesting a way out.

Behlendorf, 24 March 1990
Feeling lousy. Today went to the doctor's in Lübeck. The Suhls left yesterday: the grotesque evening with them in Lübeck's Schiffergesellschaft, crowded with tour organizers, very bourgeois. There was soup, corned beef mash, red fruit compote, red wine . . . and the Travemünde Seamen's Chorus singing sentimental oldies: "Come back soon, my bonny boy."

Since the election everything is crumbling, becoming trivial and stale. Stoltenberg and the interminable submarine affair. The unknown number of former Stasi agents who are now deputies in the East German parliament. The wavering of the SPD-East between opposition and coalition (without the DSU). And

Oskar's inadequacy as a candidate, because the only position he knows how to take is to say no. To make things worse, growing nationalism in Lithuania and Romania, and among the Serbs and Albanians.

Am trying to get back to "The Call of the Toad." Bargain Eastern cremations in Potsdam for West Berliners; thus burials in Poland (in the German cemetery) could be cheaper than a normal burial in the West, even with transportation costs. Role reversal: the widow is the practical one, the widower unworldly.

Tomorrow I am off to Berlin.

Berlin, 26 March 1990

Mountains of mail again. Beatrice big-bellied and contented, expecting the baby any day now, if not any hour. Ingrid seems rather dejected: her sister's death coincides with other problems. Yesterday took part in a television round table in East Berlin: Stephan Hermlin in profile next to a beautiful Russian harpist. I secretly asked a photographer to take a picture for me. The most convincing speaker was old Heym, while Heiner Müller came across as lukewarm and habitually cynical. Rolf Schneider well informed, neither fish nor fowl. I could have spared myself the attack on Kant, particularly as he was not there. For Ute I ordered the theme music of *Aktuelle Kamera,* now off the air.

Before the show I made one call after another, as if it were the most normal thing in the world, to Ingrid, then Veronika, then Ute, and finally Anna. Not until later did I realize what I had done. Nele wants to get her hair cut short.

In the Schleswig-Holstein local elections the SPD picked up a bare 2 percent of the vote, making it the strongest party, because the CDU lost accordingly, though not appreciably; it must have benefited from the election in the GDR.

Behlendorf, 1 April 1990

Bruno is turning twenty-five and wants to come by this afternoon with his daughter, Ronja, and Susan, the mother, to see the first fruit trees in bloom. Everything is blooming too early and all at once: daffodils, cowslips, tulips . . .

The week in Berlin was quite something: Ingrid Krüger caught between the death and the funeral of her sister, the mountains of mail. Long-distance call to the harpist in East Berlin, the reading on Friday at the State Library (*Show Your Tongue*) before a cultivated bourgeois audience from East and West Berlin, the visit from the Links brothers, my loan of 10,000 marks to the one who is a goldsmith, the evening with Veronika and Helene: dancing with my blooming daughter, who led. Up late with Katharina and Stefano.

And then the Federal Bank announces that the probable exchange rate will be 1:2, and Kohl's election scam becomes unmistakable: the GDR turned to charkohl. To make things worse, the never-ending Stasi revelations. I am supposed to go to Poland with Weizsäcker. Receive an honorary doctorate in Poznań. And then Stephan Lohr asks me to come to Loccum for the annual meeting of the Academy; perhaps I could pick up where I left off in the Tutzing speech, under the heading of "Politics and Obstinacy," thereby proving my own obstinacy: first, the mindless annexation; second, the deutschmark election; third, homespun nationalism in a period of great mobility; fourth, the erstwhile loss of the German colony in southwest Africa and the recent gain of a colony, Germany East; fifth, the battle over Articles 23 and 146, the blessings of a constitution for our times, a multicultural nation; sixth, how one moves from a confederated, constitution-generating state to a federated constitutional state; seventh, only at the end, the rule of the deutschmark.

Behlendorf, 7 April 1990

Am writing this after the trip to Göttingen on 2 April, where I worked with Steidl until two in the morning, setting the captions for *Dead Wood,* an almost playful process, because he has the technology to enlarge or reduce the font effortlessly. We took a break for two hours so I could have supper with Franz, whose latest idea is to pipe the whey from his cheese-making operation into his bathtub, because of its health-enhancing properties.

Went early the next morning to Munich, where I met with Walter Höllerer at Hans Werner and Toni Richter's place to lay plans for the Group 47 trip at the end of May. Richter's feat of forgetting the beginning of every sentence as he is reaching the end. The way he plays up his senior moments. At the same time, a perfect memory for the period when he was a bookseller's apprentice in Berlin in the 1920s. In the end, he admitted he was looking forward to Prague.

After that (return flight to Hamburg, dinner with Ute and Bruno), back in Behlendorf. Peace, solitude, awareness of the futility of my political endeavors: resolve to speak out from now on, only because something absolutely must be said. That goes for the Wewelsfleth Discussion. Astonishing how quickly Björn Engholm has turned cynical. Apparently political power fulfills the clichéd image we have of it. Already, despite some verbal hedging, he is coming around to supporting Article 23 of the Basic Law, the annexation clause. The way he brushes off the young leftists. Also the way he dismisses my own objections as "literary comments." On the other hand, the young Social Democrat from the GDR (Matschie) so refreshing.

"The Call of the Toad" will have to wait. Am still doing large-scale drawings of dead wood. P.S.: On 1 April, Bruno's birthday, Rosanna was born. Weighing four kilos three hundred grams. The very next day Raoul brought his Beatrice home to the house on Niedstrasse.

Behlendorf, 8 April 1990

I am drawing my way back into the Upper Harz, into the Erz Mountains. Meanwhile, mixed news reports: the newly elected Volkskammer is meeting for the first time (on 5 April). A Norwegian ferry catches fire in the Oslofjord, 140 killed. Elections going on everywhere: in Peru, Slovenia, Bulgaria, Hungary.

I hope that between Cottbus, Spremberg, and Senftenberg I can free myself of the dead wood obsession.

Have accepted the invitation to Loccum, but will not outline my speech until the end of April (Berlin), and will then write it between the beginning and middle of May. Make my point in seven pages.

Yesterday Günter de Bruyn came to supper with Pastor Harig: asparagus, boiled potatoes, smoked ham. Ute and de Bruyn immediately got into an animated conversation about heliotropes and other plants mentioned by Fontane. (Whenever I am not working regularly on a manuscript and drawing has the upper hand, my spelling gets shaky.)

This evening the discussion with de Bruyn and Loest is scheduled to take place at St. Peter's: Germany ad nauseam, singly and times two.

Behlendorf, 9 April 1990

And that is how it turned out. In cold St. Peter's with a miserable sound system. Loest felt compelled to call me "the nation's pessimist," but then went on to describe developments in the GDR in bleak terms. Günter de Bruyn made a point of taking a position different from mine, despite our fundamental agreement. Is this an instance of writers vying for attention? The minute the discussion goes public, two even-tempered colleagues, of whom I am fond, emphasize the distance between us, which in turn provokes me into emphasizing the distance they have talked into existence. A dispirited and dispiriting trio. No less depressing when I woke up this morning.

Behlendorf, 11 April 1990

On the telephone: Ingrid is dejected. After her sister's death, she and Nele went to celebrate the eighty-third birthday of her mother, who is unable either to register her daughter's death or to recognize her living daughter and her daughter.

Tomorrow the government of the first freely elected Volkskammer is to be sworn in.

In the next-to-last issue of *Der Spiegel* an article about market-savvy funeral parlors: postmodern coffins.

And tomorrow it's time for a change: am off to a football game with Bruno: St. Pauli against Stuttgart.

From Büchen to Berlin, 16 April 1990

On the road again after twelve days in Behlendorf: near Cottbus in the soft-coal region. Perhaps by drawing the landscape here I can work my way out of my preoccupation with dead wood. The last twelve large charcoal drawings, plus two drawings in ink extracted from unusually early inky caps found in our orchard, actually make for a nice conclusion.

I am only moderately curious to see how the GDR has fared since the 18 March elections. In the meantime, the "Grand Coalition" has formed, and I am not especially hopeful that it will develop sufficient backbone to assert itself against the Bonn government. Now that Lithuania probably cannot escape a trade war, the next few days will most likely bring a crisis. The Americans' stereotype of the enemy might well prove accurate again. The Georgians and the Ukrainians will also try to take advantage of Moscow's weakness — a situation that could spawn a whole litter of dangers.

Bruno, Malte, and Hans were in Behlendorf for Easter. Ute managed to shoo the boys and me out into the rain-soaked garden to hunt for Easter eggs. Bruno, who had left earlier, would certainly have joined in. Spoke with Laura on the phone: it looks as though Ralf has a good chance of landing a regular job with Bärenreiter: one less thing to worry about. I remind Laura of the trip to America we took together almost a year ago.

For "The Call of the Toad," the increase in nationalist fervor in Lithuania and the risk it poses to the Polish cemetery should be taken into consideration: only the German cemetery is flourishing!

Cottbus, 17 April 1990

Was met at Zoo Station. Two-hour drive to Cottbus. We eat with Metag (Jimi) at the Hotel Lusatia. Later sat and talked with Metag's girlfriend at the Cottbuser Hof. She is the head bookkeeper for a company that deals in bull and boar sperm. They both agree with me that the currency changeover (on 1 July?) will backfire because the West German marks (so fervently longed for) will immediately be spent on Western products and trips to the West — Paris, Italy, Spain — and will thus flow straight back to the West without stimulating the East German economy. On the contrary: all the goods produced here will become unsalable, companies will go under, including those that had the wherewithal to become profitable.

West German "investors" who come to look over GDR businesses are interested only in their sales figures. We can expect an army of West German corporate lawyers to swarm over the country (when the new states are established): colonial administrators. The people of the GDR will be duped yet again.

In the pedestrian zone a poster recruiting people to work on commission selling West German products, and advertising for warehouse space. Lovely (and as if from another planet) the art nouveau theater in Cottbus.

Cottbus, 18 April 1990
Made drawings on both sides of the village of Pritzen in two large soft-coal pits: the village, still in existence, perched on a land bridge. But the houses are crumbling, the village overdue for demolition. Pritzen lies just off the road to Senftenberg. When we drove to Senftenberg in the evening for the reading (*Plebeians*), I caught a glimpse, just before we reached the town, of the overgrown but still recognizable soft-coal pit near which I was wounded on 20 April 1945 on the way to Spremberg.

The sandy soil typical of the Brandenburg March. The pit in stark contrast to the lovely landscape. I dash off five drawings in the sun, which comes out between rain showers. Not until afternoon did I notice how intense the sun's rays were. Even the setting sun was alarming. I am certain that the protective ozone layer has been damaged more than we suspect, know, surmise. The lilacs are in bloom everywhere, six to eight weeks early.

Reading in Senftenberg, in the House of Culture. A good, thoughtful discussion afterward.

Written in the evening: today another five drawings near Spremberg, opposite Black Pump and Hoyerswerda. Large open-pit mines in which the power shovels disappear into the blackness like giant insects. The burning sun. The gas fumes from the Black

Pump works. I am worn out from drawing. Today Nele and Ingrid are coming with another woman, a friend of Ingrid's. An intense evening with Baby Sommer on the drums.

After a nap: my face is burning.

Cottbus, 19 April 1990

The performance with Baby Sommer almost fell through. He did not want to appear in a "dismal hole" like the youth center; that was asking too much of him. Egged on by Heidrun, he refused to step out onstage. She thought I could read some other selection to fill the time. Metag asked me for help. It proved not all that difficult to change Baby's mind, especially once Heidrun kept her mouth shut. A good (last) performance. Nele sat in the front row.

The first days under an overcast sky. Nele and Ingrid are coming along to see the soft-coal mining. Ingrid is still depressed, full of frenetic activity. Why does this intelligent, beautiful woman, difficult only because she is uncompromising, live alone? She has Nele, of course, but even so, she has to rely entirely on herself.

The last drawings in the large soft-coal pit to one side of the road to Senftenberg, ending with two drawings from the edge of the pit near the village of Altdöbern, an inviting spot with its castle and grounds. I plan to settle in there for a few days (with no car) and draw on-site. The large pit — impossible to miss, forty to forty-five meters deep — has seized hold of my imagination. Ingrid and Nele came along, and we had a cheery picnic on the rim of the pit, right by the garbage dump, where Nele discovered half of a dead horse.

Now an hour of peace and quiet — Nele and Ingrid have left — before I have to go to Hoyerswerda for a reading from *The Rat*.

Cottbus, 20 April 1990

Today it is forty-five years since I was in this area as a seventeen-year-old. Maybe it was not the exact spot, but I saw the very soft-coal pit, just outside Senftenberg, next to which I was wounded on Hitler's final birthday. The name of the village where a lance corporal and I were locked in a cellar, for being "absent without leave" (Schörner's orders), had stuck in my mind as "Peterlein," but its real name is Petershain, and it is located between Cottbus and Senftenberg. Here, on several days and in various places, it became clear that it was only by sheer chance that I survived.

Back to Berlin today on the Reich Railway.

From Berlin to Büchen, 21 April 1990

From one birthday to the next. Nele's table piled high with gifts: an only child. I arrived shortly after eight with *Brehm's Life of Animals,* the children's edition, then caught the train at 9:35. Ah, if it were not for this child, whom I love . . .

Stayed up late yesterday with Raoul and Beatrice. They don't want to get married until December, because of the government child support. Beatrice loved the silver necklace from India that Ute and I gave her to celebrate Rosanna's birth. I gave Raoul five hundred East German marks, my earnings from the readings. At first he was disappointed — only Western marks count! — but then he realized how special this gift was.

I am looking forward to the next two and a half days in Behlendorf, and to being with Ute. I will try to work on the fourteen sketches. The "Obituary" for *Dead Wood,* checking the page proofs. The German-German unification process is turning into a provincial farce, thanks to a pervasive paucity of ideas and political imagination. I am losing interest, and only anger keeps me involved. Nonetheless, I plan to find lodgings in Espenhain, near

Leipzig, and in Altdöbern next to the soft-coal mine. (I am fixated on drawing.) At the end of July, the beginning of August, let us say. My gaze is still drawn to the soft-coal pits. The cone-shaped slag heaps. Lakes formed by ground water. Above the entire scene the clanking of the conveyor belts. The excavators like giant insects. You see hardly any human beings, or only rarely. Then, suddenly, over the loudspeaker, a clear voice announcing, in a slight Berlin/Brandenburg accent, which conveyor belts are stopping or starting up. Two bucks in the midst of this lunar wasteland. I wonder how it looks here in a gale, a thunderstorm, at full moon. My eyes are tearing worse than they used to. Ever since Calcutta. Or is it a symptom of age?

Behlendorf, 22 April 1990
Exhausted after the birthdays and probably also the intensity of the short trip to Lusatia. The fourteen drawings, when I spread them out on the floor, look odd to me, but tomorrow I want to do one or two large-scale versions in pencil.

A rather long telephone conversation with Antje Vollmer. We want to meet in Loccum and hatch some plans.

Outside, spring has arrived, too early but obviously unimpressed by human dislocations. I recall the stillness in the soft-coal mines, which includes the constant noise of the conveyor belts; somehow they don't impair the stillness (because subordinate to it). I haven't had the energy or time to add sketches to this journal.

Lithuania ad infinitum: now under blockade. How is Poland reacting? With silence.

Behlendorf, 23 April 1990
Yesterday and today started on two large-scale drawings, in pencil and charcoal, of the soft-coal pit between Spremberg and

Hoyerswerda. Tomorrow back to Berlin. There I plan to draft the speech for Loccum: "The View from Suckers Square." First, the setting and the elections; second, the rule of the West German mark; third, the knee-jerk reactions of the political parties; fourth, the assertion of unity; fifth, the headlong rush to the currency union; sixth, the consequences; seventh, final suggestions from the perspective of the suckers. Growing familiarity with the GDR and alienation from the Federal Republic should also be worked in.

From Berlin to Büchen, 27 April 1990

A lively evening with Helene and the Schröter clan, but Veronika looked strained, especially next to her blooming daughters, Jette and Katharina. Stefano is sinking more and more into silence. Christoph, Veronika's first husband, a man of few words. The next day, dinner with Nele and Ingrid. Our friendly relationship thrives on distance. Then, on television, the news of the assassination attempt on Oskar Lafontaine, as if putting the final seal on the political situation. Later I had a hard time seeing his narrow escape as a blessing in disguise. Still unclear whether Oskar will have time to demonstrate that Emperor Kohl has no clothes. He lacks a clearly formulated position. When it comes to the political issues of the day, he is increasingly living from hand to mouth.

I had just dictated almost the whole speech for Loccum when Ute informed me that the conference there had been called off. Now I will revise the speech and make it an article. It still lacks a description of the sadness hovering over the entire GDR, which has also seized hold of me.

And yesterday a boys' night out with Peter Schneider and Delius. Schneider describes German shepherd dogs posted on the GDR's borders who are not alert because they have had too many handlers (the result of constant shift changes). Our conversation was relaxing because for the most part we think alike, which makes for a friendly atmosphere such as seldom occurs among writers.

And today, as I was organizing my papers in preparation for turning them over to Trautwein at the Academy of Arts, as my so-called living bequest, I found folders containing early plays — *The House of Cards, The Table* — texts I had completely forgotten. Also folders with unpublished poems. Some of them I should work into the studio volume.

Ingrid brought photos of the soft-coal pits. Also one with a red banner for the first of May that we found in the garbage dump on the edge of the pit.

Airport Holiday Inn, Cologne/Bonn, 1 May 1990

Flying out to Poland tomorrow with Weizsäcker. Since German Wings, a Burda airline, went bust, all I could get was a Lufthansa flight to Düsseldorf, and from there the CDU delegate Würzbach (formerly state secretary in the Ministry of Defense) gave me a lift in his chauffeured car.

A strange feeling to be all alone in the hotel, as Ute almost always comes with me on longer trips; even stranger to have dinner by myself: Argentine steak with Idaho potatoes, wrapped in aluminum foil and served with sour cream.

But actually I am still preoccupied with my drawings — soft-coal landscapes — and with the text of "The View from Suckers Square," which I revised over the past two days for publication next week in *Die Zeit*. My objection to implementation of the currency union at this particular time and without any economic adjustments in advance is based on the disaster I foresee. If the opposite should occur — that is, if the money stays in the East and the economy there begins to revive — I will be happy to admit that my political judgment is seriously flawed.

Am I looking forward to this trip to Poland? Hardly. No matter how strenuously the federal president tries in his speeches to reassure Poland, he can offer it no guarantees vis-à-vis Germany. Still, I am willing to be surprised. Nervous about the visit to Treblinka. The sun today disturbingly intense, as in Lusatia. More and more I am convinced that the damaged ozone layer is the cause. My eyes are watering, but it is probably a sign of age.

On the plane from Bonn to Warsaw, 2 May 1990
I am seated next to Dedecius. These strangely configured delegations on state visits to Poland: one or two people from the literary world — when Brandt went, it was Lenz and me — then representatives of the Church and the Prussian aristocracy, including this time, surprisingly, Countess Dönhoff, and no fewer than two Bismarcks, one of them a former director of the Goethe Institute, the other the chairman of the Pomeranian refugee organization. Interesting the way little brochures are handed out with instructions on protocol. All of us packed in like sardines. I am looking forward to hearing the Polish national anthem, the only one, so far as I know, that you can dance to. Dedecius says that Dombrowski, the marshal or general hailed in the anthem, had a German mother and spoke only broken Polish. Weizsäcker strolled through the cabin to chat with the guests. I wonder whether "The Call of the Toad" will come to mind again?

Upon our arrival, the usual military dance. We follow the limousines in a minibus. At ten forty-five to the Tomb of the Unknown Soldier, the laying of a wreath and an officer's speech about the Poles' defeats and victories. The tomb is all that is left of the former Saxon palace. Then we drive to the monument to the 1944 Warsaw Uprising: another wreath-laying. After that, for the guests only, to the Ministry of Art and Culture, and following that to the Parkova Guesthouse for lunch. Then a rest period. I catch up on sleep. Read Laurence Sterne's *Sentimental Journey* — and promptly the German-Polish lovers bring "The Call of the Toad" into view. This is just the kind of style I am looking for, one that slips easily from narrative description in letters into paraphrases of letters. The narrator would thus be in a position to depict the couple's end, the automobile accident: since they have both been robbed before the accident (with their letters among the things stolen), the police find no identification on them, nor any indication as to who they are. For that reason they are buried anonymously in a village cemetery. The narrator might find the letters at a flea market where stolen goods are fenced; or he is an Italian intellectual who has fallen on hard times and survives by stealing; or the story is simply told by the spirit of narrative — nothing is clear yet. But Sterne points in the right direction!

Poked my head into the minibar, which contained three bottles, nothing else. I thought I was pouring a glass of mineral water and found myself downing vodka, and a minute ago, instead of my cigarillo, I stuck half a pretzel stick in my mouth and sucked and sucked on it.

Went walking with Dedecius in Saxon Park, a generous expanse with many fine old trees, branching paths, lovers, everything well tended, reflecting no signs of Poland's economic condition. The palace of the kings of Saxony is being restored. The pleasant smell of tar. The obligatory Chopin monument in Polish sentimental style: the genius under a storm-tossed tree. Dedecius keeps whistling a passage from *Tannhäuser* and talks about his department at the university. We run into one of his colleagues who has a Polish wife; both teach in Darmstadt.

The subject of German-Polish cemeteries could produce a cheerful, impudent, easy-to-read book! Now off to dinner at the Hotel Victoria. Jaruzelski is our host.

On "The Call of the Toad": perhaps Reschke authored a historical monograph with the title *Connections Between Polish Immigration to the Ruhr Region and the Flowering of German Football.*

Warsaw, 3 May 1990

After the wreath-laying at the ghetto monument (with memories of Brandt kneeling there in December 1970) and at the monument on the square where Jews were loaded onto trucks, the drive to Treblinka in summery May weather. Shortly before we get to Treblinka I see, on the side of a wooden barn, a gallows, painted white, with a Star of David hanging from it. Maybe the horror, the incomprehensible reality of organized genocide directed at the Jews, can be sensed from the numbers, rough estimates that are not in agreement: one calculation says 800,000, another 1.3 million. The frenzied horde of journalists, milling around the idyllic landscape with their photographers, made it hard to concentrate.

After that, a late lunch, put on by the Europa Club at the Palais Jablonna. Adam Michnik splendidly drunk. Weizsäcker's overly beautiful speech, and Mazowiecki's grander speech. Both speeches would have benefited from critical discussion afterward. Quotation: "Not what Germans have done to the Poles, but what human beings have done to human beings."

After that, the book exhibition, once we had paraded across the marketplace in the Old Town, where gawking, clueless Poles surrounded us. Strange to see the underground edition of *The*

Tin Drum displayed behind glass like a precious relic. Then a packed reception for the Germans and a press conference by Weizsäcker, skillful but obviously cool to the core. I am wondering what the purpose of this visit is. Since it achieves nothing besides mutual expressions of a friendship that could fall apart tomorrow. Amazing to see the Poles, who must depend entirely on themselves, managing to keep going despite a host of problems that show no sign of diminishing, though there is certainly an element of con-artistry involved: the reception and banquet in the palace, the well-trained waiters, the grand old men of letters, their resistance — still in jail the day before yesterday, today the new aristocracy, shabby yet dashing. Would I want to be a Pole? I would rather be neither a Pole nor a German, just free to work on my drawings. Am going to have another vodka as a nightcap, and tomorrow Danzig/Gdańsk, where I was hatched.

From Warsaw to Danzig, 4 May 1990

Another lovely day, with a reprise of the military ballet at the airport. In the morning we drove in convoy to a civilian cemetery on the outskirts of Warsaw. There, surrounded by Polish civilian graves, a simple birch cross: apparently, in the course of construction, scraps of German uniforms were dug up, then buried here for the time being, since Poland has no German military cemeteries. Now visiting statesmen like Weizsäcker can lay their own wreaths in the presence of the press; woe to any politician who passes up this absurd cultic ceremony. Quite possibly the uniform scraps come from a Polish partisan, since the resistance fighters, lacking uniforms of their own, dressed in whatever they were able to capture from German soldiers.

Too little sleep. Woke up with puffy eyes.

It will probably be necessary to write "The Call of the Toad" from the vantage point of the year 2000, looking back at 1 November 1989 and the development of the German-Polish cemeteries after that date.

Landing at the Kashubian airport; Aunt Anna's farm was supposedly located where the runway is today. Lunch with Weizsäcker at our table: he is relaxed, and in conversation with a pastor immediately falls into the official Lutheran Church Convention phraseology with which he is so familiar. Afterward a short stroll with Dedecius and others, with me as the tour guide, to the Frauengasse and the Brotbänkengasse. Then on to St. Bridget's and the Solidarność monument. Pastor Jankowski, corpulent and smug. Wałęsa also bursting with self-satisfaction these days. The president's discussion with students at Oliva University. Good questions, the answers too pat. In front of the Oliva cathedral my Kashubian relatives are arrayed: Marija and her husband, Kazimir and his wife, joined a bit later by Agnes with her husband. We chat and laugh in the sunshine, while inside the concert is in progress.

What will stick in my mind is the excursion to the Westerplatte on a naval minelayer. There the German national anthem is played; I am horrified. The ocean liner *Schleswig* was anchored here in '39, but where exactly? The Bismarck brother jabbering military nonsense.

Danzig, before departure for Mohrungen, 5 May 1990
Please, no more after-dinner speeches that assign every problem to a united Europe for solution. More and more optimistic platitudes, leaving no room for ironic asides.

Stayed up late drinking vodka with Antek and Max.

Flight from Danzig to Cologne, 5 May 1990
Traveling all this sunny day on the presidential bus through the lowlands, across the Vistula and through the Werder — magnificent pollarded willows, the sense of breadth, of childhood, green and more green, then passing Elbing on the way to Mohrungen, to the Herder Museum in Dohna Castle and on to Frauenburg, where we climbed the Copernicus Tower and lunched with the bishop. To cap off the visit, the dedication of a new waterworks near Elbing, and then to the airport.

The view from the tower across the Frisches Haff toward Kahlberg, and on the right toward the Soviet border. (This part of East Prussia will be cut off as soon as Lithuania becomes independent.) The storks around the monastery church.

East Prussia, the Werder, the area where time has stood still. Friendly rural folk in Mohrungen, clapping for us, the children with faces out of a picture book.

Now we are flying over Rügen and Hiddensee because the air force plane is not yet allowed to fly over the GDR. As they serve us dinner, we are over Møn for a second. (I miss Ute.)

On the train from Cologne to Hamburg, 6 May 1990
The flight from Danzig to Cologne yesterday, at time-gobbling speed, did not allow for a proper arrival, for which reason at the beginning of my conversation with Tomáš Kosta (in the Mondial) I felt as if I were not all there. Hans Werner Richter has had a fall on the street and may not be able to travel to Prague. Kosta tells me that the Czech writers are reacting with increasing jealousy and envy to Havel's work as president.

Returning to the Federal Republic means registering my growing alienation from "greater" Germany. This cannot be my country. I will probably have to take leave of it (literally).

It is pernicious the way Kohl's hasty actions are exacerbated by the thoughtless travel mania of his foreign minister, who, if not clever, is certainly sly; it is as if the two were trying to outdo each other. Weizsäcker's wife is endearing; on my return flight in the presidential cabin I noticed that she keeps a travel journal. (The pretty blond female Polish security officer whom Frau Weizsäcker repeatedly took by the hand and drew out of the crush when people crowded around us.) Everyone in our party agreed: three quiet days in Frauenburg would have been the best finale to our journey.

People: the differences between the Bismarck brothers, Claus von a year and a half older, the younger Philipp still nattering on about "the right to our homeland" or basking in his military reminiscences.

The Bundeswehr officer accompanying the president as his military escort forgot to salute when the national anthems were played; when the German anthem was played at the Westerplatte, he almost failed to salute as well.

At the water project: the Polish boy of about thirteen with a plucked bass and the girl of about twelve who took up a position beside him, stroking the strings: a pretty pair.

I danced a few steps with Barbara, the president's secretary, when the peasant band struck up a mazurka. The band's costumes come from Kraków. The project director, who played the concertina, brought them along, transplanting them to Elbing.

Agnes receives a pension of 300,000 zlotys. A loaf of bread costs 2,300 zlotys. While I was in Gdańsk, a 50,000-copy edition of *Dog Years* was published and promptly appeared on the black market.

I am looking forward to Ute, Behlendorf, the drawing I started before I left, even to the dog — certainly not to the results from today's local elections in the GDR. Everywhere the rape is in bloom (too early), and blooming its heart out on both sides of the Vistula.

By train from Behlendorf to Berlin, 11 May 1990
I have put the presidential trip (not Poland) behind me by drawing, alternating between charcoal and pencil. Yesterday *Die Zeit* carried my polemic against the currency union, under a different title. In the meantime, *Der Spiegel* has also discovered the deutschmark scam as a topic, and for now Augstein is sparing his readers the German nationalism that has become the trademark of his Monday editorials. Yesterday the proofs of the afterword to *Dead Wood* arrived. I will sit down and do the proofreading right away.

The death of Irmtraud Morgner, snatched away in the middle of the third volume of her trilogy. I have to go to Berlin for the funeral. After Johnson (or along with him), she is the only novelist of real quality to have found her material in the sediment of the GDR.

I suppose I shall be compelled to write about Germany for a third time, after the currency union. Everything is becoming a matter of leave-taking or detachment for me.

Flight from Berlin to Hamburg, evening of 11 May 1990
With Ingrid from the Paris Bar to Lichtenberg Central Cemetery. Not many mourners, considering Irmtraud Morgner's importance. For instance, the new chairman of the Writers' Union, Rainer Kirsch, was absent (not to mention Kant and the other GDR literary bigwigs). Gerhard Wolf spoke well, but too softly and mumbling, then Alice Schwarzer, who talked, with Morgner's mother present, about the tough, deprived childhood of the deceased.

After that, to the funeral reception at the Hotel Unter den

Linden (without Ingrid, who had a meeting with Rowohlt–Naumann). Soon, too soon, the topic of future collaboration between the Aufbau and Luchterhand publishing houses came up. Faber unwilling to commit himself. Gerhard Wolf supports my suggestion that the tradition of collaboration be continued for the paperback editions. Christa Wolf claims she understands none of this.

In the house on Niedstrasse Eva Hönisch and Trautwein have found many of my old play manuscripts. Now Bruno is coming to pick me up.

By car from Behlendorf to Rostock, 12 May 1990

With Ute and Bruno. Both have this usually endearing but occasionally also insulting way of smiling at my distractedness, at my allegedly unshakable self-confidence, at me.

Yesterday a conversation about choosing where to be buried. Ute, who wants to sew her own shroud, does not have a location in mind yet. I have decided on the little Friedenau Cemetery in Berlin. The conversation was sparked by my description of the Morgner burial: at her request, she was placed in a row that puts her diagonally across from her first husband, Paul Wiens, supposedly a Stasi agent. Wiens is directly across from the grave of Herbert Nachbar; the letter N is missing from his metal nameplate.

In Rostock the Bremen collection of my Calcutta drawings is on display. I plan to read from *Show Your Tongue*. Tomorrow, elections in the states of North Rhine–Westphalia and Lower Saxony.

In the car from Rostock to Behlendorf, 13 May 1990

A nicely mounted exhibition of the Bremen collection at the Kunsthalle: seventy Calcutta pieces. An attentive audience for the reading. Rostock in better repair than Wismar and Stralsund. The director of the Kunsthalle spent five years in Africa (Kenya), where she became an expert on the art of the Makonde. The folks from Bremen, as the opening remarks revealed, are still embarrassed about the 1960 literary scandal when *The Tin Drum* was denied the city's prize. Funny, this contrition so long after the fact.

I should put together a paperback with a third essay on the two Germanys, including interpolated texts from my trips to the GDR, to Poland, to Prague: sixty or seventy pages.

For "The Call of the Toad," work in the euthanasia initiative, a means of bringing about deaths that will further the cause.

Behlendorf, 15 May 1990

The elections took an unexpected turn. The slight margin of victory in Lower Saxony will make possible a Red-Green coalition and a majority in the Bundesrat. But whether the Social Democrats will seize this advantage remains dubious.

And yesterday the discussion with Pörner from Leipzig, moderated by Stephan Lohr from North German Broadcasting's Channel 3. We agree that the results of the currency union will be ruinous. The discussion was broadcast this afternoon.

Around noon we visited a masonry supplier in Ratzeburg to find granite for the terrace and the steps, and the whole subject of headstones, along with my time as a mason's apprentice in Düsseldorf, forced its way into my plans for "The Call of the Toad": two masonry and gravestone businesses owned by Germans employ Polish journeymen. The displays of both companies feature old German headstones from before 1945. One will carry the inscription "All earthly things one day / shall crumble away."

If I wanted to use this journal as the basis for a book, the period from November 1989 (the Day of the Dead) — i.e., from the opening of the Wall to the pan-German elections — in the planned work, "The Call of the Toad," would have to develop in batches, fragments, and reflections. Several texts from this period could be incorporated, from my speech at the Social Democrats' party convention to the "Short Speech by a Rootless Cosmopolitan" and "The View from Suckers Square," as well as a speech yet to be written. The final version of "The Call of the Toad" could be appended — or that story could appear at the same time as a separate book.

Behlendorf, 18 May 1990

On television I just saw the State Treaty being signed by the economics ministers, Romberg and Waigel. Yet another "historic moment." The document was spread out on Adenauer's desk, on which the signing of the Basic Treaty took place back in Willy Brandt's time. The Greens refused to attend. Vogel claimed to have a "prior commitment." Apparently the Social Democrats will vote for the treaty in the Bundestag, and likewise in the Bundesrat. If that happens without significant amendments, my days as an SPD member are numbered.

Yesterday in Lübeck the event sponsored by the SPD voters' initiative, with the ministers Jansen, Bull, Klingner, and Böhrk present. An example of good information. But typical that the GDR was mentioned only in passing, and not until West German interests came up: the nuclear plant in Greifswald, §218. I spoke at the end and left no doubt as to my growing alienation from the SPD.

The day before yesterday at the urologist's. Blood test, urinalysis, all fine and normal. Just some sponginess in the left groin; apparently the incision from the operation did not heal properly. A minor irritation I can live with.

Today finished the twelfth large-scale image of the soft-coal landscapes. Six charcoal, six pencil pieces. In mid-June I want to go to Altdöbern and settle in for three days on the rim of the pit.

Behlendorf, 21 May 1990
Motivated by Steidl's visit, I again drew two large-scale lithos on transfer paper: tree stumps in vertical format. One of them will become a poster for Oskar L., in case — politics rears its ugly head — he decides to remain a candidate. With good reason O.L. made rejection of the State Treaty in its current form a condition of his candidacy. Vogel is trying to bring the caucus and the SPD-ruled provinces together. So, a poster subject to recall and only for this situation: "To the dead forest with Oskar."

Tomorrow we are driving to Prague by way of Dresden. Let us see what remains of Group 47.

Over the weekend, Maria Rama and Fritze Margull came to visit. Maria's memory, which stores everything relating to my family, and my women, in chronological order. The story about Franz, who, as a form of protest against the atom bomb, hangs himself from a tree with a device of his own invention and shakes hands with a horrified Turk, who shyly touches him. Or the prayer spoken by sixteen-year-old Franz when he gets lost in Lapland: "Dear God, don't let me die. I'm still so young." Or the way Franz decides he does not want to be a Grass anymore and picks a new name from the telephone book (in vain).

Prague, 22 May 1990
Between nine-thirty A.M. and six-thirty P.M., Ute drove us the seven hundred kilometers to Prague by way of Berlin and Dresden, with only brief stops. Tomáš Kosta and his wife were already settled in the Hotel Atlantik. We ate together before the two of them went off to a concert of the Prague Philharmonic, conducted by

Václav Neumann for the first time in twenty years. We strolled through the Old Town. (By the way, when we arrived, a taxi piloted us to the hotel.) Along the Graben, a main street, pillars display the history of Czechoslovakia on posters: from the country's founding after World War I to the Prague Spring and the brief Dubček period in 1968. Seldom have I seen history documented so impressively: the Slánský trial; young Pavel Kohout still siding with the Communists.

When we decide to have a cup of coffee, the hotel's porter invites us to join him at his table out on the terrace, where he and his wife and son are enjoying a glass of Crimean sparkling wine after work. His uncritical, boundless admiration for the West Germans, his disdain for the East Germans, Poles, Russians. In the end, because his son allegedly has a birthday tomorrow and is supposed to be given a Braun electric razor and a cassette recorder, he wants to exchange some money for deutschmarks. He is disappointed when I am willing to exchange only 100 marks. Apparently he invited us to his table only on account of the Western currency. Ute is disappointed. I see how easily people can be corrupted.

But the Old Town, where I have not been since '68, does not disappoint. On the other hand, the trip from the border to Prague: a state of decay more obvious than in Poland and the GDR, in contrast to the expansive, heroic-seeming landscape, which, to be sure, has a haze of industrial smog hanging over it. On the Czech side, the Erz Mountains' ridges look even more wretched than the East German side. A desire to get back to my drawing right away.

Prague, 23 May 1990
Where the Kafka family lived, where the father had his business, what is left of the house where Kafka was born, the portal. Then

to the oldest synagogue and on to the Jewish cemetery, the grave-stones crowded together. It was established around the turn of the century, when a new residential area was laid out and the graves were moved to this "collective cemetery" from several others. I draw the stones, leaning at all different angles, and their staggered rows. The relationship to the memorial cemetery at Treblinka. Between the grave mounds, acacias. If only I could spend three or four days there and draw these eloquent stones.

A reading from *The Plebeians* at the Realistic Theater with actors, and an hour and a half of discussion afterward. In the audience for a little while Stepán, the youngest son of my deceased friend Vladimir Kafka, and František Herný and Josef Hermák. I find myself thinking back to that time more than twenty years ago. No sense of strangeness. With Herný the familiar, skeptical, cheerful tone. The Bohemians are stick-in-the-muds. After that, to the theater, which is full, because the play *Urban Renewal,* by Havel, the president, is being performed. We stay only until intermission because it is a work in which the characters do nothing but talk.

Prague before the elections. Everyone hopes the Civic Forum will win. That may be the case in Prague, but in the rest of the country? How fortunate this poor country is, relatively speaking, not to have a wealthy brother.

Dobříš, 24 May 1990

Back to the Jewish cemetery for three sketches, then up to the castle, taking our luggage with us. After lunch in a restaurant decidedly not catering to tourists (pork roast with dumplings), we drove to see the president. Various mix-ups before we were announced, a whole succession of Rococo chambers, all white with gilded stucco ornamentation, until finally — after the Italian radicals have left — we get to sit down with Václav Havel. He recalled that in 1967 Anna and I had given him a rabbit en croûte that I had cooked; I reminded him of the meal he had hosted in the mountains: chicken with pig's feet. The conversation was unproductive, because Havel, despite all his merits, has already become one of those politicians who are poor listeners. He never looks at the person he is speaking with, whoever it is. No interest in social problems. As president he enjoys getting out and taking the people by surprise, so to speak. At the point where a real conversation (including an argument) could have developed, it was disrupted by Walter Höllerer, who (foolishly) cast everything in terms of Berlin (his Literary Colloquium) and Prague as cultural neighbors. When I think back to the Havel I knew in 1967–68, the obstinacy is still there, as both a strength and a limitation. Nonetheless, it remains a remarkable and admirable achievement that a people in a situation as difficult as the Czechs' should have chosen a literary man (with a literary staff of advisers) as their president, an achievement Germany never pulled off. (I remind Havel of Heinrich Mann's futile candidacy during the Weimar Republic.)

Then by way of the almost deserted highway to Dobříš: a castle (the seat of the counts of Mansfeld after the Thirty Years' War) with a labyrinth and a timeless beauty. Hans Werner Richter was already there, his memory full of gaps. Others arrived: Jürgen Becker, Jochen Schädlich, Milo Dor . . . Melancholy is tearing at me. I can hardly sustain conversations and long-ago friendships. As far as I am concerned, this meeting, no matter how fitting, should be the last.

From Dobříš to Berlin, 28 May 1990
It went well after all, this meeting. And at the end Hans Werner Richter commented, "Till next year, if my health holds up."

Berlin, 29 May 1990

Dobříš in retrospect. After Peter Bichsel's reading — two excellent stories, completely new, yet unmistakably Bichsel-ish in style — my interest in literature revived, the more so as the readings that followed were of superior quality, including those by the Czech writers. Really hopeless (yet again), the reading by Buch: pretentious ineptitude. Delius's piece was interesting: he pulls out all the rhetorical stops to describe, from the perspective of GDR citizens, the planting of a pear tree in their town of Ribbeck by West Germans — five busloads of whom show up. Czechowski found it offensive that a "Western writer" had the temerity to write from an Eastern perspective.

On Saturday the Friedrich Ebert Prize was conferred on Havel (together with Janka). No German speaker mentioned the Group 47 writers, but Havel did. Not a word from Börner, whose speech was empty rhetoric, about Hans Werner Richter — the usual lack of respect.

In five and a half hours Ute drove Helga Novak and me to Berlin. Helga lives in Poland, in the Tuchola Forest, and apparently has a poacher as a lover (hence the nature-intoxicated love poems). They fish trout and pike out of a brook with hoop nets.

Helga Novak: she is living her own life (still with an Icelandic passport), drinking less, has become plump, more womanly, almost affectionate.

Today wrote a longish letter to Björn Engholm in which I gave reasons for agreeing with O.L., also for my possible resignation from the SPD if Oskar is forced to withdraw his candidacy.

The singing Ludvík Vaculík and his *Cat and Mouse* story. Too much fruit brandy the last two evenings. The quarrel between Bichsel and Schindel. Havel's campaign speech (three minutes) in the packed market square in Dobříš. Seeing Vladimir Kafka's sons,

Tomáš and Stepán. František Herný, slated to become the cultural attaché in Bonn. Pushing Hans Werner Richter in his wheelchair. Ute and Helga Novak, possible women friends. Smiling like a sphinx: Ilse Aichinger.

From Berlin to Büchen, 1 June 1990
Even before reaching the intersection with Lietzenburger Strasse, we get stuck in traffic. Ingrid boldly changes lanes. We park, unload the luggage, and run, rush, stumble, shove our way toward Zoo Station. Arrive three minutes before the train is due to pull out, get into the wrong car — Helene is waiting for us. Ingrid laughing on the platform, although earlier she was stone-faced, furious at Nele, who is taking it all calmly. We have to fight our way through four packed cars, with luggage and all, to find our reserved seats. Well past Potsdam and I am still out of breath and dripping with sweat. Now my daughters are seated across from me, chattering away. Helene barefoot, festooned with chains from forehead to ankles, Nele with her doll, adorable, and fascinated by Helene. Yesterday Ingrid, Nele, and I went to the Roncalli Circus (with complimentary tickets). Sitting beside the child, I was completely relaxed and could lose myself in the performance, as lighthearted and spirited as it was artistic.

After reading the draft of a screenplay based on *The Rat* by Tengiz Abuladze, a mystical, reactionary bullshitter, I had to write him a harsh rejection letter. And today an equally curt letter to the publisher E. Raabe, who is carrying on her jealousy-fueled confrontation with Steidl in public. A lot of aggravation, and the days in Prague and Dobříš seem so far behind.

Yesterday in *Die Zeit,* Greiner's unfair polemic against Christa Wolf, and a defense of her by V. Hage. The revolting attacks and self-righteous ravings are starting. Lafontaine is being isolated more and more. I assume he will throw in the towel as a candidate shortly, or might he be sufficiently calm to bide his time, which will come in the fall, when the damage done by the union of the currencies will become apparent?

I am looking forward to Ute, Behlendorf, my studio, and the drawings and lithos I started before the trip.

In November, an exhibition is scheduled for Reinickendorf: one hundred images on the topic of dead wood: "Clear-cutting in Our Heads." Agreed to Maria's proposal for it today.

Well, not only aggravation: my daughters sitting across from me are sweet, lovable, funny, and well worth my sins.

Behlendorf, 5 June 1990
Yesterday Helene and Nele left. I was preoccupied with both of them, especially Nele.

After the attacks on Christa Wolf by Serke and Greiner, the *Frankfurter Allgemeine* has now printed a hostile account by Schirrmacher, pages long. I am considering a response, under the heading "Tying the Noose." I would make my way from Reich-Ranicki's large hank of hemp to the delicate web spun by Schirrmacher and Greiner to Herr Serke's threaded filament, thus tracking down the material used by the noose-tiers. At night I often toss and turn, haunted by images of a Germany that can no longer be mine. This Kohlian abomination: egomaniacal, bombastic, jovial, tough, condescending, domineering, feigning harmlessness.

Am leafing through old folders. Plays and drafts from the fifties, written in Berlin and Paris. Titles I had forgotten. As I am rereading, various things come back to me. Unfinished material that later turns up in scenes in *The Tin Drum,* for instance: "The Last Tram," "The Table," "Carpet-Beating," "House of Cards." Not to be published in book form! Odd to encounter oneself as a stranger this way. At the same time the desire to be uncoupled, someday soon, from the train of history, so laden with social freight, and just live an artist's life, in the moment, se–ing pleasure in watercolors, feeling clay between my fingers, doing delicate, brittle drawings, and getting back to poems at long last. Maybe, if I can pull it off, after "The Call of the Toad." Will I ever manage, after Calcutta, dead wood, and those soft-coal landscapes, to be playful, lighthearted, free of purpose again?

B>ind the roses on the studio trellis a blackbird is sitting on three eggs. My sons Franz and Raoul beg me not to view the situation too pessimistically. I find it amusing that they see themselves as pragmatists.

Behlendorf, 9 June 1990

Ute has a meeting with a veterinarian called Jobst from Rostock. I am off to Berlin, so that tomorrow, after the dedication of the Döblin Library at Urban Hospital, I can continue on to Altdöbern for four days in the soft-coal region. Maybe as a byproduct a "Letter from Altdöbern." Also as part of my preparation for the meeting taking place on 16 June in the Reichstag, when the oppositional caucus for a "constitutional congress" is to be established.

For "The Call of the Toad," a narrator who tells the story of the German-Polish couple, basing the account on their found and salvaged letters and quoting from them. I am determined to write this book (as the capstone to the Danzig books), but I am still in search of a concept that will dictate the narrative point of view.

I am cultivating my "solitude," protecting it by means of irony, if necessary by a display of good cheer that can even escalate into merriment.

As I am packing—my bag, the satchel with drawing materials, my three-legged folding stool, the portfolio with paper, and my books: Döblin, my *Plebeians*—I realize that packing and unpacking are characteristic activities for me. In between, temporary settling down for longer or shorter periods, with baggage always close at hand. By way of contrast, the houses in Berlin, B>lendorf, and Portugal, and the cabin in Denmark, waiting, patient, their feelings a little hurt because their invitations to sit down and stay awhile are so seldom accepted, and only between arrivals and departures. I would not want to change a thing!

On the way from Büchen to Berlin by train

On the train I draft my short speech for the dedication of the Alfred Döblin Library at the hospital. I am reading, for the first time in years, my essay "On My Teacher Döblin." It is worth reminding ourselves of him at this particular time. At the end of my remarks—Döblin today—I want to bring up the ideological witch-hunt against Christa Wolf, provided the audience seems receptive.

Altdöbern, 10 June 1990

After my speech for the library dedication, which I delivered largely extemporaneously, taking my cue from Döblin's outspokenness and the pleasure he derived from polemical exchanges, I launched into an equally outspoken defense of Christa Wolf.

The man who prints lithos for Steidl brought me a proof of my "For Oskar" poster. This at the moment when Oskar might withdraw his candidacy, tomorrow or in the very near future. Then Nele and Ingrid come to tea, and shortly after four P.M. Jimi Metag, my GDR driver. We set out in pouring rain, which has not stopped since yesterday morning, and reach our destination in about two hours.

Altdöbern is located between Finsterwalde and Cottbus, near Calau and Senftenberg. Jimi has arranged for me to stay with old Frau Schreck and her handicapped daughter: a room with a double bed on the second floor. The bathroom is in their living quarters on the ground floor. I promptly hear that Altdöbern has "five thousand inhabitants, some say, but, well, by now it's only just over four thousand."

The daughter says, "It all started when we voted wrong, on the eighteenth, I mean." The mother adds, "Everyone was saying, Go with the CDU, they have the money."

Many inhabitants of Altdöbern took some of the topsoil when the soft-coal pits were being excavated. "But it had coal mixed in. Nothing would grow in it. My tomatoes were tiny."

"The only thing left will be the co-op grocery store," the daughter says. "People will be trampling each other after the first of July. You won't be able to get a shopping basket, the place will be so crowded."

The open-pit mining is supposed to continue for another half year. "They're hoping someone from the West will buy it. Everything else is gone. In the old days, we had a sawmill here."

I eat at the Fox's Lair, diagonally across the road. Both the friendly waitress and the Hacker-Pschorr beer came from Bavaria. GDR beer can no longer be sold here. Only the solyanka soup and my entree, Bulgarian stir-fried meat with risotto, are left over from East bloc days. The innkeeper tries to project an optimistic attitude: "The people in this area drink a lot, you know. Things will pick up here, even after the first."

While I am eating, Jimi Metag comes by to say hello. His concert business, too, will stagnate after the currency merger. Later, from seven P.M. on, I sit in the living room with four women and watch the World Cup match between Germany and Yugoslavia: 4–1. Apparently the four ladies enjoy my presence: cock of the roost.

Altdöbern, 11 June 1990

In the morning, it began to rain again shortly before noon. I sat b>ind the children's hospital, where Altdöbern's dump is located and the earth's surface breaks off at the edge of a forty-five-meter precipice. On the new, blackish gray bottom of the pit a lunar landscape dotted with conical slag heaps has formed around a lake. I made two charcoal drawings and a sketch, the latter at the spot where the narrow road from Altdöbern to Pritzen suddenly ends, and from deep down, the steep bank rises from the lake in steps, suitable for a vertical composition.

On the way back, I go by the church square. Circle the remarkable church, which has an art nouveau feel to it. To the left, a World War I memorial. Bearing right at the church, you come upon a carefully tended Soviet military cemetery with a good forty-five tombstones, each one displaying the star and emblem for several soldiers.

The community notice board promises, for 16 June, a last bus excursion that can be paid for with Eastern marks: to Soltau Heath for 100 marks, plus 12 Western marks for admission to the park. In front of the town hall, on the church square, the results of the local elections of 6 May: an absolute majority for the CDU. The second-strongest party, but far b>ind, is the SPD. One of the old women said yesterday, "It's not the old folks, no, it's the young ones who are buying like crazy, only products from the West, and they don't realize that they're wrecking everything." My landlady, Frau Schreck, comes from Grünau, in Silesia: "We had a farm there, almost seventy-five acres . . ."

Altdöbern, 13 June 1990
Am drawing as if intoxicated. Yesterday five, today four pieces. After charcoal, pencil has taken over. Have not yet got back to the "Letter from Altdöbern" I started at the Park Restaurant as a "Report from Altdöbern." This text could be suitable for my short speech at the Reichstag. After (1) Introduction: Altdöbern and the pit, (2) could be the pit as an image of destruction, analogous to the GDR, and (3) would comment on the clearance sale in the Altdöbern manufactured-goods store; all stores have to be cleared out by 1 July so the shelves can be stocked exclusively with products from the West. From that follows (4) the revelation that the whole free market economy is a scam, and (5) the last word on those responsible: Kohl, Haussmann, Pöhl, all those who, following the Adenauer rule of "chancellor's democracy," have bypassed the democratic institutions to cobble together the abominable State Treaty, leaving (6) Article 23 to administer the final blow. But how can (7) a pitiful band of valiant radical democrats reactivate Article 146? Can it be that outright annexation under Article 23 is unconstitutional? Should a constitutional challenge be mounted?

From the marketplace and Marktstrasse I can see atop the chimney of a closed factory an inhabited stork's nest. One positive thing at least. In the manufactured-goods store, where a shovel was selling for 7 marks, a scythe for 3, I bought three large pads of wood-free drawing paper for 50 pfennigs apiece. The newspapers in the store were all from the West, with the exception of the *Sachsenspiegel.*

A reading yesterday in Guben before a good audience. A long discussion followed. Except for one couple who did not want to give up hope, the rest of the audience shared my reservations about the State Treaty. Up till late in Cottbus at the Hotel Lausitz, surrounded by cars from the West.

The noise from the road starts at five in the morning, cutting my sleep short. Every day at eight Frau Schreck and her daughter have my breakfast on the table. In the meantime, word of my presence in the village has spread; the mayor wants to meet me.

After the old church burned down, the new one was built in 1921. The castle is said to have been inhabited at one time by a von Witzleben, until he went bankrupt and had to sell. Four young men doing alternative military service are now cleaning up the park.

Altdöbern, 14 June 1990

I finished up today with two lithos on tracing paper, and now have thirteen drawings and sketches in my portfolio. The reading from *The Plebeians* yesterday, in a full hall, was also good. The discussion free of rhetoric. Before the reading I had my meeting in the park with Mayor Thierbach, on the CDU list without party affiliation. He is full of optimism, but doesn't know why. In the manufactured-goods store I bought two more drawing pads and two pencil sharpeners from the great GDR closeout. My last honoraria in Eastern marks. Jimi Metag wants to buy me 350 marks' worth of Wilthen brandy.

Looking down into the pit. A landscape that seems scarred for eternity. Yet here, too, the mayor tells me, in about three years' time a lake will form in the hollow, just as in Senftenberg. I still have the noise of the excavators in my ears.

Berlin, 16 June 1990

This afternoon in the Reichstag (south wing) I used my "Report from Altdöbern," which I wrote yesterday, as my address to the caucus for a new constitution. Then Ullmann gave an excellent speech. After that, everything threatened to drown in vague jabbering about fundamental democratic principles. Here, too, the famous question from the hope addicts: Herr Kästner, where are the positive elements? This after I had spent the evening before with Ingrid, who is full of despair for herself and for Nele, who, according to her, hates school and has no desire to learn. In the end we watched football on TV. Now I am about to join Veronika and her clan at a Greek restaurant.

Berlin, 18 June 1990

Yesterday in late afternoon to the literary center on Fasanenstrasse to read poems to children. At the end, I read the poem "Marriage" to children too young to understand and their helplessly amiable parents. Conversation with a journalist from East Berlin. I invited her out for chanterelles and dumplings. A Sunday-afternoon flirtation, how relaxing. I should allow myself such follies more often.

Today mail again. My talk has not reached *Die Zeit* yet. Franz still doesn't have a visa. Altdöbern seems far away, although I had wanted to draft a poem: "Looking into the Open Pit." Maybe when I get back to drawing in July. Ute has arrived with Maria. Tomorrow to Poland.

Poznań, 19 June 1990

Am writing this after a four-and-a-half-hour drive in sultry summer heat from Berlin to Poznań. In the morning wrote letters to Klaus Staeck, criticizing the lack of substance in his call for participation in the elections; to Oskar Lafontaine, to whom I sent the

Altdöbern speech, along with a demand that he offer an alternative to his alternative-less no: a "Federation of German Lands" on the foundation of a new constitution. Since *Die Zeit* was unwilling to print the Altdöbern speech either this week or next, I called Eisermann at *Der Spiegel*. Some interest there, although in the next issue Karasek is apparently going to go after Christa Wolf. As a precaution (and on the basis of experience), I made sure the piece will be offered, if need be, either to the *Frankfurter Rundschau* or the *Süddeutsche Zeitung*.

In the letter to Oskar, I suggested the formulation "Show pity, for heaven's sake, for the people in the GDR," because it is the pitilessness of the prevailing policy that disgusts me; it is characterized by the strength of conviction of those devoid of pity. It cares for nothing but the deutschmark economy.

Even before the Polish border, the barren landscapes. And so many Poles on the road in Western cars. At the border we discover that Ute's identity card runs out tomorrow. I am happy to be able to get away from the German agony for a few days. Want to write something about the ugliness of this unification.

Poznań, 21 June 1990
As chance (chance?) would have it, today, while the honorary doctorate was being solemnly conferred on me in Polish and I was sweating under my robe and four-cornered velvet tam, in the Bundestag and the Volkskammer the western border of Poland was finally being recognized — and at the same time the calendar marks the official onset of summer.

Franz arrived by train at five A.M. Helga Novak, who was still with us in Gnesen and had stuck it out through the two and a half hours of the reading and discussion, has apparently done a disappearing act. At any rate, she has made herself scarce, without saying a word to anyone, probably off to her hideaway in the Tuchola Forest.

A day as fine as it was strenuous. The congenial Polish Germanists, trying to be clever at all times. The ambassador had come from Warsaw, bringing forms and rubber stamps to extend Ute's identification card. At the end of my acceptance speech (in academic regalia and black gloves), I mentioned the new economic and political challenges confronting the Poles and the Germans: the deutschmark at the Oder. Will Poland, practiced in resistance, now be able to summon the strength to develop a modern state, economically and socially stable? Will the Germans have the wisdom to put a brake on their economic power and their expansionist tendencies? I have my doubts on both scores.

Inflation dominates everyday life in Poland. One deutschmark can be exchanged for 5,300 zlotys. Franz is working on our Kashubian family tree. At the end of the ceremony the academic choir sang "Gaudeamus Igitur."

From Poznań to Gdańsk, 22 June 1990
The Tuchola Forest begins only once you pass the town of Tuchola, a wooded area dotted with junipers. People in festive dress: the Feast of St. John? We drive along on a beautiful summer day. In 1970 Anna and I traversed this same stretch with Franz and Raoul.

Gdańsk, 23 June 1990
Showed Franz and Ute the city. Here it becomes evident that despite all the revolutionary changes, Poland has nothing to replace its crumbling political structures; whereas the GDR, in the grip of external forces, is compelled to be or become something that has not yet taken shape; for its own, similarly crumbling structures

may still be around, but they are being withdrawn from economic circulation.

The GDR: I should write something about the threadbare phrase you hear day in, day out — "with decency and dignity" — because the annexation currently taking place is both indecent and undignified. In Gdańsk, by the Kran Gate and on Warehouse Island, new Gothic and warehouse-style buildings are going up. Everyone is trading in everything, but fewer and fewer are prepared to actually produce anything. Late in the evening we decide to go to the actors' club on Frauengasse for a glass of wine. People recognize me, and I drink to three waitresses who have just passed their university exams in Old Church Slavonic. Franz describes his farm to everyone, thereby describing the world.

Driving through Kashubia yesterday on secondary roads. Franz is considering moving his farm here.

We also went to see the Polish post office. I showed Franz the plaque with the name of his great-uncle, Franciszek Krauze. Now we are driving to see the Kashubians. On Monday at noon I have a meeting with Wajda. He wants to film *The Plebeians*.

Gdańsk, 26 June 1990
The last three days were packed. On Saturday with Franz to visit the Kashubians. First a hospitable spread at Hannes and Lucie's. Then to Agnes and Josef's, where a similar spread awaited us. Then, it was already late afternoon, to Kazimir's new apartment, where again the table was piled high with cake, sausage, and tomatoes, as well as chicken and schnitzel. Finally Sigismund also wanted us to see his apartment in Rumia. The table was groaning there too, of course. Late that evening we took Lucie back to Brösen, with Sigismund's help.

A good thing that Marija and Kazimir did not arrive until late. That way we had Hannes to ourselves for three hours. He gave a lively account of his childhood and his time as a Wehrmacht soldier, peppering his narrative with dirty jokes. His interest in Franz's farm insatiable. He sits on the edge of his bed with the blanket slipping off, smokes five or six cigarettes a day, also drinks a glass of vodka or two.

His work as a cobbler during his captivity with the Americans. Had never seen Negroes before. His return to Danzig. How his reichsmarks and his photos from his time in the military were taken away from him. The photos were burned. How, on the advice of an officer, he spent the night in Langfuhr and only then made his way on foot to Bissau, where he learned that his father was dead, the farm burned down.

Franz is working on his family tree and wants to track down his most distant relatives.

At Kazimir's the children receive us with flowers and songs. Gratitude for the apartment, which I bought for a modest sum. They give us a handmade wooden model of a Kashubian house. Before that, at Agnes's place — she is in Firoga and does not get back until later — Josef is there to make strawberry preserves. The open jars are next to the toilet. He wants to shave, but doesn't get around to it because we have so much to talk about.

Because it is St. John's Eve, children have made piles of wood everywhere for bonfires. Later it starts to rain. The smoky fires. The forest just behind the identical new apartment buildings in Rumia. Kazimir's apartment is on the ground floor, and from the balcony you can go right into a small garden planted with vegetables. Sigismund, who lives three houses over, has a larger garden nearby, three hundred square meters, which his wife tends. Many beautiful, quiet children. Unavoidable vodka. When they press him, Franz describes his farm for the hundredth time, the number of cows, the cheese-making operation, shows family photos.

The drive from Brösen, by way of Oliva and Zoppot, to Gdynia. After the spa, elegant yet crumbling, still charming with its conservatory buildings, we pass through the hideous industrial landscape of Gdynia and its outskirts. Hard, cold, foursquare, and unwelcoming, tearing up the once beautiful landscape of the terminal moraine. Devastation that can never be repaired.

The family congratulate me on my honorary doctorate and are genuinely happy for me. I try to be happy, too.

On Sunday, in unsettled weather, we first drive to Heubuden (Stogi), ruined by urban sprawl, then try, in the seemingly unplanned, chaotic industrial area, to find the crossing between Neufähr East and West. We do manage to get through, catch glimpses of this once untouched landscape, still recognizable in the sixties, eventually cross the pontoon bridge by the mothballed ferry, see the iron pyrite slag heap next to the stagnant Vistula — an ugly mountain rearing up amid the flats — immediately locate the ferry when we reach Schiewenhorst (Swibno), find Nickelswalde, likewise wrecked by urban sprawl, travel by way of Stege — its beautiful church with old frescoes — Stutthof, past the concentration camp museum, and after Fischerbabke onto the Courland Spit as far as Kahlberg. The landscape of the spit on either side of the road still almost unscathed. We walk through the woods along the shore. We are four kilometers from the Soviet border and find several chips of amber (Franz takes some for Gianna), but we dare not venture into the Baltic. We drive back, seeing herons above the Courland Lagoon, cranes flying in formation, then turn off at Stege toward Tiegenhof. Both villages appall me. Dilapidation, squalor, incompetence, none of which can be explained by poverty or Soviet domination; rather, it is continuing and apparently persistent ineptitude, for nothing can excuse the decay of the old farmsteads, among them houses with East Elbian porticoes, especially when the Old Town of Danzig has been rebuilt so successfully.

Yet we are all, including Ute, enchanted by the flat Werder landscape, with its neatly staggered rows of trees (willows, poplars).

From Neuteich we drive back by way of Dirschau, Praust, and Ohra. Here, along the road, some portico houses are in relatively good condition.

Now, after this trip, sadness creeps over me in anticipation of the misfortune to come (for Poland, for all of us). Toward nine P.M. we take Franz to the main station, just as in 1944 my father took me, sixteen years old, to the main station. Back then I had my call-up notice and a cardboard suitcase; today Franz has a better destination. On television we watch the football match between West Germany and Holland: 2–1. After that, the news. Wałęsa's struggle with Geremek and Michnik is coming to a head.

On Monday, breakfast with Zeidler. Discussion of the Chodowiecki Prize. After that, to my publisher's on Breitgasse, where I discover that I am owed 64 million zlotys (12,000 marks) for the edition of *Dog Years*. I can open a bank account, which is what we did today, with 55 million zlotys. *From the Diary of a Snail* is scheduled to appear later this year; it is at the printer's. The translation of *The Flounder* is done. I suggest having *The Plebeians* translated.

At noon we meet Andrzej Wajda at the hotel. Until May of next year he will be tied up with his duties as a member of parliament, but by then he wants to have the script for the filming of *The Plebeians* ready (screenwriter: Kohlhaase from East Berlin?) and other preparations in place: financing and so on. I am surprised that he wants to work exclusively with German actors. Wajda is even thinking of shooting in the Theater on Schiffbauerdamm. We speak briefly about Poland's mounting problems — declining productivity, the absence of foreign investment, the absence of capital altogether, the struggle inside Solidarność, the intractable old structures. I explain my fears about how things will develop in the GDR. Our conversation is calm, that of two experienced craftsmen who do not have to pretend or prove anything to each other. Our (muted) happy anticipation of working together.

Afterward Ute and I walk through the city. On Frauengasse, German tourists stare at me as if I were one of the sights. (I could always become a tour guide here.) On Langgasse, a conversation with an old Danziger who returned in '46 from American captivity (in Holland) and went looking for his parents, both of whom were dead. He stayed. Married a German woman from Dirschau. Asks me to give him money "for a cup o' coffee." Shortly before that he said, "Danzigers won't try to con you."

Then with Zeidler again in the gallery; later I ask him to drive us to the Grosse Allee. Opposite the House of Sport, now the opera house, is the brick structure that served as the entrance to the former municipal cemeteries, though in 1968 the cemeteries were bulldozed and turned into a park. This setting is ideal for "The Call of the Toad," both for its size and its historical background. The nearby Mennonite cemetery goes with it. An avenue of linden trees extends all the way to Mirchauer Weg.

Later we drive to the French cemetery, also to possible sites on the other side of the Bischofsberg. Up above, by the former Hitler Youth hostel, are the old Napoleonic barracks, crumbling away. Across from the barracks at the Oliva Gate, where the road to Karthaus passes the filling station with lead-free gas, likewise next to the Soviet military cemetery, an old German cemetery, used by Poles until the mid-fifties. It could be purchased later by the cemetery association for expansion.

My couple visits this area (old German tombstone: the Zielke family, 1934). Here, too, the right historical background.

After that, to the Leege Gate. By the ruins of the old Gothic tower a group of drunken sailors along the Mottlau, a view of warehouses and the Cow Bridge.

In St. Peter's an Armenian choir. In Poland the Armenian Church is merged with the Catholic Church. Around forty Armenian families in Gdańsk. Only the nave of St. Peter's has been restored. The special beauty of the whitewashed walls.

Details: the pastor of St. Peter's has his little dog with him in the church. Electric golf carts to transport tourists around the city. Opening my account at the old Danzig Bank. We buy pizza at the covered Dominican Market. A German tells us about the difficulties encountered by General Health Insurance, which wants to invest in Poland, in hotels and sanatoria for Germans. Only leases available, limited to ten years.

Later went with Zeidler to Oliva. He shows us the ruins of the inn in Schwabental. I see the Silberhammer Mill and Freudental. The valley is crammed with allotment cottages and wooden A-frames. In Schwabental, an old man with eight dogs guards the ruins of the old tavern. Later with Zeidler and his wife in Adlershorst (Orlowo). On the boardwalk. Hordes of swans in the dirty water of the Baltic. Dinner in a restaurant with waitresses dressed as Playboy bunnies. Later "entertainment": dancing, striptease, Russian music. Everything (including the prices) geared to German and Scandinavian tourists. Zeidler describes how he pretended the German Order of the Knights Templar wanted to invest in Poland "for purely humanitarian reasons."

Back to the hotel late. On television the struggle between Wałęsa and Geremek continues.

I think I have found the perfect locales for "The Call of the Toad"!

Gdańsk, 27 June 1990
Yesterday at eleven to my publisher's. The reassuring feeling of having a proper publisher here who provides reliable information on printing and release dates, delivers author's copies, and pays royalties. Afterward with Max to the old town hall, which survived the war unscathed and is as charming inside as out. An exhibition of Javanese art is taking place there. The museum's director pressed us to visit often. Then we drove back to the Grosse Allee because I wanted to pin down details in my journal about the once and future cemetery. The burial ground stretching from the technical university to the polyclinic — where I was operated on for a middle-ear infection when I was three — measures a good kilometer.

Then out to see the Kashubians in Brösen once more. Again the table was set with cake, greens, dumplings, mushrooms, chicken giblets, and so on. Later Agnes and Josef joined us. When we got ready to leave at seven P.M., of course it was "far too early!" Hannes told stories again "from the old days," when he was transporting bricks and wanted to swap meat and butter for tobacco at a tobacconist's by the Halbe Allee tram station and was stopped by one of the "secrets." Or how, during the time of the free city, he was called a "stupid Swabian" by the Polish border guards and a "dumb Polack" by the free-city border guards. When he asked his father, Uncle Josef, why he was catching it from both sides, his father said, "We Kashubians wear our coats sometimes this way, sometimes that." We gave Hannes the remarkable flowered carpet from Posen. Jolla, Marija's daughter, recited a poem in German for my honorary doctorate. Vodka made the rounds yet again.

Then Zoppot (near the former border of the free city), the Jewish cemetery, located in the forest. The tombstones without inscriptions, blank, as if eradicated, effaced. The maintenance is paid for by Americans. No memorial plaque. Just as there is no plaque at the site of the synagogue in Langfuhr. Instead a Chopin plaque, because a music conservatory occupies that handsome building. We are about to leave.

Behlendorf, 28 June 1990

Helene is turning sixteen and naturally cannot be reached by telephone: rehearsals. The drive yesterday from Danzig by way of western Kashubia, through Karthaus to Stolp, Küstrin, Kolberg, difficulty finding lead-free gasoline, then on to Cammin, where Uwe Johnson came from, and Swinemünde, where, after crossing on the ferry, we experienced a bit of drama: the officer at the Polish border recognized me, knew about the honorary doctorate, and immediately let us through, although the crossing is reserved for GDR Germans and Poles. The GDR border guard, on the other hand, had to put in a call "to headquarters" for instructions. At last we were allowed to drive on, but not until I had given away two copies of *Dog Years* in Polish translation, with dedications. By way of Wollin, Usedom, Anklam, Stavenhagen, Güstrow, where we had supper at the Castle Restaurant. Conversation with a West German refrigerator salesman and his Brandenburg associate. Then on through Schwerin, the border, Ratzeburg, and home. We got there around eleven P.M. The last part of the drive was stormy, with heavy rain and fog, and this on Seven Sleepers Day.

This trip, with the four days in Altdöbern, the interlude in Berlin, and the journey to Poznań and Gdańsk, highlights for me the contrast between the prevailing misery here and the still un-spoiled landscape that extends across the borders. Trees lining the road. Good secondary roads in Poland. An insight that came as quite a shock in Swinemünde: here the enlarged Federal Republic will soon butt up against Poland, the demarcation line between European wealth and poverty.

Today I found out that *Der Spiegel* is willing to publish my "Report from Altdöbern," but in censored form, without the first page, where I defend Christa Wolf; so now the text will appear next Saturday in the *Frankfurter Rundschau*.

In the next few days I plan to make drawings based on the im-ages I captured in Altdöbern. I should do a new outline for "The Call of the Toad" soon, working in the locales I identified in Gdańsk. Only once that is finished will it become clear whether I will write a classic narrative or whether this journal can serve as the basis for chronicling a transformation that, like the narrating, or rather co-narrating, text, merits the title "The Call of the Toad."

Behlendorf, 29 June 1990
Title for a polemical piece yet to be written: "A Bargain Called the GDR," in which the cliché of the bargain basement, newly popular in Germany, will stand for the current mindless capitalist greed. This compulsion to snap up a bargain wherever an opportunity presents itself, with "decency and dignity," of course.

Behlendorf, 30 June 1990
On large-scale Bristol board I have made my way back to Altdöbern, using gray-toned charcoal. So tomorrow the moment will have ar-rived: while in Arizona and California whole landscapes are ablaze, generating temperatures of close to 50 degrees Celsius; while the gazillionth world environmental conference is taking place, at

which the decision to end dependence on fossil fuels is postponed yet again; while the World Cup is going into the quarterfinals (tomorrow Germany takes on Czechoslovakia); while I have to adjust to my new glasses, picked up yesterday in Mölln: the deutschmark is on the prowl, West German products are rolling over the leveled border, bargains large and small are to be snapped up, and from tomorrow on, money will rule throughout Germany. (Would it not have been a good idea in "The Call of the Toad" to take advantage of the clearance sale and for a song empty out the coffin warehouse of the People's Own Earth Furniture Cooperative?)

Behind the United Cemeteries on Grosse Allee, between the technical university and the polyclinic, was Albrecht Forster Stadium, named for the gauleiter (from Fürth) of the Reichsgau of Danzig–West Prussia. Next to the Church of the Abdication, the crematorium, today shut down (Poland is Catholic). But it could be reactivated for the German-Polish Burial Association if the Orthodox Christians in the Church of the Abdication could be persuaded to move to a new church, donated by the cemetery association.

Behlendorf, 1 July 1990
On Day X, I compose an image from Altdöbern in vertical format: "Next to the Women's Hospital." The nation's attention (and mine as well) is fixed simultaneously on the World Cup and on the introduction of the deutschmark. Quite an accomplishment: to have the currency on site, ready to be distributed in an orderly fashion at the appointed time; goods will follow the money, coming hot on its heels, so to speak. This much people have learned; this much they can do. But whether work and wages will follow this distribution of the new money remains uncertain, the more so because the actual wares will come from elsewhere, while domesti-

cally produced goods will not be for sale, and the wages paid for producing them will be kept low.

A telephone conversation with my Helene, now sixteen, whom I will see acting in a play tomorrow. She is in a hurry, wants to get out and see what people in East Berlin are doing with the new money.

A hard-fought football victory for the Germans over the Czechs: 1–0.

From Behlendorf to Berlin, 2 July 1990
My first trip to Berlin without checkpoints manned by sullen army types. In my compartment is a retired couple from Frankfurt on the Oder: "For us, things can only get better." The husband, a 650-mark pension each month; she still waiting for her disability pension.

It is all I can do to maintain my membership in the SPD. Aside from saying NO in capital letters, O. Lafontaine has no ideas to offer. His influential supporters, Engholm and Schröder, are apparently not prepared to represent Lafontaine's position effectively in public during his absence. I don't want to think about Brandt.

In today's *Spiegel* Augstein first gallops through a thousand years of history like an old-fashioned schoolmaster (veering between a right-leaning liberal and a German nationalist point of view), always focusing on the "greats"; then, in the final section, he picks out my oppositional stance for attack. The usual omissions. His rejection of morality as a measuring stick for politics. Basically it is little Moritz's unquestioning belief in history that keeps this professional cynic going. Should I respond? Probably not.

"The Call of the Toad," the first two thirds based on the journal, could in the last third turn into a "lean" narrative, having written its way into the clear, so to speak, by uttering toad calls on the current political situation. A slow and by no means painless separation from Germany, with the help of the German language. For that is what seems to be going on here.

Crossing my fingers for the Czechs during yesterday's game, or hoping, until the final whistle, that Cameroon would succeed in beating England, whereupon the team would show the Germans in the semifinals what a former colony can achieve. (The whole thing, of course, not without backsliding: Klinsmann and Littbarski are good, no doubt about it. I hope Matthäus won't pick up a second yellow card.)

From Berlin to Behlendorf, 3 July 1990
After two hours of back-and-forth: Luchterhand's plan of creating a company to promote paperback editions. Faber's insane notion of launching a paperback series when the market is already saturated: "Our classics!" This is the same Faber who (according to a *Frankfurter Allgemeine* reporter waiting to see him), when Gerhard Wolf pressed him, admitted that he had had the letter firing Wolf on his desk for four days, and that Wolf was only the interim director of Aufbau. Now decisions had to be made quickly. Even Christa Wolf, usually quite hesitant, was prepared to accept the charter of Luchterhand's Authors' Council, and sought Christoph Hein's advice. I hope it's not too late. I advised her to consult the intellectual-property lawyer Hertin, who had been helpful to us. On the table were plates of Bahlsen cookies, arranged in an unusual symmetry: all the wafer rolls were pointed toward the head of the long table, like cannon muzzles. For the first time I took an East German taxi to West Berlin (the driver still unfamiliar with the streets), deposited my bag at the house on Niedstrasse, and half an hour later took Nele with me to Helene's theatrical debut at the Droste-Hülshoff School. A successful performance. Along school

corridors, up and down staircases to the auditorium, and the same on the way back. The first part comically absurd. A text by Botho Strauss mucking around in the universal suffering caused by love proved irritating only for a short while, because the Borchert and Kafka adaptations were successful. It was clear that excellent teachers had made the months of rehearsals pay off. What good luck to have such teachers.

Helene was cast as the letter I, an ostracized outsider who wished she could sit on the bench with the other letters and flail her legs and screech in unison with them. Veronika felt compelled to interpret this portrayal as an expression of Helene's actual situation: these mothers!

Before the discussion at Aufbau got under way, I went by the Academy of Arts to pick up Peter Härtling. Was greeted there like a prodigal son (or father?). We drove to the Brandenburg Gate. Then we walked through the sparsely attended deutschmark premiere on Unter den Linden, stopped for coffee and GDR brandy (the remaining stock), and finally found our way to Französische Strasse and Aufbau (I for the first time). There, in the outer office, a lovable ghost from bygone times: Theo Pinkus.

Maybe it was yesterday's school play that suggested the idea of smuggling into my soft-coal landscapes figures and fabulous creatures, allusions to my long-ago birds, and also placing a bony fish down in the pit, since from a distance the power shovels (in reality) are the size of insects, and in their black rigidity resemble fabulous creatures.

The discussion this afternoon with Peter Glotz for the *Neue Gesellschaft* journal offered me a chance to formulate my long-repressed criticism of Brandt and Lafontaine — that is, of an SPD that has run out of alternatives — and thus to hint at my growing alienation, on the one hand, from the party of which I am a member, and on the other, from the greater Federal Republic being created through annexation and borrowing.

On All Souls' Day the widower and the widow should visit the cemetery next to the Russian memorial (across from the lead-free filling station), and there come up with the outlines of their plan.

Behlendorf, 4 July 1990

Yesterday Italy was knocked out. The boot is weeping. But the Argentines were better, surprisingly: up to the penalties. These proxy wars do serve a purpose; and if England beats Germany today, and the final round pits England against Argentina, we could see a replay of the Falklands War — this time without bloodshed.

Today I agreed to a *Spiegel* interview (for tomorrow), with Karasek, whom I have come to dislike intensely. Bissinger advised me to do it. I plan to bring up the Christa Wolf situation.

At noon Carlo Feltrinelli came by; he and Bruno are friends. He has taken over leadership of the publishing company, bowing patiently to pressure from his energetic mother and the legend of his father. He wants to get me back in the fold — ironically with a political book; after all, it was a political (Social Democratic) book that his politically rigid father refused to publish that made me leave Feltrinelli and go to Einaudi. A likeable young man, maybe a bit too friendly for the business he is in.

At last Albania is beginning to quake, too!

Behlendorf, 5 July 1990

The first of the old birds now have the new landscape as a backdrop, as if it had been waiting for them. These pieces convey something of a "heroic landscape," with the enormous pits in the background. Should I position the abandoned blackbird's nest with the four unhatched eggs in the foreground of a vertical composition?

The game yesterday ended with penalties and the Germans won. I caught myself crossing my fingers for the Germans when the English team had a chance to shoot. Oskar L. offered a postgame commentary like a pro. The *Spiegel* interview today with Karasek and R. Becker turned out to be fairly civilized. I am curious to see how much of that will be left in the edited version. Apparently the Bundesrat is intervening now in the drafting of the second State Treaty, the one that will bring about unification of the two states: strengthening the rights of the individual provinces.

Behlendorf, 6 July 1990

This morning I found a four-leaf clover under the walnut tree right away and put it on Ute's plate at breakfast.

This afternoon I am supposed to attend the village festival: Behlendorf has been named the "prettiest village." Am supposed to read from *The Flounder* at the inn. Between the concert of the fire brigade band and the mayor's speech.

After that we are driving to Hamburg to see the Nevermanns.

Have some of my toad calls been nothing more than toad calls, the mistaken predictions of a notorious pessimist? Is the absence of the buying craze I had anticipated for the GDR population a first positive sign? Is it possible that the Bundesrat, with an SPD majority, and O. Lafontaine, now politically visible again, could nudge things in the direction of a German federation or a federation of German provinces after all? Do the cautious moves of NATO and the Warsaw Pact toward each other suggest the possibility of a new European security system? If Poland's western border is guaranteed by treaty, would that not ultimately set limits to economic expansion across the Oder? Would eighty million Germans intent only on achieving prosperity constitute an acceptable risk? Am I, with my fears, anxieties, and toad calls, merely a captive of the past, a dinosaur?

What speaks against such an explanation is that from one day to the next it becomes more obvious who will own the means of production, from beer to cinemas, from coffee-roasting operations (Tchibo) to automobiles: the gentlemen from West Germany. The conditions of ownership are already settled for the long haul.

After the village festival — a Herr von Suchandsuch spoke on the topic of "Structural Changes in Rural Areas" — I finished the large-scale drawing of "Old Birds in a New Landscape." "Old Fritz," the chapter from *The Flounder* that I read aloud, apparently struck a chord with the completely unliterary audience.

Behlendorf, 7 July 1990

It was grappa and kirsch (after a lot of red wine) that enabled Jürgen Flimm and me to get properly plastered — without a hangover — for the first time in ages; consistent with our perpetual jousting over *The Plebeians,* I threatened in jest to impose a moratorium on performances of the play in the German-speaking and theater world (after a grace period of six months); he was determined to work up "something new" for the stage with me. Yes, I said, but only after he produced *The Plebeians.* And so forth. An enjoyable evening, especially since Naumann (Rowohlt), who wants to buy up Aufbau before Suhrkamp (Unseld) snatches it, was also shocked when I told him in no uncertain terms that the Aufbau authors, on advice from Härtling and me, intend to shield themselves from the arbitrary actions of publishers by adopting an authors' council statute.

Our host, Knut Nevermann, who in 1968, as a confirmed leftist, categorically refused to support my "revisionist" plan to participate in a Social Democratic voters' initiative, has in the meantime become so loyal to the government and so mannerly that I keep having to kick myself. But he is lovable, as is his Marie. And besides, I predicted at the time that we would encounter the leftists again when they reappeared several years down the road, smiling amiably as they approached from the right. Now Knut Nevermann is not a right-winger. He has become neither-nor, but is still lovable. And Ute was beautiful all evening long (in purple).

In the afternoon we had company from Schwerin: Herr and Frau Ürkwitz. Both complain, like everyone in the GDR at the moment, about the high prices, especially for groceries, which are far more expensive than in West Germany. Up to now the last remaining East German companies, HO and Konsum, had a monopoly. Now SPAR and other cut-rate companies from the West are about to break this monopoly. But for now people are going over the former border and to West Berlin to do their shopping, which could drive up prices here. Cooperatives are forming, sending someone with a car or a truck and shopping lists across the border. This is a development even I, the pessimist, had not foreseen. No wonder they complain, given their low wages and salaries: this is worse than before! At the cobbler's, Frau Ürkwitz says, the prices are higher and the waiting time is just as long as in the old days. In the coming months this is likely to be the predominant tone: moaning and groaning.

Behlendorf, 8 July 1990
After a long sleep, so long that no dreams stayed with me, I switched from charcoal to pencil: a vertical format, in the foreground the

blackbird's nest Ute brought me. The drawing has been sketched and must now wait for when I am home again. Tomorrow, off to Berlin.

From Behlendorf to Berlin, 9 July 1990
So that was that: the Germans played better and are now world champions. Afterward the celebrations took place in true German style: all through the republic, and louder and more joyful than when the Wall fell. In the meantime, the deutschmark has had its one-week anniversary in the GDR and has lost some of its luster. Indeed, it is revealing itself as a hard currency in both senses of the word.

The three large-scale drawings done in a week left me exhausted. Am wondering whether "The Call of the Toad" should be narrated in the present tense.

In the next few weeks I must send off my papers to the Academy for the archives and endow and launch the new Chodowiecki Prize. All this in light of the unsettling prospect that Berlin will become the capital — of what? The Greater German Federal Republic? The German Federation? Or, as I would prefer, the Federation of German Provinces?

Berlin, 10 July 1990
When I picked up Nele, cheerful as always, from school at noon, we went first to the bank — Nele said "to rob the bank" — and then sat on a small bench across from the Italian restaurant, Nele with an ice cream cone. I explained to her, keeping my words simple, the conflict between Ute and Ingrid, and the reasons for it. Nele understood the whole thing and did her best to make talking about it easy for me.

After a few hours of dictating letters, I went with Maria to

Rheinstrasse for an Italian snack. Maria is a good listener. Now off to see Jurek Becker and his Christine. The day before yesterday the baby arrived: Jonathan.

Behlendorf, 13 July 1990
Back from Berlin, exhausted by mountains of mail, family squabbles.

Jurek Becker as a father. The apartment, which used to be neat as a pin, almost interior-decorated, ideal for life as a couple, now looks like a battlefield. With Manfred Krug having turned all nationalistic on us, too, Jurek feels he has lost a friend. Anticipating that for the next ten years Berlin will be one enormous construction site, and because in Berlin all the little children will be suffering from "Krupp," he wants to have a second home on the Schlei River near Kappeln, a waterfront property.

And Ingrid has found a house — what a relief! — in the Uckermark, and bought it with a simple handshake. Apparently in a half-abandoned village in an area inhabited by former residents of Stettin now convinced that as a result of German unification Stettin will soon be "ours" again. History as a process of regression: toad calls.

Right at the beginning of the story, when the widower and the widow are visiting the cemetery next to the Russian monument and across from the Hagelsberg, once a German, later a Polish, burial ground but unused since the mid-fifties, they could come upon a tombstone with a German inscription that the widower recognizes as that of his maternal uncle.

In the GDR social chaos is erupting. Even Raoul, who wanted to reassure me pragmatically, now sees my "grim predictions" confirmed. Being proven right in this way leaves me feeling morose. Worked yesterday and today on editing the *Spiegel* interview, which has been cut several times, and the interview with *Neue Gesellschaft:* sent off the former and did the latter over the telephone.

Ute is picking me up in Mölln.

Behlendorf, 14 July 1990
Two weeks since the introduction of the deutschmark in the GDR: the horse that fled when the barn door was opened has been declared guilty.

Behlendorf, 15 July 1990
It took us only fifteen minutes to reach the former border crossing at Mustin. The GDR begins with a stand of dead birches. We drove by way of Schwerin and Sternberg, passed Dabel and Borkow, then took a left turn, and after another kilometer reached Woserin, where Christa and Gerhard Wolf live in a remote former rectory, with two linden trees flanking the entry to the courtyard: just a two-hour drive through a sweeping landscape that near Woserin resembles the area around Behlendorf, but the large stretches of farmland cultivated by collectives make it appear more monotonous. The gray villages now look even more so in contrast with the signs advertising Western products — Camels, Langnese ice cream — and the freshly painted names on the stores.

A writer from Hannover, Elisabeth Lenk, is staying with the Wolfs. The visit began with several varieties of crumb cake in the garden. Later, in the kitchen, Gerhard Wolf pulled a roast duck out of the oven. On the overgrown property, a married daughter of the Wolfs also lives with her husband and two children, Anton and Helene. Anton addressed our harmless Kara timidly as "you big dog."

Never have I seen Christa Wolf so relaxed and unguarded. Yet it seems to me that she is tearing herself apart, brooding over herself and the uproar that refuses to subside. Her (understandable) failure to resign from the Party when Biermann was expatriated. Whereas several writers who protested this action were expelled by the Socialist Unity Party, among them Kunert, Sarah Kirsch, and also Gerhard Wolf, she was let off with a reprimand. She never withdrew her signature from the protest. The role Kant played as Hager's errand boy.

Apparently she cannot get past the undifferentiated and clearly unjust accusations heaped on her in public, accusations intended to destroy her. The problem is that these accusations overlap with certain things for which she can never forgive herself, such as her silence when the Soviets marched into Czechoslovakia in August of '68.

Our visit to the Wolfs confirmed that I was right to come to her defense in the current campaign directed at her, as I did most recently in the *Spiegel* interview, which appears tomorrow.

It is striking how she dominates the conversation. Although Gerhard Wolf is the clearer thinker, he usually keeps his opinions to himself: obviously their tried-and-true pattern. In between, snatches of conversation about dreams, grandchildren, the man who fishes in the nearby lake but can no longer sell his fish to the local restaurant because, since the introduction of the deutschmark, no one eats there anymore. Shortly before we leave — an exchange about cars — she thanks me, superfluously, for my solidarity and support.

I really should look over my defense of Christa Wolf and make sure to provide solid justification. The questions Karasek or Peter Glotz posed did not get to the heart of the matter; and crude attacks tend to result in a crude, that is to say massive, defense.

It was after eleven P.M. when we drove back along the deserted road. Distracted from our own concerns, Ute and I chatted away. I want to get back to drawing.

Behlendorf, 17 July 1990
I am drawing. Starting with the large-scale pencil drawing I began before the trip to Berlin, it was easy to go on to a piece in charcoal. It is as if I wanted to bury myself in that lunar soft-coal landscape, among the slag heaps, the more so since the major political events hardly leave me much choice.

Kohl is celebrating his triumph in the Soviet Union. The miserable economic situation is forcing Gorbachev to accept united Germany's membership in NATO in return for 5 billion deutschmarks, an embarrassing capitulation. A decision with major implications for the future (until past the year 2000), leaving Poland squeezed between two giants. What is to prevent us, with West Germany a member of NATO, from insisting that the territory between the Elbe and the Oder be kept free of troops, if NATO allegedly no longer sees the Soviet Union as an enemy? Our Western neighbors are nervously celebrating Germany's "successes," so as not to fall into the coarse tone being struck by the British. The Greater German Republic already seems to be in charge, setting the pace, establishing deadlines, and flaunting its economic prowess. At the same time, the chaos in the GDR is spreading. Oskar Lafontaine is making his first cautious appearances there, speaking of Kohl in a congratulatory vein to demonstrating construction workers and dishing out criticism in little bites.

After an almost sleepless night: reading a book that describes the final phase of the Thirty Years' War in Germany, the role played by the electoral princes.

Told Ute for the first time about my plan of working this

journal into the "Call of the Toad" story, in a tighter, expanded form.

Today the Two Plus Four discussion on Poland is taking place.

Behlendorf, 18 July 1990
Ute has gone to Freiburg to be with her mother, who is ill. Afraid it may be cancer. She intends to stay a week or longer. I like being alone with the dog. I went back to the *Signatur* drawing project, which has been lying fallow for too long: the first sheet (charcoal) shows birds in the foreground of a landscape. The text, "My ancient birds are back," is situated in a new landscape this time, between Cottbus and Senftenberg, where the lignite comes to light. Ease into my letter from Altdöbern, which could fill half of a double leaf.

It looks as though "unity" has "moved full-speed ahead," to use the current terminology. Now billions in loans are supposed to prop up the collapsing agricultural sector and the impoverished cities and towns. Long live the free market economy! Now Poland, like the Soviet Union, wants to conclude a general treaty with united Germany, but of course it must not be called that, for the sake of the economy. No sooner is the Oder-Neisse Line recognized than it is supposed to be Europeanized, or, in other words, made porous, so the economy — that is, the German economy — can expand freely.

Write a portrait of the Germans: how this time they cross the border peaceably, armed only with consumer goods and cheap loans. To be sure, this will not work unless the countries in question adopt legal provisions allowing the establishment of foreign firms. The advantages of location will require guarantees. Thus the politics will determine the plot of my "Call of the Toad" story, still in the conceptual stages. (Might one not use the generally understood term "Europeanization" to describe yet another partition of Poland into zones controlled by different economic interests?)

Behlendorf, 19 July 1990

What if the narrator of "The Call of the Toad" had such large literary ambitions that he found a straightforward narrative repellent, character descriptions ridiculous, factual information trivial, and for that reason, his taste shaped by the fifties, fluctuated between the *nouveau roman* and concrete poetry? A comical fluctuation, repeatedly thwarted by external events dictating the course of the action? Thus right at the beginning the establishment of the topography and the detail-obsessed analysis of the flower stands at the Dominican Market could run wild until finally — of necessity — the purchase of the flowers takes place. The widower and the widow buy rust-brown asters from a peasant woman squatting off to one side.

Behlendorf, 20 July 1990

Yesterday Björn Engholm came from Hamburg with Nilius to pick up the keys to our house in Portugal. My supposition is gaining strength that he would like to get out of politics as soon as he has a chance. At most, he says, he might be tempted by the opportunity to serve as prime minister of Mecklenburg and rescue that province from its dismal economic prospects.

His happy anticipation now that he, too, has written a book. A generation of politicians, to which O.L. also belongs, who lack passion; they have other choices: returning to private life, running an art gallery, etc. On the other hand, precisely this lack of commitment makes them human.

Am working on a vertical-format drawing and on the *Signatur* project. In East Berlin the coalition may fall apart because of the voting system.

For the Oslo conference at the end of August I must prepare a ten-minute speech: "On the Hate of Those Left Behind." On the belated victory of the losers: Germany and Japan. Social injustice as fertile ground in which hate grows. Two different kinds of Germans. And next to the second-class Germans we will soon have third- and fourth-class Czechs and Poles, consumed by hatred of the Russians. Over eighty million Germans as the object of envy and hate. The brevity of the text calls for propositions. Hate based on racist (the Jews) or religious (Islam) reasons and centuries-long political dependency (Poles and Russians), added to which are ideological reasons (Communists and capitalists) and, last but not least, social factors.

Behlendorf, 21 July 1990
Being alone suits me, the more so since age is becoming impossible to ignore, yet being alone in company is not tolerated. Also ignominious defeats (not only the political kind) become more and more unavoidable.

Drawing for the *Signatur* project lets me go back to old motifs: today, in graphite, the flounder.

In a little while the Nevermanns are coming to take me to a birthday party near Behlendorf Lake: Kuhbier, Hamburg's senator for the environment, is turning I am not sure how old.

As irrational as any form of hate seems, it still has a basis in reality. (For Oslo.)

Behlendorf, 22 July 1990
Was back by midnight: a gathering, in a hospitable farmhouse with an unpretentious addition, of nice public officeholders, in-

dividually also interesting, architects, ministers, and their wives. Homemade cake. A walk down to the lake (across from the village of Behlendorf). A small bay with a beach for swimming. An old-fashioned wooden diving platform. Some of the gentlemen go swimming. Later I fall silent, because there is laughter all around at local-government inside jokes, and the observation that the GDR lacks properly trained notaries fails to amuse me. A gathering of comfortable left-wing liberals: hard-working, disturbingly even-tempered. The after-dinner speech by Kuhbier's older brother in which he describes their monster of a father and what he did to them; then my brief speech defending the father, who is dead and thus incapable of speaking up for himself, and criticizing fifty-year-olds who persist in blaming their parents for the damage they suffered in their youth. (That, too, is received amiably.) The family's adolescent daughter: amusing in a straw hat, a gangly redhead.

And today, after I had composed a drawing for *Signatur,* Bruno, Susan, and my sweet granddaughter Ronja arrived. An affectionate son. We took Ute's bicycle and the tandem and rode to Berkenthin, where we ate Königsberg dumplings and then pedaled along the canal, under the poplars, to the Behlendorf lock. Lovely summery weather, windy but persistently dry.

Behlendorf, 23 July 1990

The gardeners are coming early. Ingrid Krüger announced on the telephone — after some back-and-forth — that Nele would be arriving in late afternoon. So there was still time for another *Signatur* piece. Because I am focused on the *Signatur* format, at the moment I lack the impetus for large-scale pieces. I am witnessing with nothing but chagrin (and also waning interest) the coalition squabbles in East Berlin. This wrangling motivated purely by party politics fails to address the population's very real problems. Now potash mining is collapsing, too: pressure from West German competition.

One of the gardeners sums it all up: "Kohl is getting his way." The other gardener says, "The people in the GDR wanted this. So I have no sympathy for them." The roles have already been assigned: the East Germans are going to be the failures, the losers yet again.

Before Ute gets back I want to try to come up with an outline for "The Call of the Toad," or to list the elements. Also a chronological table of parallel developments.

Behlendorf, 27 July 1990

Yesterday Nele left. Three pleasant days, father and daughter: a trip to Lübeck, walking through the woods to Behlendorf Lake, swimming. I teach Nele the backstroke, proudly show her my dive from the two-meter board, cook for her: zucchini, apples with fried potatoes and diced ham. I will still have time to spend two or three hours working on *Signatur*. Only the outline for "The Call of the Toad" will have to wait. Moments of happiness: walking hand in hand with the child through the woods.

A visit from Stephan Lohr with his wife. As Wolfram Schütte (*Frankfurter Rundschau*) already did on the phone, Lohr now tells me about Greiner's unspeakable article in *Die Zeit* and an article in the *Frankfurter Allgemeine* that defends me in a spiteful manner against H. Kant's insinuations. The unanimity between those two papers makes both Schütte and Lohr uneasy, but it does not bother me anymore. Now that my conversation with the *Neue Gesellschaft* has appeared today in the *Frankfurter Rundschau*, the attacks will only increase. I plan to save all this material, wait for the second State Treaty, and then draw up an interim balance sheet, if not at the beginning of August, then in Denmark.

Typical the way they treat Christa Wolf: her achievement as a writer, set against those judgmental, prejudiced cultural functionaries Greiner and Schirrmacher. The first moves toward declaring the entire GDR population guilty. The treatment of Germans by Germans. This businesslike brutality betrays the new lordly tone in dealing with the Poles and Russians as their economic weakness persists. Perhaps I should include on this interim balance sheet the four pages of text I plan to write in Denmark for Oslo.

Behlendorf, 31 July 1990
Today Ute left for Freiburg again to be with her mother, who is to be operated on at the end of the week.

A single one-page drawing and thirteen double-page drawings for *Signatur* with the title "Letter from Altdöbern" are now finished. Surprising to see how, without a predetermined plan, simply with the benefit of distance from earlier creative phases, but sparked by the soft-coal landscapes, one image after another took shape. The question remains whether a last double leaf as an addendum, with a reference to Calcutta, is possible and necessary.

For Oslo I plan to examine social deprivation as a source of various forms of hatred. The National Socialists' seizure of power and the rabid racism they unleashed would hardly have been possible without six million unemployed. American racism, especially toward the blacks, parallels the social deprivation of the lower classes, especially of the blacks themselves. Thus the persistent and growing impoverishment of Third World peoples will also result in an increase in various forms of hatred, at first directed at those closest to the group in question — members of other tribes, religious groups. The predictable impoverishment of large swaths of the population in the Soviet Union and Poland will occasion hatred combined with nationalism. Despite seemingly more favorable conditions, within the GDR population the initial anticipation of the miraculous deutschmark will give way to disappointment. Unemployment growing by leaps and bounds, the arrogant, supercilious behavior of the West Germans as they "take charge," the likely prospect of yet again being the duped, the eternal losers, and now also the failures, could allow hatred to sprout, not without self-hatred. After the collapse of the repressive Communist regime and the economy of scarcity, the capitalist system and its ideology, the free market economy, and the power of the banks are being put to the test.

In the GDR, four weeks after the introduction of the deutschmark, reports of catastrophes are multiplying. Today Labor Minister Hildebrandt spoke of the collapse of the economy and the increasing departures of trained workers and apprentices for the West — all developments that I predicted, and which, now that they are actually occurring, are not calculated to lift the spirits.

Yesterday and the day before, Antje Vollmer was here with her Johannes. We observed how little remains of the hopes expressed at the Tutzing conference, modest even then. It is scary to see the debates raging on television about Berlin as the capital or about the proper way to conduct elections, while the financial hole — currently 30 billion — keeps growing.

Behlendorf, 1 August 1990
A hot day and burning eyes. Neither my new glasses nor eye drops do any good. I wonder whether even out here in the country the ozone pollution is to blame. Or should I attribute this annoyance (since Calcutta) to old age?

And yet a serene day of quiet, concentrated work. In the morning one more double leaf for *Signatur,* the last: an addendum bringing in Calcutta (cheek by jowl with Altdöbern), a charcoal drawing.

Then, after several false starts, I sketched the double snail with the soft-coal landscape in the background, using graphite on Bristol board in horizontal format. It is as if this creature, too, had been waiting for this particular region and its horizon.

And then, already tired from drawing, I began laying out Plan 2 for "The Call of the Toad," using one of the five drawing pads I snapped up on sale in Altdöbern. The five-part structure begins with the exposition, but I am not yet sure of the narrator's point of view or tone. There is still time before the end of the year to get the opening sentence right.

How present Ute feels in the house, and at the same time so far away.

From Bonn the GDR ministers receive warnings not to spread bad news. The dollar has fallen to 1.59 deutschmarks. This coming weekend I plan to go to Berlin and then on to the Uckermark region to take a look at the house Ingrid has bought. I am glad the two have found a place they can call their own. Ingrid on the phone: hectic as always. What if I did not have my drawing boards, large and small! My eyes are burning.

Behlendorf, 2 August 1990
Iraq's incursion into Kuwait. The way wars of conquest take place now, as in earlier times, under the protective shield of the great powers.

More work on the double snail. A hot day. I spent an hour relocating the sprinkler hose. Painstaking work on the outline for

"The Call of the Toad." The wretched Election Treaty is signed. I doubt whether I shall participate in these elections, and if I do, I will vote for Alliance 90 instead of the Greens. First reservations being voiced in Karlsruhe over the Election Treaty.

In the evening the Bissingers came to visit, later Eva and Peter Rühmkorf. We had a great time bemoaning Germany.

Behlendorf, 3 August 1990

Now the headlong rush toward a unified country begins. Allegedly at the behest of the GDR prime minister, de Maizière, Kohl moves the elections up to 14 October. This is how he intends to cheat his way out of the economic and social chaos. Given the continuing weakness of the SPD, I fear his calculation will pay off.

The "Double Snail at Her Destination" is finished. Now I want to concentrate on the outline for "The Call of the Toad" and draft an outline for another text, which I will dictate in Berlin: "A Bargain Called the GDR."

Late in the evening, Lafontaine, speaking from Paris: combative, serious, with pointed criticism, yet still offering nothing in the way of alternatives. "The Call of the Toad," now mapped out conceptually, could develop into a slight, bitterly comical story of 180 to 200 pages.

In the afternoon my sister came to see me for an early celebration of her sixtieth birthday, which falls on 23 September. Then Ute's first husband, Bruno Grunert, came by with Annette and two children, as well as their dog with six puppies, 1,000 deutschmarks each. They were on their way back from Møn: the Baltic stinks of rot. Persistent, no, increasing heat. The ozone levels high in the north.

Why am I concentrating calmly on my drawings? Yesterday

Norbert Elias died, one of the last "learned men." In the evening I ate one of the twenty-five trout Herr Lübcke fished out of the pond this morning, with scrambled eggs.

Behlendorf, 4 August 1990
It keeps getting hotter. Franz, our organic farmer, complains on the phone about this third dry summer in a row. And beneath this dome of heat German unification is taking place, a declaration of bankruptcy. Nonetheless, from Monday on, when I am in Berlin I plan to get started on the text "A Bargain Called the GDR." These would be the main points:

1. The bottom line after only one month of bankruptcy: empty cash registers, unemployment.
2. Headlong rush toward violation of the constitution: elections on 14 October, the form of the elections.
3. Second-class Germans: the consequences are hate, jealousy, inferiority complex.
4. The newly burnished ideology: free market economy.
5. Without decency and dignity — no ideas, just a bargain.
6. The way Germans treat other Germans does not bode well for the Poles.
7. Democracy is taking a beating: violations of the constitution, bypassing the parliament, persecution of intellectuals, while the Stasi is spared. The press singing in unison. Need to warn against the Germany that is taking shape. Contempt for the opposition.
8. Blitzkrieg mentality. As if Germany and Japan had won the war. No sign of culture.
9. Ozone alert. General obliviousness.

The whole thing still lacks a compelling introduction and framework. Twelve pages would be about right. Maybe my trip to the Uckermark region will provide further insight.

My drawing, the hours and days spent at the large drawing board, northern light falling on it from the side, is at an end for now. Once I am back from Berlin, it will be time to leave for Møn.

Gorkow, 5 August 1990
The trip to Berlin resulted in a declaration by two older women in my compartment that Kara was a dog who should be on television. Maria met us at Zoo Station. The usual commotion there heightened to the point of absurdity. A drunk, naked from the waist up, bawling a repentant sermon to the diners seated on the sidewalk terrace of the station restaurant. I showed Maria my drawings for *Signatur.* How cautiously she responded to them. Later at the Greek restaurant: Kara, the country dog, enjoying the smells of the streets of Friedenau.

This morning at ten Eike and I drove through heavy traffic on the autobahn out to the Uckermark. Striking numbers of GDR residents driving cars from the West. We turned off near Pasewalk, reaching the tumbledown village of Gorkow twenty-five kilometers farther on. There a single-family house with stables and sheds on an overgrown piece of land, already occupied, as it turned out, by Ingrid and Nele. A young man by the name of Richter — the director of the Reclam publishing house in Leipzig, the successor to Marquardt since Opitz, that nonentity, was voted out — has also bought a house in the village, a bargain, of course. Swimming in the lake. The people on the beach like something from the fifties. The changing cabins on knee-high stilts. Many women, still young yet already chunky, lying around like manatees. Late in the afternoon through the Randow Gap with the stocky female leader of an agricultural cooperative to see Haflinger horses in a paddock. Should I buy a gelding for Nele, who is horse-crazy, just as Laura used to be? I like this level landscape — poor, sandy, seemingly forgotten, likely to be bypassed by future prosperity.

Despite my distracted state, I am happy for Ingrid and Nele, who have found a place for themselves here.

During the car ride, Eike tells me about his current project, a film about a former Mercedes assembly plant that was operated during the war with concentration camp inmates and forced laborers from Ukraine and is now scheduled to be revived by Mercedes for truck manufacturing, with the nonbinding promise that four thousand of the current seven thousand workers will be kept on.

Back on Niedstrasse late in the evening, when Raoul returned from Elskop, I noticed he is developing a paunch. I felt annoyed, as if my sons should not be allowed (or not yet, at any rate) to imitate their father's paunch.

This evening Christoph Hein and his wife are to come by. They live twenty kilometers away, likewise in a single-family house, built in the fifties, which he was able to buy cheaply shortly before the currency union and is now adding onto. I saw him in work clothes there, gaunt, fragile, yet tough, sitting at the table with masons who earn 4 marks an hour at the agricultural collective, whereas on the weekend he pays them 15 marks an hour. One of the masons has already been lured away to the West. Contracts in the construction industry are few and far between because the towns have no money, so even construction firms are facing bankruptcy.

Behlendorf, 9 August 1990
The three days in Berlin (with the dog) kept me hopping. At last it is raining.

All eyes are riveted on the Near East, where war could break out any day. On close inspection it becomes apparent that the white industrialized countries (now including the Soviet Union) are aligned against the Third World nations poor in natural resources. In addition, in the double Germany, soon to be single, there is conflict over the elections and accession. Lafontaine is beginning to fight. At the moment the SPD is backing him, but for how long? During a late-night discussion with Peter Schneider over wine and fruit brandies, we considered giving our support in September to a future SPD–Greens–Alliance 90 coalition.

Because I had to dictate a five-page text for the Paris event on 25 September, I could not prepare for Oslo. A project for Møn.

Sent *Signatur* off to Rommerskirchen.

Behlendorf, 10 August 1990
The Bundestag debate yesterday had only one high point: the short speech by Antje Vollmer, who argued confidently that the Germans' behavior toward each other and among themselves would be an indicator of their future actions, for instance toward the Poles. She cited the democratic process that began in 1968 as giving legitimacy to the claim of political leadership being voiced by Alliance 90 and the Greens. Lafontaine's speech, while right on social policy, as usual lacked anything new. Now the elections are scheduled for the original date after all: 2 December.

Steidl's visit: I signed the last tree lithos and copies of *Dead Wood*.

Am editing the piece for Paris, and will rewrite it tomorrow. Ute arrived late. Was looking forward so much to seeing her.

Telephone conversation with Laura and Ralf: housing problems. I doubt I'll find sufficient concentration in the next few months to make progress on "The Call of the Toad"; the political situation is too turbulent. I would almost have preferred having the whole thing over with on 14 October: the ensuing bleak silence would have made work appealing.

Behlendorf, 12 August 1990
Am exhausted. From what? From large-scale drawing? But also from this new Germany taking shape, as if there were no other possibilities, civilized ones. Why does it always have to be so grand, so Wagnerian?

And tomorrow we are off to Møn, where I can take refuge in the woods.

Have coated seven copper plates. Plan to do more drawing with lead and graphite. The typewriter must come along. For Oslo I should also write a passage about hatred and "holy war." The text for Paris, "Some Warning Signs," is finished, very much to the point and unambiguous, as warnings should be.

Am reading about Chodowiecki: what lifelong diligence on a small scale!

Ulvshale/Møn, 13 August 1990
The Baltic lay leaden beneath motionless muggy air. The Vogterhus was waiting for us (our fifteenth summer here). The grass yellow, the birches yellow, the blackberries shrunken. Although the sun is hidden behind haze and veils of clouds, it stabs the skin and is so intensely hot that I had to give up working at the table outdoors, in the past always cooled by a slight breeze.

Ute forgot her bag on the ferry's sun deck. We did not miss it until we were already down on the car deck. I ran to the loading area, had an announcement made over the loudspeaker about the lost bag, searched the sun deck, all in vain. In the meantime, Ute drove the car off the ferry and parked, then ran back to the boat, and returned half an hour later with the bag: someone (from the GDR, she thinks) had come across it and brought it to the lost-and-found office. Of course we had to pay a reward of 100 deutsch-marks.

No sooner had we arrived than I set up my little study, which looks out over the ocean, complete with northern light — pencils, brushes, charcoal, tobacco, cigarillos, matches, pipes. On a shelf the seven coated copper plates. The Olivetti, on a little chest, still too low. Left here from last year, a bunch of gull and wild goose feathers for drawing. Above the house and the woods behind it, above the meadow stretching to the dunes, gulls are in constant motion, but silent: restless against the pale yet blazing sky.

Two years ago I did the first *Dead Wood* drawings here, in the copse in back of the house. In a few days the book will be reaching the bookstores.

Ulvshale, 14 August 1990

After a night of tossing and turning, battling the unaccustomed mosquitoes, and after the first refreshing plunge into the Baltic near Klintholm Havn, where we bought fluke and herring right off the boat, I went to the woods and tried to get back into the swing of drawing, returning to the motifs that have been so familiar for the past two years. Using lead and graphite I managed to come up with an image in vertical format that will lend itself to further development, perhaps even (after the pencil phase) to compact charcoal drawings; but I want that to be the end for this topic — if, indeed, it can ever end.

The three drawings in my sketchbook from the Jewish cemetery in Prague could provide the impetus for engravings; lithos would be merely translations.

I am having a hard time settling into the Ulvshale Vogterhus this summer. Whole bundles of thoughts related to the GDR (Altdöbern, the Uckermark region) need to be headed off. The nagging question remains: Would it not have made more sense, and been more logical, to find a place to stay for two weeks in Saxony or in Lusatia, rather than coming here as a favor to Ute?

Am going to fire up the typewriter and write my way back.

Ulvshale, 15 August 1990

Could not get to sleep. For ten minutes around midnight large drops of rain fell. Unfinished thoughts going around and around like a mill wheel. Then this chicken coop that keeps us huddled together year after year, as if made for love. And Ute, who year after year combs the four walls and the ceiling for mosquitoes. The traces of her swats. My reading before not falling asleep: Rilke's *Malte Laurids Brigge.* How out of step with our time and yet so apt, because this book already voices in vain the longing, no, the demand, for a death of one's own. How precise and far removed from vagueness Rilke can be. A book that will survive, insofar as books survive.

After swimming, despite being exhausted, bought live herring right off the boat. The fishermen skin the fluke while they are still on board and toss the skins to the gulls: a population without a pecking order — unless the strongest one gets its way, behavior so similar to that of humans.

A scandalous development in the Persian Gulf war that might occur any day, and as early as tomorrow, could be an Iraqi attack on Israel's cities with poison-gas warheads — which would make the Germans, of whom the world allegedly no longer needs to be afraid, responsible for the annihilation of Jews, because the Germans were the original suppliers. The very possibility should set off protests, if not in Germany, then abroad.

The forest exhales mugginess, is stifling. Nonetheless, did some drawing in pencil, a horizontal composition.

Hundreds of wild geese, their formations constantly dissolving and coming back together, are passing over the meadow in front of the house, heading for the open sea. Their honking becomes audible and just as suddenly is swallowed up.

Might not the widower and widow leave behind their diaries, as well as their correspondence? How would it be if both sent their papers to the narrator, when they are in Italy and on their way back from Naples, suggesting that he "do something with the material"?

Ulvshale, 17 August 1990

At last I have found my Møn rhythm: drawing in the woods, picking blackberries on the heath, the typewriter in the north-facing room. Also a thunderstorm today, followed by rain that brought coolness and wind. We are living on fish from Klintholm Havn: herring, fluke. The news on German radio reports a falling dollar (1.55), escalation of the Iraq conflict, and the dismissal of the SPD ministers by de Maizière. All this seems close, as I have started working on my speech for Oslo.

At some point — next year, I hope — I want to let myself relax, perhaps with the help of "The Call of the Toad," and shake off the obligations I have imposed on myself. I have been driven too long by a sense of duty.

Today went biking with Ute on the tandem.

Ulvshale, 20 August 1990

The days flow into one another; harvesting the blackberries is the only thing that imposes a schedule. When was it that, out where the heath borders on the sound, in the section by the overgrown bulwark from the days of Napoleon's continental blockade of England, we saw those seven chimney sweeps — adolescent apprentices and journeymen — drinking beer on their company outing. Of course there was one girl gamboling gracefully among the blond boys, who, in their black caps and head-to-toe black outfits, fit the guild image perfectly. Several of the boys had blackened their faces. A story that can be told in a number of ways and does not need to be written down. We could hear them for a long time.

Breakfast in bed, because since early morning it has been raining, sometimes pelting down, sometimes falling evenly. Above the sound of the rain, Radio Germany: the Gulf crisis is intensifying; the GDR-SPD has dropped out of the coalition (finally). Two circumstances that at first glance have nothing to do with each other, but the stock market is twice as volatile as usual.

The five-page piece on hatred (the Oslo conference theme) is finished. I drew far-reaching conclusions from the German-German and German-Polish reasons for hate, and pointed out that with the development and establishment by German companies of poison-gas factories in Iraq, the Germans were once again culpable, the more so since they have also been decisively involved in the development of long-range rockets and, possibly, Iraqi nuclear warheads. (I should, or could, try to combine the Paris piece with the Oslo piece in a third, expanded text.)

By now five medium-sized pencil drawings are hanging on the walls of the north room. All uprooted trees, their roots exposed. In the course of one year the decay of the fallen trees has progressed to such a degree that the woods smell of rot. I am plagued by mosquito and ant bites, without minding very much because the plea-sure of drawing is so intense. Since the temperature dropped the Baltic is icy cold; only our dog is not put off.

Ulvshale, 22 August 1990
Our summer rituals: standing at the Dutch door in the evening, drinking a shot or two of aquavit and looking across the meadow to where the wild geese are resting. Or, after dusk, stepping out of the house, where we are immediately pinned by the zigzag flight of bats. Flying low and in tight formations, they speed by us so fast that it is hard for the eye to follow them.

Buying fish in Klintholm Havn: this time gar in addition to her-ring. Berry picking is becoming a mania: when I close my eyes late at night and wait for sleep, I see bushes full of outsized, gleaming blackberries, close enough to reach out and grab.

Or in late evening, because my eyes are smarting from the fire, stepping outside, walking a short distance, and looking back at the thatch-roofed cottage with its two candlelit windows against the dark background of the forest. We have an exclusive life here, in the true sense of the word.

And only Radio Germany and the newspaper that arrives by mail give us an inkling of the rest of the world.

However grim my predictions for the GDR after the currency union, the actual effect is worse, more ruthless, more botched, and uglier than my worst imaginings. Even investments that had al-ready been promised, such as those by Mercedes, are being with-drawn. (If the West Germans had a chance to restore conditions to the way they were before the opening of the Iron Curtain, presum-ably they would do so, to be rid of this costly "unity," which brings nothing but annoyance.)

Today I completed my seventh drawing. But I am still lacking a drawing that shows an uprooted tree from a foreshortened frontal perspective.

Ulvshale, 23 August 1990

As we were crossing the big meadow on our way to the beach, walking through herds of heifers and calves (with bulls), about two hundred wild geese took off, as if on command, coming down again in the dunes and landing among other wild geese. Year after year they gather here, which explains why the currently grazed-over meadow is dotted with goose feathers and down. I can still vault over the wire fence with the electrified top strand.

Breakfast without mushrooms, because of the drought. Today the accession of the GDR to the Federal Republic has been scheduled for 3 October: yet another historic moment. Public expressions of dismay because the announcement seems to engender no enthusiasm.

This morning, as I set out to pick blackberries, Ute smiled at my passion for hunting and gathering. Yet nothing relaxes me more than hunting for mushrooms, picking berries, or (in Portugal) looking for unusual seashells along the wide beach or poking among the flint stones at the foot of Møn's bluffs, always hoping to come upon a petrified sea urchin; and over the years I have made a number of lucky finds.

Tomorrow I plan to write the final draft of the piece for Oslo.

Ulvshale, 25 August 1990

Yesterday and today, to the north of the grove of birch, elder, and sea buckthorn and just before the dunes, I found the first young birch boletes — and behind the house, toward the woods, under spreading bush boughs, young parasol mushrooms, exactly where I found them last year and the year before. After trimming the gills, I sliced the crowns in quarters and sautéed them in butter, then added the sliced birch boletes: a superb appetizer, followed by the marinated gar.

Now the tenth drawing (in graphite) is finished: a successful series, because after charcoal and ink, lead and graphite offered further (final) possibilities. Uprooted trees, each lying in a different position. Some of the pieces are to be included in the Reinickendorf exhibition; I am thinking of five to seven.

As we move toward early fall, the number of birds flying over the meadow bordering the sea is increasing. The wavering, then reassembling formations of the wild geese. The moment herons land, they take off.

Finished *Malte Laurids Brigge*. The last third makes for disappointing reading: the precise observations and previously mentioned oddities drown in sentiment and in the vagueness more typical of Rilke. The scenes set in Denmark are as strong as I remembered them: the loud dying of old Brahe, or the mother's fear of needles. Remarkable how the book's demand for a death of one's own contrasts with the illness (cancer) of Ute's mother, which will probably result in death. She is experiencing all the torture stations of a modern, well-equipped hospital, and all the glitches: the lung injured in the course of a biopsy; the wrongly positioned ostomy. For weeks now she has been unable to eat or drink and has to be nourished intravenously. Our nightly agonizing discussion about euthanasia. Yes or no? Only if things get really critical will this question be unavoidable, and starting next week Ute's mother will be with her middle daughter, Undine, receiving private nursing. I could never take such a step on my own, at most at the request of the dying person.

The situation in the Gulf region still hangs dangerously in the balance. Apparently the Americans, having invested so much time and effort, are intent on armed conflict. It is grotesque how political bungling on a grand scale (America) relates to political bungling on a small scale (Federal Republic); for instance, there the American reservists are being called up, here the two Germanys are at odds over the right to abortion.

Tomorrow we fly to Oslo, leaving the dog with Danish friends, the Bagges.

Oslo, 26 August 1990

I hope this conference turns out nearly as clear (and farsighted) as the view during our flight from Copenhagen to Oslo, over the Baltic where it meets the North Sea. Because the invitation to this conference, "The Anatomy of Hate," was issued by Elie Wiesel and the Norwegian Nobel Peace Prize Committee, Israelis and Scandinavians are overrepresented among the participants. But Nelson Mandela, György Konrád, Adam Michnik, Geremek, Havel, Rybakow, Nadine Gordimer, and so on are also here.

What a topic! And how great the danger that everything will drown in well-intentioned appeals. The opening speeches, including that of Elie Wiesel, unfortunately suggest as much. Then a panel of short presentations: four women. First a French woman who offers the interesting thesis that children do not experience hate, and are taught to hate only by the example of adults. She talked about studies she had undertaken with children in Marseille. Then a Japanese woman spoke, a leader of the opposition and chair of the Japanese socialists. She suggests that the United Nations impose a new economic order on the world. Rita Süssmuth spoke next, noble, helpful, and good — as always. Last came a woman from India, who took as her point of departure the Hindu-Muslim conflict.

Oslo, 27 August 1990

The discussion yesterday following the speeches unfortunately remained vague, except for the contribution by Sakharov's widow. After dinner I spoke briefly with R. Süssmuth and told her that in staying such a brief time (she took an early-morning flight today) she was being unfair to the other participants. Her plan of inviting Christa Wolf was absurd, I said, so long as she did not speak out to denounce the campaign being waged against her. A woman who displays a burst of courage but is too quickly intimidated, Süssmuth will be incapable of using her position as parliamentary president to go on the offensive (say, for a new constitution). Late in the evening we had a glass of red wine (my first in two weeks) in the bar with Per Wästberg and his wife.

A bad night, mild toothache.

Now Jimmy Carter is speaking. He invokes Cain and Abel, as did the Norwegian foreign minister yesterday, with quotes from the Bible.

A very informative contribution by Moncef Marzouki from Tunisia, who presents an Arab point of view and relays the Arabs' fear of a new crusade, for instance when American aircraft carriers steam into the region.

Later, hate was compared — both meaningfully and meaninglessly — with cancer.

My short speech was not discussed, but later, during the two-hour cruise on the Oslofjord, people expressed agreement, including the Poles Geremek and Michnik.

My toothache is gone (I hope). Now Nelson Mandela is speaking: at once sturdy and delicate, dressed with conservative elegance. Apparently he is a candidate for the Nobel Peace Prize. The white foreign minister of South Africa, Wessels, offers a constructive response to his speech. And now Nadine Gordimer is speaking: small, girlish, plucky. Sixty-six whites were killed, but on the other hand, ten thousand or more blacks. Nonetheless, she says, there was anger, bitterness, but no hatred toward whites. Among the whites, too, fear of the blacks' revenge, not hatred, is the dominant emotion. Two Israelis (Urbach and Olmert) demand that Mandela dissociate himself from a UN resolution that condemns Zionism as racism. Mandela answers magnificently, pointing out that the blacks always have to include the arguments and interests of the whites in their thinking.

Oslo, 28 August 1990

The banquet last night in the Akershus Castle. The host was the prime minister. It was a civilized occasion, with speeches, and music by Grieg, the Norwegians' Chopin. Across from me sat one of the Chinese women from Tiananmen Square, now a well-groomed young lady who speaks excellent English and accompanies her speech with poetic gestures. Next to her a Scandinavian rabbi whose family has produced rabbis for generations. He drifted off, then woke up, not embarrassed in the slightest. My toothache is gone, and the conference continues. Unfortunately the Israel-Palestine debate is not up to the level of Mandela's speech yesterday. Familiar arguments and security demands are repeated. And then Mitterrand offers a sort of school-radio speech on Europe, Eurocentric to the core, though there are hints he will fit in a few brief sentences about the Third World toward the end.

And here it comes, the obligatory reference to the Third World. Clever, insightful even, with references to the stock market and falling prices for cacao. And now, after Mitterrand disappoints as usual, Václav Havel is speaking: "Hate is more important to the hater than the object of his hatred." A precise analysis that here and there sounds academic. The Eastern European nations' susceptibility to collective hate, especially because these nations are young, inexperienced, and not "mature." Geremek speaks intelligently, with experience, but remains strangely abstract when it comes to Poland. Konrád is more concrete, but also more at a loss for suggestions. Landsbergis tries to come across as statesmanlike (Christian).

Oslo, 29 August 1990

The last day. Unfortunately the conference degenerated yesterday into an Elie Wiesel fest. It started with Mitterrand's naming him a knight of the Légion d'honneur at the French embassy. The concert in the evening with a potpourri of a program, which took a bombastic American turn (with Gregory Peck and Audrey Hepburn). But ironically, the flood of superlatives also betrayed helplessness. Today the topic is supposed to be prisoners of hate. The Chinese students are to be the prize exhibits again, but no one wants to respond to their political questions.

Yesterday I spoke up twice during the discussion, criticizing the inflexibility of the Israeli and Palestinian positions and citing Mandela as a positive example. Then I reproached Mitterrand for giving a speech that was merely rhetorical and therefore hollow. Reminding everyone of the postwar Marshall Plan, I demanded that he put forward a Mitterrand Plan for central Europe, and compared the situation of the countries in that region with the crushing debt burden in the Third World countries.

Today Jack Lang tried to get in touch with me (before the president left for Iceland).

It disturbs me to see Václav Havel getting caught up more and more in the presidential circus. Stayed up late with Per Wästberg and his wife in the hotel bar.

In bed, a dream I was speaking French.

In the face of Polish anti-Semitism (without any Jews in the country), Adam Michnik speaks of a "magical anti-Semitism."

Ulvshale, 30 August 1990
Flying to Copenhagen with poor visibility. A good time as always with Vagn Grosen and Per Øhrgaard. I like the Danes' ironic style, their consistent ability to see themselves as European — in contrast to the Swedes and the Norwegians.

Shortly before we reached Ulvshale, at around midnight, a fox unfortunately ran in front of the car.

With the help of the blackberries I managed to get back into the swing of things and started on large-scale close-up charcoal drawings of the bushes: black on black, reflecting the general state of affairs.

In retrospect, the "Elie Wiesel Festival" seems absurd. On the one hand, he succeeded, with the special talent he certainly has, in bringing together prominent politicians, from Mandela and Mitterrand to Havel and Geremek, but the sponsors of his foundation, American Jews and Israelis, were unmistakably in the majority. As a result, the Soviet Union — that is, communism — was repeatedly fingered as the source of all evil, while the United States remained free from criticism. Even the priest from Honduras did not dare to name the Americans as the instigators of terror in his country.

It was annoying how at the end of the conference Wiesel contrived to pull out of his sleeve a prepared resolution "Against Hate," giving us no opportunity to discuss it: a text in which sentimental lyricism set the tone, and the social and political responsibility for hate all over the world went unmentioned. As indeed the conflicts in India and South America were hardly discussed.

The Iraq crisis drags on. How long will the Americans hold their positions in the desert? With such a display of force, this major power is expected to achieve a decisive victory. Grotesque the way the German unification process has run into a snag over the question of abortion, and so soon before the treaty is to be signed.

Today, at last, we are having turbot.

Ulvshale, 1 September 1990
No, we had the turbot today, after I had conjured it up for luck by drawing it, for Erling Bagge informed us earlier in the day, with apparent casualness, that next Monday the Vogterhus is to be sold to the government by the fourteen farmers; there is even talk of tearing it down. Ute cried; she is very fond of this thatch-roofed cabin. But I, too, have spent fifteen summers here, after all, worked here on *The Flounder* and *The Meeting at Telgte,* and spent many hours drawing in the forest, year after year, the last three summers. Now I will try, with the help of Niels Barfoed and Per Øhrgaard, to get a long lease. We are leaving tomorrow, because Ute has to take care of her mother, who is going to live out her last weeks in Dobersdorf, where Ute's sister lives: a torment that would be even more inhumane in the hospital. No etchings, but ten drawings in pencil and graphite and four large-scale charcoal drawings are finished. And fifteen preserving jars of berry compote, made with blackberries instead of the usual red ones, are coming home with us, our August harvest.

Since yesterday hunters have been banging away all around us: hunting season has started. They have scared off the wild geese. I am fascinated by the spiders that have spun their webs around the house but also deep in the blackberry bushes, and sit in the center of the webs waiting for prey.

Am reading an interesting Chaplin biography as well as *The Kreutzer Sonata.* By now I am up to Chaplin's third marriage and *Modern Times.* A comedic perfectionist. Tolstoy's novella: alarming in its deliberate artlessness.

Behlendorf, 3 September 1990
On Sunday we drove home by way of Dobersdorf. In the Cavalier's House, next to the castle where Laura started her potter's apprenticeship when she was sixteen, Ute's mother is now waiting for death; or rather, she is not waiting, merely worrying over whether — "when this here is over" — she should go to see a doctor in Stralsund or Greifswald; only places she knew as a child and a young girl still mean anything to her. She has become emaciated, almost transparent, and her face has regained some of its former beauty. Didi and her husband, both doctors, give her only a few weeks, or perhaps just days.

But today she was apparently more alert. I assembled the drawings for the exhibition in Reinickendorf: thirty soft-coal landscapes and another twenty-five dead wood pieces.

Even though "The Call of the Toad" remained entirely in the background during our time in Ulvshale, I did sketch a toad from all angles: studies for an etching that could provide the jacket illustration for the book yet to be written.

With barely a week remaining before my departure for Berlin, I want to write a longish text, "A Bargain Called the GDR," which could be finished in time for the "Day of Unity" on 3 October and draw on the theses I presented in my short speeches for Oslo and Paris. I owe myself this final accounting, and want to offer it to *Die Zeit,* if only out of stubbornness.

The blackberries on the other side of the pond are even larger and juicier than those on the Ulvshale Heath.

Behlendorf, 4 September 1990

No sooner had Ute set out for Dobersdorf to be with her mother — and left me to take advantage of the peace and quiet in the house — than the telephone started ringing off the hook. First it was Lafontaine, who apologized for not answering my letters (he said he preferred the telephone) and then wanted me to be in Bonn on 1 October for the publication of his book. Politicians who write books — spare me!

Then Walter Höllerer called in a state of utter confusion; after four weeks in the hospital he no longer knows whether he is already crazy or still normal. He asked me to come at once, since I am the only one he can talk to. He hinted darkly that I had been right and he had been wrong. But about what? So tomorrow I will drive to Berlin with Fritze Margull, who is coming by at noon, though I am by no means certain that I can be of any help.

I started another soft-coal drawing after all, with two black hens in the foreground.

It has been raining for hours, as if making up for lost time.

On the telephone, I urged Lafontaine to focus positively on the future: constitutional convention, worthwhile sacrifices for solidarity, a new, emphatically federalist Germany. He promised to speak out more clearly on the problem of political asylum.

Berlin–Behlendorf, 6 September 1990

After a drive of two and a half hours, we passed the empty, silent checkpoint buildings and were in Berlin. I found Walter Höllerer in a pitiful state. He, always so generous, so ready to help out notoriously impecunious poets, now sees himself and his family — "the poor children!" — facing a financial abyss. After four weeks of torment in the hospital, he has lost the sight in his right eye, and the left is at risk. He is incapable of finishing a sentence. Often makes no sense. The effect of too much cortisone? I patiently advise him to walk away from his unsalaried commitments in Sulzbach (the literary archives) and Berlin (the Literary Colloquium) and to end his lease on the apartment in Sulzbach. His papers (letters, manuscripts, material for the journal *Akzente*) should be organized and offered to the Academy for sale as a living bequest. After three hours — during the last of which we were joined by Renate Höllerer, who, he tells me in a panic, is "throwing money out the window" — he seems more relaxed, even smiles.

I want to try to get started on "A Bargain Called the GDR" after all. The night too short, too little sleep.

Discussed the book fair with Steidl yesterday: the exhibition of the *Dead Wood* drawings will open on 3 October, the "Day of German Unity." Delighted it will provide a contrast to all the hoopla.

The consequences of debt in the billions: the GDR is being wantonly turned into a basket case. Flowery speeches used as a cover-up.

In Behlendorf, 6 September 1990
Maybe it helped that I was tired: I came up with a possible opening for "The Call of the Toad":

The widow and widower were standing next to one another at the flower stall. I do not know why they sent me later, much later, all those papers, tied up in bundles — letters, receipts, newspaper clippings. Strangers to each other, the widow and widower just happened to be standing in front of the almost sold-out flower stall. Because he and I, he claims, shared a desk at the Petri Secondary School for a while? Only a few bunches of cut flowers, asters and chrysanthemums, were left in buckets. The widow decided on asters. Their bundles of papers included his diary, with the dated entry, "No wonder the flower stall next to the market hall had so few bouquets left; after all, today is All Souls." So it was on All Souls' Day that the widow and widower were standing in front of a flower stall next to the Dominican Market hall. I really cannot recall having him next to me at the desk in school. I had to change schools too often. But that is my story, which does not count here. When the widow pulled two or three still presentable asters out of the bucket, the widower began to pull asters from the bucket, too, rust-red ones, just as she had pulled out rust-red ones. In his diary he writes poetically, "Apparently she has a special fondness for rust-red asters, which smolder quietly to themselves." Perhaps the bucket had nothing more to offer. There were not enough flowers for either the widow or widower to have a proper bouquet.

That is how "The Call of the Toad" could begin. But it is still too noisy for writing: too much unity, too much Gulf crisis.

Behlendorf, 7 September 1990
I could begin by enumerating the terms — "The Soviet Occupation Zone, the other Germany, the state in quotation marks, the GDR, the ex-GDR, East Elbia, the country of Luther" — and then continue with a quotation in which Thomas Müntzer said something, at the time of the Peasants' War, that still holds true today: "The gentlemen bring it upon themselves that the poor man becomes their enemy. They have no wish to remove the cause of the uprising. How can it go well in the long run?" And after that I could work in the main ideas of the Oslo speech and make a transition

from "German poison gas factories" to the Paris speech, whose topic is fear of the Germans.

I am waiting for Laura, Ralf, the grandchildren, and Ute, who is coming from Dobersdorf. I picked blackberries yesterday and today, to have plenty on hand.

Since I got the opening sentence and the following ones down on paper yesterday, I have been itching to start on the first draft of "The Call of the Toad." Have to think through the narrative perspective again, to make sure I don't end up on a tempting but possibly wrong tangent.

Before the horde of children bursts in, I started a vertical-format charcoal drawing that will be here when I return: a fish skeleton in the soft-coal pit.

Behlendorf–Berlin, 9 September 1990
Counting Bruno's Ronja, there were four grandchildren keeping us on our toes. The parents unsure of themselves, leaving everything to the children's whims or moods. Then a pleasant walk to the lock; only the dog seemed irritated by the constantly shifting groupings. I looked on from the sidelines, a loving grandfather without responsibility. Ute took refuge in her kitchen.

Have decided to help Laura, whose long-suffering, smiling patience I admire, chip away at her husband's mountain of debt.

Yesterday, after five weeks, off came my black-gray-white holiday beard, once I had had a chance to scare the children with it. A favor to Ute, who, on the one hand, is glad to see that while the hair on my head remains dark, at least my holiday beard is shot through with gray, and on the other hand does not want my chin to be overgrown. Still, I would like to draw myself with my next holiday beard. Besides: no shortage of long-beards!

On the train, a conversation with the Saxon-accented Mitropa waiter, who serves his coffee — a small pot still costs 4.50 — with two packets of sugar, labeled "40 Years GDR, 16th and 17th September 1989 (6th Rositz Market Days)," and under that, again "40 Years GDR." Under the Rositz Market Days banner is a green fruit platter on which, in addition to pears, wine grapes, and cherries, one can make out the coveted bananas. The fruit platter and the two celebratory phrases "40 Years GDR" look as though they had been applied with potato stamps. The green of the platter with the red of the anniversary lettering. The waiter complains, but he ends every complaint about the plight of the GDR — he hopes Mitropa will survive, for the sake of the familiar name — with the cliché "We'll get through this." The train is crawling past barren harvested fields.

In the afternoon the discussion with Pörner and Lohr for North German Broadcasting's Channel 3. Our third conversation: the first in November '89, the second in May '90, and this time looking forward to October and back to 1 July and the currency union. We all come to a similarly negative conclusion, though on the basis of different experiences. We spoke upstairs in my former kitchen, which has now been cleared out. At teatime we had Nordhäuser, a GDR brandy.

After that a cheerful meal with Ingrid, Nele, and her girl friend. Later, on television, I saw again the impressive GDR movie *Trace of Stones,* which was banned in the sixties.

Driving from Berlin to Leipzig, 13 September 1990
Three stressful days in Berlin are behind me. There was no time for writing, although various ideas for "The Call of the Toad" occurred to me, always after midnight, when I couldn't sleep. For

instance: the narrator's critical attitude toward the widower, who occasionally waxes poetic. Or gravestone inscriptions such as: "Only in death does he return to his homeland" and "Final resting place in German soil." Inscriptions, in other words, that promptly provoke Polish objections. The story brings together the political events to which the widower alludes and the German-Polish Burial Association. Perhaps the story should be narrated looking back from the year 2000?

The mountains of mail have been leveled. I hope to finish the first draft of "A Bargain Called the GDR" tomorrow. With Maria I put together the Reinickendorf exhibition: ninety-three drawings and eighteen lithos.

Yesterday in Moscow at the Two Plus Four conference a treaty was signed that is intended to restore Germany's sovereignty on 3 October, on ten conditions.

Yesterday Jurek Becker and Peter Schneider came at eight P.M. for red wine, cheese, smoked ham, and rye bread with caraway seeds. We discussed the elections scheduled for 2 December and agreed to come up with some "Theses on the Germans' Election Choices" that we will publish in *Der Spiegel*. Peter Schneider, who is about to go to America, will send his suggestions from there. Jurek and I will meet in Behlendorf. Tired though I was, a pleasant evening.

Perhaps the widower and the widow should not be the same age. He could be sixty-two, she fifty-four. This old concrete-slab highway from Hitler's time makes writing difficult.

Berlin–Büchen, 15 September 1990
What a week! Not until today, toward noon, did I finish the first draft of "A Bargain Called the GDR." Leipzig seemed unreal. The

road leading into the city is still called German-Soviet Friendship Avenue. Will that name remain? The gray façades looked even grayer in contrast to the colorful signs advertising West German products. In the Theaterpassage Gallery the *Dead Wood* originals were hung in three parallel rows, one above the other. The overcrowded room where the opening took place was halfway through the exhibition. I read the "Obituary," made candid comments. What a nervous reaction! Also gratitude, because I was expressing what many find troubling. This is how, without wishing to, one becomes a spokesman. I persuaded Steidl to invite all of us, including the gallery owner's family, to Auerbach's Cellar, which in the meantime has been bought by a man from Hamburg: higher prices, poorer quality, many empty tables. Erich Loest, who came to the opening, left early. I would have liked to ask him whether he still sees me as "the nation's pessimist." After a two-hour drive there, we made it back in two hours, with Jenö, the Hungarian litho printer, at the wheel (and his girlfriend). Along the highway automobile dealerships are springing up, and wrecks from accidents litter the side of the road. The suicide rate, already high, is mounting. Interesting to see some GDR artists trying to adapt to Western art.

Yesterday I read the "Obituary" to Petra Meyenburg and answered some of her Berlin-accented questions. Remarkable the way she manages to hold her own in the rough-and-tumble of East German journalism, weighing all of forty-eight kilos and contending with illness and raising a small child.

Then, starting at ten P.M., the talk show *Friday Night* with Lea Rosh, on the topic of "right-wing radicalism in the GDR." My first talk show after a long period of refusing all such invitations. My goal was to use the few televised minutes at my disposal to talk about the causes of right-wing radicalism. Impressively old-fashioned in his style of argumentation: Gustav Just. Clear in his summing-up: Erwin Leiser. The two neo-Nazis: one, an Austrian, has managed to make his mouth look just like Mussolini's. The wine awful.

And finally, this afternoon, something not on the program: with Beatrice, Rosanna, Raoul, Ingrid, and Nele I went to the National Gallery to see the Carl Blechen exhibition. A painter who produces splendid surprises time and again, but only a few of his works can compete with Friedrich and Turner. Then Ingrid and Nele saw me to the train. A few minutes on the platform as a little family. Ingrid looks worn out next to the blooming child.

During the train ride I slept for an hour, breathing in the familiar smell of Lysol. I want to write a book as light-footed as it is uncompromising. The Germans' and Poles' compulsion to live up to their respective clichés. Inescapable roles.

Behlendorf, 16 September 1990
Hans met me at the station. After a long sleep, we hear just before noon that Editha ("Mausi"), Ute's mother, died early in the morning, apparently in her sleep. Ute and Hans have driven to Dobersdorf. The dog is lying in the studio doorway. Outside it is Old Wives' Summer. Spider webs, clouds of pollen. I am organizing my folders. I still have fifty dead wood images lying around. Am going to put a sheet of paper in the typewriter now ...

Behlendorf, 19 September 1990
Despite a cold and waves of flu, I have finished the final draft of "A Bargain Called the GDR." After Antje Vollmer called, I decided to use this text as the speech she invited me to deliver before the

Greens and Alliance 90 Bundestag members, assembled at the Reichstag on 2 October. Ah, my beloved Social Democrats, look at the company I have been driven to keep! At least the Greens and Alliance 90 rejected the State Treaty and the Unification Treaty and demanded a new constitution.

Am debating whether it would not make sense to publish the following texts as a paperback (before the elections in December): "Short Speech by a Rootless Cosmopolitan," "Letter to Augstein," "Some Comments on Suckers Square," "Report from Altdöbern," and "A Bargain Called the GDR." Either with Luchterhand (too slow) or with speedy Steidl.

The last text is to be published in *Die Zeit,* on 4 October, after all the bell-ringing. Greiner is offended because I criticized him harshly, but he has agreed to publish it. Ellen, Ute's sister from Freiburg, has arrived with the children. Tomorrow Ute's mother, Mausi, is to be buried in Behlendorf.

Gave GDR television an interview yesterday on the topic of unification. From start to finish, nothing but closing remarks.

Behlendorf, 21 September 1990
Yesterday the burial. At noon we saw Mausi one more time in the open coffin. The absence of her voice and that coquettish smile she kept into old age. An empty husk. The grandsons and sons-in-law served as pallbearers. Ute had imposed tight restrictions on the pastor. Hymns by Gryphius and Paul Gerhardt. A sonnet by Gryphius, which the pastor read well. Ute's clear voice, which faltered only now and then. Since only the family was present, we stayed together until evening. The three sisters who all turned out so differently.

Today I finished the text of "A Bargain . . ." The paperback will be brought out by Luchterhand after all. The ladies promise to do their best.

Lüdenscheid, 23 September 1990

My sister's sixtieth birthday got off to a moist and merry start yesterday: Bruno and his friend Tim picked me up at the main station in Hamburg. We made the drive in a delivery van that was formerly a police vehicle, a fire department vehicle, possibly also a hearse, and now can hardly get up to 100 kilometers an hour. The antenna held on with tape. An overpowering reek of gasoline inside. Nonetheless a pleasant trip with the two young men. When we stopped at one point I filled my pockets with beechnuts, a passion from childhood.

Got to Lüdenscheid shortly before five P.M., where Kazimir and his wife, along with Irmgard, had arrived after an eighteen-hour bus trip from Gdynia. Irmgard Krause is the eldest daughter of Franz Krause, the Polish post office official who in 1939 was condemned to death by a German judge, a man who was still active in Schleswig-Holstein long after the end of the war. Krause was shot along with other postal officials. I had last seen Irmgard and her brother Gregor fifty-three years ago. She went to the Polish school on Weidengasse.

Then calvados was served. After a walk through the town — everything properly set up for consumerism, the small Old Town like a doll's house — we ate far too much at an Italian restaurant. After the red wine came the obligatory grappa. And starting at midnight Waltraut's birthday party got under way in earnest, with dancing, champagne, headstands, and Kashubian merrymaking. It was a treat to watch Bruno and Tim, who have not experienced such parties. Waltraut was in fine fettle. Eventually she "baptized" me with champagne. Almost one role reversal too many. Just when

I was about to get really furious, it occurred to me to ask for a hair dryer. So my champagne-soaked hair was dried, and the day saved.

Irmgard, who has no use for the Church and its priests, said, "When end is near, priest can come. Nothing to be done then anyway."

Paris, 25 September 1990
At first the actual birthday party had trouble living up to the pre-celebration. But then my sister's charm came into its own as she took things in hand, always provocative: "I need stress!" Toward noon Franz, Gianna, and Laura arrived, Laura by herself because Lucas, Leon, and Luisa were sick. Maybe she was glad to be free of the children for a change. Dancing until three in the morning. In between, skits, poems, etc. A good buffet. And in the midst of the celebration Franz was selling cheese from his farm. Quite the businessman! Initially reticent, the Kashubians became more and more self-assured. The one who impressed the children and me most was Irmgard. In my little speech I talked about how the family had split in the years '36 to '39, and then mentioned the first German-Kashubian encounter after the war, in 1958. Unfortunately without my mother. Got to bed too late!

Charlie and Helga drove me to the airport. Flight to Paris in a prop plane. From the moist and merry petit-bourgeois birthday party to the Méridien Montparnasse hotel. My television interview with Tournier was framed in the usual clichés.

Shortly before eight P.M. Helene arrived, no longer depressed, as Veronika had said she would be, but rather relaxed and pretty (without baubles and bangles in her hair). We ate at a Breton restaurant: crêpes and red wine. Helene spent the night with me in my luxurious hotel room. She asked for a wake-up call at six-thirty and went to school from here. How calmly she accepts luxury, whereas it still embarrasses me.

Paris, 26 September 1990

The conference in La Défense — a horror show! — can be described in few words. What had been announced as a round table for the morning turned out to be a series of twenty-minute presentations, without any discussion between speakers. The only interesting bit was the extemporaneous speech by Cohn-Bendit, after whose contribution Mitterrand had trouble getting his empty blandishments (like his speech in Oslo) to fill the allotted time of half an hour.

La Défense is a de Chirico landscape translated into architecture. Is there such a thing as brazen kitsch?

In the afternoon I spoke off the cuff, as my speech had already appeared in print in *Libération* under the title "Some Warning Signs." I called my contribution the "Speech of a Nest Besmircher," and intervened several times in the discussion. I would not have thought that so many French consider themselves second class in relation to the Germans, and accept that position proudly: no reason to fear the Germans, whom they consider their preceptors in the subject of economics.

In the evening with Helene. We went to the Mabillon, my regular café back in the fifties. Dinner in a little Senegalese restaurant. I showed Helene, who arrived at the conference center looking quite depressed, several of my favorite nooks and crannies in the Latin Quarter. Toward midnight I fell into bed, dead tired: the aftereffects of the strenuous German-Kashubian birthday celebration are still with me. Sweet, sharing the hotel room with Helene. A chaste couple.

The things Helene loves: the smell of the Métro, tea, those curiously shaped buildings located on street corners, having lots of friends, her papa, honey in her tea ...

We went to the Avenue d'Italie. And again I was surprised (as last year with Laura) at how quiet, how cozy the little rear-courtyard building, No. 111, seems. Beutler, the current owner, was away. I described for Helene the tiny niche, next to the furnace, where I wrote *The Tin Drum*.

A splendid fishmonger's on the avenue. By Métro and then on foot, and finally through the Jardin du Luxembourg, where I found the carousel (not where I remembered it), on which Franz and Raoul had their first carousel experiences. Unfortunately no white elephant came along, only a grayish-blue one.

We went out to eat with Anne Freyer. She promised to stay in touch with Helene. Was surprised at how good her schoolgirl French is. The child is disturbingly advanced for sixteen. After that we rode to the Place de la Bastille and then walked along the Canal Saint-Martin, covered over at first, then out in the open. Boules players, but only elderly ones. The open canal with its bridges is still unexpectedly beautiful, but the automobile traffic does not let up for a moment. The Hôtel du Nord is crumbling. Shameful.

Back to the hotel (from the Gare de l'Est). A short rest for our throbbing feet. Then we ride to the Gare du Nord and from there by suburban railway to Helene's host family. She was not exaggerating: the cramped apartment is revoltingly tasteless. Large, framed jigsaw puzzle of a landscape in the Dolomites. Knickknacks. Hideous wallpaper. The couple, both teachers, with their four children form a typical family, friendly enough but they ask no questions, have no interest in hearing about anything outside France. The endless meal, five courses.

In this setting Helene obviously sticks out like a precocious foreign body. Nonetheless, I hope she will come to feel at home; if she simply gave up, it would be understandable, but her pride would interpret it as a defeat.

Helene takes me to the station. Just before we set out I want to give the child some money, and in the process misplace my wallet, which Helene finds just before the train pulls in. I interpret this tendency to lose things as a sign of age. Am exhausted: Paris on top of my sister's German-Kashubian birthday was just too much.

Behlendorf, 27 September 1990
Back home, and promptly in the thrall of the house and garden. In the morning, still in Paris, some time after breakfast with Anne Freyer, the eternal beloved without opportunity. She wants to discuss the "ugly unity." Then to the airport. There I see a fat madame carrying through the concourse a life-size cutout of Charlie Chaplin, jammed aslant under her arm. Or yesterday the respectably attired man on the platform in the Gare du Nord: he is sitting on a bench with his shoes next to him and under his stockinged feet a section of the same newspaper he is reading, while a dark-skinned janitor mops the platform with sweeping gestures.

Now to let my arms relax, shake off the dust from my travels, and stiffen my resolve: after 3 October the topic of Germany will not be closed, but it will no longer be worth commenting on; time to start on the manuscript of "The Call of the Toad" in Portugal.

Ute tells me Greiner found "A Bargain . . ." impressive and of course wants to publish the text in the 4 October edition.

Behlendorf, 29 September 1990
Another head cold and cough — and now Ute has caught it, too. Luchterhand is supposed to bring out a quick paperback after all,

at the end of October. My attempt to write a preface yesterday failed because everything has been said. So the subtitle that came to me spontaneously, "Last Speeches Before All the Bell-Ringing," will have to do. Enough is enough.

A telephone call yesterday from the office of the federal president: because he has been criticized harshly, the president wants to have my joint reading with Günter de Bruyn take place in Bonn, not in Berlin. I refused and suggested Weimar as an acceptable alternative. On television I watched the SPD party convention, feeling detached. Since Kohl's successes (historic hours, moments, days) are past, Oskar, if he could stick to the topic, might roll up a few advantages; in '69, too, before the elections only a few people believed in the possibility of a socialist-liberal coalition.

Visit from the *Mecklenburg Awakening*. A likeable woman who is struggling to keep her paper — with a circulation of barely fifteen thousand — afloat.

Long live the Federal Constitutional Court! It has overturned the election law.

Filled three baskets with drops from the orchard, apples and pears, for cider-making. Last year we were drowning in fruit; this time the frost we had during blossom time reduced the yield.

Behlendorf, 30 September 1990
The cup of blackberries yesterday was probably the last for the year. Steidl stopped in briefly: of the portfolio *Clearcutting in our Heads,* an edition of 35, 21 copies have been sold. And today I did a major tidying up so when I am back on 5 October there will be no more German unity cluttering my work area. Room for new projects!

Then looked through my folders for the Academy archives, reading unpublished poems from the years '51 to '75. Some of these poems are suitable for the artist's studio volume Steidl plans to publish; something from the Anna-Vladimir period, or the Veronika-*Flounder* period, three or four from the early fifties. I could insert them in the narratives that provide background on my works. Some texts from the *Rat* period will certainly turn up as well.

Ute has gone to Mölln with her sister from Kiel and her husband: Mausi's estate.

Any minute now there will be a conference call with the Luchterhand Authors' Council people. Frau Vitali announced that there would be changes to the rights provisions.

Tidying up the studio has put me in a good mood. Should continue this project.

For the paperback of "A Bargain Called . . ." the large-scale pencil drawing "Double Snail at Her Goal" should serve as the jacket illustration.

In late afternoon a conference call (my first) with the publishers, with Härtling, Bichsel, Max von der Grün, about the implications for Luchterhand if Aufbau is bought out by Holtzbrinck. How will Christa Wolf and Christoph Hein take this? If not even these well-known writers dare to challenge the West German colonial masters, how can we expect courage of the general population?

Behlendorf, 1 October 1990
Ingrid's comment on the telephone, "Both of us are in the same line of work, after all," deserves to be noted. Yesterday the Bissingers' visit. Manfred seems worn out. His capacity for hard work — first he gets *Natur* out of the red, then he increases the sales for *Merian* impressively — is doing him in. Now he wants to get away with his daughters for a week in Vermont and a week in Jerusalem, at a time when war could come at any moment.

Just raided old poem files. From the early period, 1950 to '53, not much is left: three or four poems from the cycle "The Stylite," an early prefiguration of Oskar's role as an observer. Also two or three short poems from my Italian journey: "Aurora's Garden . . ." Finally a handful of poems from the pre-*Windhens* period. But then from the years '70 to '76 many poems turn up, first versions, fragments, and a complete cycle, "Eulogy for Vladimir," which I did not publish at the time because it was too personal, but whose existence I hinted at in the *Snail* book. In addition, several poems marking political events: the death of Allende, Brandt's speech to the UN, the meeting between Nixon and Brezhnev. Now I want to see what I can fit into the text of the studio volume. Maybe one or two short prose fragments as well. I want to have the first draft of that text done by year's end, so the next year will be free for "The Call of the Toad."

Outside, the gardeners are taking advantage of this sunny first day of October. Must write to Helene.

I wonder whether soon, very soon, I will be able to free myself up for new poems, poems new to me.

From Büchen to Berlin, 2 October 1990
My last trip on the Reich Railway through what is still, for one more day, the GDR. Ute comments on the dirty toilet. Both of us find the chilly temperature in the compartment hard to take. Outside, the villages rush by as if forgotten. Collapsed barns, crouching church towers, the whole thing like a last refuge. This land of scarcity will stay that way for a long time: faithful to the snail, because the phases skipped by history and its assertions of fact cannot be rushed.

Reading the papers: *Frankfurter Allgemeine, Süddeutsche, Frankfurter Rundschau.* Wishful thinking: the end of the postwar period is announced, and with it of postwar literature. Schirr-macher, about thirty, a Reich-Ranicki disciple, sets the tone, imploringly, as if he wanted to swim out of range of the older generation, my generation, yet at the same time stay close to shore, because you never know.

In Berlin I still have the Reichstag event to get through: the Greens and Alliance 90. Can my gray-tinged speech possibly make them feel warm and fuzzy? After that, for television, Channel 2, last words before the unification, featuring Bahr, Schäuble, Stürmer, and me. Then a hasty escape from the mounting hoopla to Friedenau and my safe haven on Niedstrasse.

These recidivists! They are about to proclaim yet another zero hour!

Frankfurt am Main, 3 October 1990
This man Kohl can do anything! Even a full moon on the Day of German Unity.

Yesterday, chilled to the bone, we pulled into Zoo Station half an hour late. From there to the Reichstag, where the Eastern Greens and Alliance 90 were convening with the Western Greens. I delivered my essay as a speech; it is appearing today in *Die Zeit,* having been moved to the head of the line. After me, Antje Vollmer, who spoke well, emphasizing the personal: "Saying Goodbye to the Federal Republic." The discussion that followed started out in the usual way: "Where can we find something positive?" although in my text I had derided this standard German question. No time limits having been set, the faults of the Greens that came to light were not only the more charming ones: a tendency to go on and on, self-centeredness. The GDR delegates' concise comments were good.

From there straight to the four-person round table with Schäuble, Bahr, and Stürmer for Channel 2. It was probably the right decision to challenge the politicians' pieties and spit in the unity soup. Later we joined Fritze Margull, Baby Sommer, Antje Vollmer, Raoul, and Hans at the Italian restaurant on Handjerystrasse. The place half full. The diners were in no mood for celebrating.

The plane was delayed getting to Frankfurt, of course. As a result, I arrived late for the opening of the *Dead Wood* exhibition, but only by twenty minutes. The hall nicely filled. Hauff, the mayor, spoke surprisingly well. Klaus Staeck, on the other hand, was disorganized, talking more about himself than about the occasion. I read the "Obituary." After that the journalists had access to me one at a time, as arranged in advance.

A strange experience to meet my son-in-law Ralf at the book fair. North German Broadcasting's sound truck like an oven: a four-person interview.

Behlendorf, 5 October 1990
Odd mixture of exhaustion and satisfaction, because everything on the subject of Germany has been said and written. Got home late yesterday from Frankfurt, where the only good, focused conversation was with the Japanese writer Kenzaburō Ōe, whom I met for the first time twelve years ago in Tokyo.

And today Ute exchanged our orchard drops for eighty-four bottles of apple juice. That, too, is a harvest, and helps us get through this German autumn.

The "Bargain" speech is "placed" well (to use the old GDR expression) in *Die Zeit*. Back to the conversation with Kenzaburō Ōe: we talked for about two hours before an audience, with simultaneous translation, and despite the language barrier and the inevitable distance between our two cultures, we were closer to each other in our views than I would be with any European cultural professional in a face-to-face conversation. The obvious similarities between our careers and our views of our profession, our futile attempts to intervene in politics, all this made it possible for the two of us "princes," formed by war, to trust each other. I wonder whether that came across to the audience.

Telephone call with Peter Rühmkorf, who is profoundly depressed. I tried to help him see how much better off he is than Höllerer. The only thing that can help him (like me) is writing.

Ute is clearing out Mausi's place, together with her sisters and their families. Outside our shed, she burned boxes that had been piled up there for years, ever since our move from Hamburg, to make room in the shed for Mausi's furniture.

I am glad the dog is back.

Read the proofs of "A Bargain . . ."

Am still tired, smoking too much.

Behlendorf, 6 October 1990

After the storm last night, which is still raging — with storm surge warnings on the radio — I collected six baskets of apples and pears in the orchard. Everywhere pieces of "Mausi's estate" are standing, lying, piled up. Clothes and coats, disturbing. Ute is exhausted, but determined to bring some order out of the chaos by Friday, when we fly to Portugal.

Why am I still in mourning for the Germany that might have been, rich in its diversity, when it was clear to me, from last November on, that things would go in the familiar old direction (and order)? I need to shake off the dead weight of politics! Forget about duty. I am nagging myself to write to Vogel before we leave and announce that I am resigning from the SPD. At the same time am blocking myself from taking this step.

This evening Baby Sommer wants to come by with new instruments. We mean to start working on the *Flounder* program. I am trying to look forward to that.

At the moment only the windfalls mean anything to me.

Behlendorf, 9 October 1990
Although I am tormented by coughing, a runny nose, and intermittent flu symptoms, two days' work with Baby Sommer has allowed us to visualize a possible program and given me back *The Flounder:* a rich book that has kept its freshness and is still waiting to be rediscovered — and can wait. Baby brought new instruments: bells made of Meissen porcelain, wooden temple boxes, drinking glasses that make different tones . . .

The program, organized around the idea of the fairy tale, promises concentration. In November we will rehearse in a recording studio in Berlin and immediately produce a record. I have suggested to Baby that he try the Jew's harp.

A conversation with Nele and then with Ingrid restored the peace. What a good thing it is (for me, too) that Nele is such a feisty child and does not let her mother, who is both strong and fragile, mope for long. I am glad I reminded Raoul, when he was here yesterday to see the notary with us about the house in Eskop and also to talk about his money needs, of his duty. He promised to be attentive to Nele and show that he is a good brother.

Yesterday, in addition to the Nevermanns (and Baby), Herr and Frau Nölling were here for supper. Nölling is on the governing board of the German Federal Reserve Bank and agrees with me in my negative assessment of the ruthless way the currency union was pushed through. We stayed up late talking, drinking.

How remote current events in Germany seem now, perhaps as a result of my working on the *Flounder* program with Baby. Poland feels closer: the presidential election. I fear the little Napoleon from Gdańsk will win the election and bring pre-democratic conditions to Poland, ruling by decree.

When I start writing "The Call of the Toad," I want to keep the story open-ended and, in the first and second eighth of the novel, leave the couple's "idea" unspecified for a long time, so it can emerge organically.

Göttingen–Lübeck, 10 October 1990
Happened again. This time it was not as frighteningly aggressive as recently in Hamburg Station, and was silent: in the dining car someone dropped a slip of paper scrawled with abuse on my table. I didn't notice it until I was paying the check. When I left the dining car and went into the adjacent first-class car, this someone shouted from the platform — the train was stopped in Hannover — "Hey there, traitor!" It is laughable, of course, but not only laughable.

The exhibition in Göttingen was well attended, the auditorium standing room only. The discussion, too brief, would have been unproductive even if it had gone on longer, because from the beginning the only opinions expressed were extreme ones, either positive or negative, followed by the obligatory call for hope. Unfortunately the academics succumbed to this hope mania and missed the opportunity to draw attention, as best they could, to the national state of emergency.

Franz got to Steidl's early this afternoon. Together we were shown the new, state-of-the-art printing setup. Then we had an excellent meal at a Sicilian restaurant. Franz wants to visit my Aurora in Palermo, with Gianna.

Behlendorf, 11 October 1990
I should stop subjecting myself to such trips and public appearances. What I am left with — aside from the enjoyable meal with Franz — is a threat with overtones of book-burning.

Now that Germany's unity is a done deal, there is more public discussion about disunity of various kinds. Even an opportunist like A. Baring, always intent on saying the right thing in public, is sounding such notes.

Am taking along a blank book. Perhaps I will manage in Portugal to get the first ten or fifteen pages of "The Call of the Toad" committed to paper. I am positively itching for the imponderable process of writing, a process with laws all its own that I am glad to submit to, though not without anxiety.

It turns out, by the way, that the Academy of Arts in Berlin cannot purchase my living bequest because it was forbidden to accept the lottery money — as it should be! Still, because Trautwein was so assiduous, I have a good sense now of what is in the folders and elsewhere. Now I am going to concentrate on myself, which is enough.

After a telephone conversation with Kurt Mühlenhaupt, our neighbor in Portugal, it has become clear that a landfill is planned for the valley, toward Monte de Cima. Preparations are under way. Perhaps Portugal will be tolerable for another two or three years. After that Ute and I will look for a house in Kashubia to which we can escape. Must not get too settled. Travel light. Goings and comings. I have already had to give up many houses. Be prepared to become a refugee.

Ute found a small grasshopper for me that has not been seen in our area before.

For weeks now I have known that Horst Janssen, so passionate about his drawing, is in danger of going blind. His balcony collapsed, and the acid he was using there for etchings splashed all over him, including into his eyes, leaving him alive but dreadfully hurt. Yet I am confident he will keep going, even if what's left of his eyesight forces him to use a coarse brush and work only on large-scale images.

Now a big piece of amber from Mausi's estate is on a shelf next to my standing desk. With it a coquettish photo of Ute as a child.

Vale das Eiras, 13 October 1990
After an absence of three quarters of a year, during which more happened than could originally have been predicted, on our return this part of Portugal strikes me as repellent and horrifyingly ugly. Certainly the hot summer, with temperatures up to almost 50 degrees Celsius, hit the area hard. But in the absence of anything to mask this reality, the destruction suffered by the coastal region from Faro to Lagos is starkly apparent. Not only has the en-

tire stretch been overbuilt; deterioration is already setting in: trash and scrap metal all along the main road. Unspoiled slivers of open space give a sense of how beautiful this region must once have been.

Even my cactuses fared badly during the summer. Many of them are limp or shriveled up, choked with weeds. Only the plants in the inner courtyard and some next to the house were watered. Dona Maria José is lovable but slovenly, with the emphasis on slovenly. Out in front of the house the street was torn up to allow an electrical cable to be laid from the streetlight to the house. Early this morning a tractor came to fill in the trench. This, too, a fiasco, because the next time it rains huge puddles will form.

The sky has been gray since yesterday. Brief rain showers. Even shopping in Lagos didn't cheer us up. After a siesta (too long), marked by sudden sweats, we woke up exhausted and decided we were here to stay. Yet yesterday, before we could finally get into the house, a toad greeted me.

At the covered market in Lagos I bought a large crab, still alive. This was the first time since the sixties in Brittany, and the beauty in every detail still takes me by surprise. The symmetrical grooves

in the upper shell. The cleverly designed joints. The claws: tools, active long before those of humans, less well endowed, so much as existed.

Vale das Eiras, 15 October 1990
Jacob Suhl had used his satellite dish (a present from his wife) to record Channel Sat-3. Although we have experienced many disappointing election results (since Leipzig on 18 March) and thought we were prepared, the outcome of the regional parliamentary elections in the new provinces and in Bavaria exceeded our worst fears. We wisely had dinner first, fish and duck, followed by a fruit compote made with mulberries and strawberries, and only then watched the recorded program. Notoriously optimistic Social Democrats will comfort themselves by pointing out that the SPD's prospects have been improving, at least in comparison to the local elections, since the Volkskammer elections in March, if too slowly and not enough. A nonsensical argument, intended to gloss over the depths to which the SPD has sunk and its utter failure. Nonetheless I was able to watch with considerable detachment.

Today, in deference to my exhaustion and insidious flu symptoms, I stayed in bed until early afternoon, when the sun finally broke through. While filling in the potholes in front of the garage, I broke into a sweat that showed no sign of going away.

Am reading Fischer-Dieskau's fat book on the Garcia family of singers. Interesting material, which the author, prone to stylistic faux pas, unfortunately lacks the skill to present effectively. What possesses such an expert and perfectionist to display his dilettantism in a field that is not his own? Yet I am skimming the content with suspense.

Am too weak to do more. The drive to write still absent. Only with difficulty am I keeping my latent depression under wraps.

Maybe I should give in to it, let myself fall? But maybe I am too weak to do even that much.

Vale das Eiras, 16 October 1990
Even on my birthday the flu kept me in bed until afternoon. Ute bought a tilapia in Lagos, which is to be served as a birthday meal for us and the Suhls, after tripe with beans. A lovely gift from Ute: an H. Bosch volume with excellent reproductions and the usual explanations of the paintings. I'll compare it with my Berlin Bosch book.

Despite all its faults, Fischer-Dieskau's tome made for exciting reading, at least for someone forced by the flu to stay in bed.

Vale das Eiras, 17 October 1990
Stayed in bed again with mild shivers (but no fever) until almost three P.M., reading from beginning to end the story *Basanti*

by Bhisham Sahni, which he calls a novel. Clearly influenced by Premchand, but without achieving the latter's dense realism. Nonetheless an accurate picture of daily life in India's cities. Published, by the way, by Reclam in Leipzig. That is all over, too, and certainly not to the benefit of Indian literature, which is hardly promoted in any case.

Only now have I become aware of the massive depression that has had me in its (unacknowledged) grip for weeks. Conditions along the southwestern coast of Portugal form the backdrop to my state of mind. I am going to get through this, drained though I am. I have no choice.

When we went to see the hog farmer nearby to order wood for the fireplace, we were shocked at the filthy state of his derelict farm. Yet most of the farms, including that of our neighbor Germano, are in the same condition.

Vale das Eiras, 18 October 1990
After a brief sleep, strange, absurd dreams while half awake: at the suggestion and urging of Walser and Handke in turn, Nicolas Born is named the "poet laureate of German unity." The Rowohlt publishing house seizes upon this nonsense for PR purposes. I polemicize against it, and also against Ingrid K., who, as an editor at Rowohlt, tolerates this betrayal of Born in silence. I decide, as a result, to give up my German citizenship and write to the European parliament to ask for a European passport. I am told I will have to wait, and eventually accept a travel document that characterizes me as stateless, a condition I feel is appropriate.

In Lagoa today, one of the few remaining pleasant Portuguese towns. Then to see the Scottish potter in Proches, who talks about his ex-girlfriend Susan's pregnancy as if he were reporting a death. Along the still unspoiled stretch just inland from the coastal bluffs and in the small bays I filch three shoots from a cactus thicket by a tumbledown farmhouse. On the beach by the bay I find some tiny sleep stones for Ute. Back through the area where we used to live, which is being taken over more and more by golf courses. Our old house is still standing, now being used as a construction company's office. What a good thing that when we returned from Calcutta almost four years ago we gave up this place, now a permanent construction site, and built our new house here, although the coastal region between Lagoa and Porches (with a view of the sea) would have been more appealing to Ute.

At night, unable to sleep, I read short stories by Premchand. Dry in tone, incisive, for all their realism subtly metaphorical. Against the fashionable grain. Ah, to be able to draw such stories from united Germany!

Read in the *Frankfurter Allgemeine,* and find myself in agreement with, Mattheuer's polemic on the highhandedness of Western art. Schäuble will survive the assassination attempt, it seems. Am regretting, though without reason, having attacked him so harshly during our television discussion on 2 October.

Still break into a sweat at the slightest exertion.

Vale das Eiras, 20 October 1990
The morning low ebb after yet another bad night. I am managing to pass the sleepless hours by reading, but the days remain bleak. My nocturnal reading: Carola Stern's *Life of Dorothea Schlegel.* A book that starts out promisingly but peters out into partisan pedantry. Schlegel portrayed as a Romantic who turned her back on the "tiresome Enlightenment" in favor of wonder-working

Catholicism. What a relevant topic for today. But unfortunately this highly consequential historical period has the misleading label of "emancipation" slapped onto it.

Around noon a (German) woman from the neighborhood stopped by to tell us about the citizens organizing to oppose the plans for the landfill. She brought a flyer written by Kurt Mühlenhaupt and translated into Portuguese. Lives here alone with her son.

Later, when we went to the Suhls', Leonore gave me two large agaves with whitish-green branches, which I am going to plant to the left and right of the courtyard entrance. She gave me a bottle of vitamin C, with instructions to take a teaspoonful every hour. For my other ills there is no cure.

Vale das Eiras, 21 October 1990
As we were sitting by the fire yesterday, the narrative perspective of "The Call of the Toad" suddenly became clear to me: while the unnamed narrator is rooted in the present, the material entrusted to him by the widower provides information extending from 1989 almost to the year 2000 and the accident in which the protagonists are killed. This span of time, and the resulting tension, ought to determine the style of the narrative. At the end of his report, the narrator might decide to check out the details of his story on location — in Gdańsk. The widower's handwriting-on-the-wallish life, anticipating the future.

Tomorrow I want to get started on the first draft. It could be helpful to work out the chronology, from November 1989 to December 1999. Europe's continental system, designed to ward off the onslaught from the south. But also the increasingly impoverished masses from the east and southeast of Europe.

At noon I planted the two white-and-green agaves. Hacked

away at the thistles. Spoonfuls of vitamin C, taken every hour, seem to be helping. Now it is raining again, for the ninth day in a row.

Vale das Eiras, 22 October 1990
A storm since yesterday, with occasional breaks. Forgot to mention the stupid attack on my Reichstag speech, "A Bargain . . . ," by Bucerius, owner of *Die Zeit,* an attack that only confirms my worst fears. A new tone of self-righteousness: "We are the motor of Europe," "We are the paymasters of the European Community," "Our example showed France and Belgium how to restore their currencies," "As a major power, we must find our role." (As yet unspoken: "Now we have finally won the First and Second World Wars.")

Probably capitalism, now that it has been deprived of its enemy stereotype, will go ideological and, logically, destroy itself. Here in Portugal it is crystal clear what land-destroying power emanates from the European Community — that is, from its headquarters in Brussels. Enormous sums are being poured into road-building. The official term is "structural subsidies," but they chop up existing structures, wreck agriculture, which was already barely surviving, push the country and its people even further back by EU standards, portray this useless construction boom as an economic upswing, squeeze out Portuguese products in favor of Spanish ones, and could teach the Poles far to the north what is in store for them once Western Europe, in the form of the EC, gets its mitts on their floundering economy.

Yesterday to the Suhls', with Jules and Mieke. Ute looks wretched. It breaks my heart.

No, not today, tomorrow I will get to the manuscript. What is holding me back?

Vale das Eiras, 26 October 1990

Wasted days. I lack the strength to face the blank page. With this awful weather and my susceptibility to small ailments, real and imagined, that only get worse, the one thing that is gaining strength is my long-hidden depression, now out in the open. My chronic need for sleep and my sleeplessness are two sides of the same coin. Even hoeing around the cactuses helps only while I am doing it. Ute is in bad shape, too. Thus both of us, feeling miserable, remain preoccupied with ourselves. For the first time I am glad that our time here is coming to an end, although nothing but uneasiness lies ahead. No mail from the children. When I cooked tripe for supper . . . But even tripe does not help. It is as if the air had gone out of everything.

Vale das Eiras, 28 October 1990

At long last the sun shone yesterday, and we had breakfast outdoors for the first time and spoke kindly to each other, even made an excursion to the lagoon down by the coast. I pinched a basketful of agave shoots from the golf course. But now the sky has turned gray and rainy again.

Now that German unity yields nothing but cleanup costs, the newspapers are feeding off the crisis in the Gulf, which also has nothing to offer but expense, and beyond that is revealing the worldwide inability to deal sensibly with the underlying causes of crises.

In the afternoon Ute called me over to the west side of the house, where a snake hardly a meter long had begun to swallow a toad as large as my fist. With its mouth open terrifyingly wide, the snake had already devoured the toad's hind legs. The front portion of the toad was pulsing in a regular rhythm. Irritated by the two of us (Ute was taking pictures, and I had started a drawing), the snake let go of the toad, then raised its small, almost delicate triangular head, darted its tongue, and coiled its tail in exhaustion, while the rear of the spat-out toad remained motionless, covered with red slime. Presumably paralyzing digestive juices. Later the snake crawled under a bush to hide, out of weakness, apparently, after giving up a second attempt to swallow the toad. By now the toad was able to move its hind legs again. I picked it up on the blade of a hoe and deposited it under a bush some distance away. Ute thought the toad would be grateful to me for saving its life. The half-moon peeping from behind the clouds. Mild air. Finally my exhaustion is lifting.

We had quail for supper, roasted in the oven, accompanied by sweet potatoes with bacon and figs.

Back to the snake and the toad: how strange, alarming, and remote from all human reflection nature is when it reveals itself in such graphic fashion. Only in idiomatic expressions do these phenomena become graspable: to be swallowed alive, for instance. Corresponding images in Hieronymus Bosch.

Over the past few days I have been doing some unscheduled reading in Gottfried Keller, the *Zurich Novellas,* and am surprised to discover their freshness and unflinching narrative point of view. Then a volume of detective stories by Seicho Matsumoto, *Murder at the Amagi Pass.* The shorter stories especially appealed to me because they are startlingly different in style from Western detective stories: the extremely clever revenge killing in the mountains.

No mail from the children.

Vale das Eiras, 30 October 1990
The day before yesterday, after the supper of quail, we got involved in a conversation so engrossing that it went on until almost

four in the morning, but took a cheerful course, with both of us tender toward each other, the main topic being Hiddensee and Stralsund — why Ute does not want to support the Links' project of preserving the old houses next to the ruins of St. John's. But incidentally the discussion, fueled by three bottles of red wine, brought to the surface an idea that has been lying dormant for some time: the Berlin-Fontane novel, my old-age project, my possible book for the 1990s. An idea that was put aside not only because "The Call of the Toad" became more urgent, but probably also because the chronological frame of 1848 to 1969 seemed too obvious; not until the changed political situation of 1989–90 came along has it been possible to situate the living, surviving, immortal Fontane in Rohwedder's Handover Trust, where he — well paid for the first time — is responsible for various castles in Brandenburg, in the Uckermark, in Mecklenburg, in Lusatia, and so forth, thus occupying a key position while at the same time shunted off to one side. The working title could be "The Handover Trust." During our nocturnal conversation, other Fontane-like biographical details popped into my head: he, who at one time served for half a year as the secretary of the Prussian Academy of the Arts, could negotiate with the presidents of the divided academies, with Müller East and Jens West. He could also write a memorandum (for the federal president) discussing the case for Berlin as the capital and coming to the conclusion (to the president's disappointment) that this function is not suitable for the no longer divided city.

In our conversation I toyed with the idea of collaborating with Günter de Bruyn and Gerhard Wolf, only to reject it, though salvaging it as a fictional motif.

How would it be if, toward the end, a Stasi notation, and finally also a dossier on T. Fontane, turned up, recording his activity in

London as an agent for the Prussian Manteuffel government? I already have an opening sentence: "They refuse to let me die."

If my health holds up, I could write "The Call of the Toad" in '91, spend '92 doing the research for "Handover Trust," start the actual writing in '93, and make myself a gift of this completed work of my old age when my seventieth birthday rolls around in '97.

Am going to write to Rohwedder, asking him to schedule a time when I can tour the Handover Trust building, the headquarters for the closeout sale featuring "bargains" in GDR properties.

Yesterday, after our visit to Jules and Mieke (with the Suhls), the Jeep was full of agave shoots and one large plant. Today I scooped out a good fifteen holes and planted the rest of my booty. I am almost childishly eager to see how the results of all my gardening efforts will hold up until next January.

This evening I brought two versions of fried potatoes to the table (sweet potatoes for myself). They were served with leftovers of marinated fish and olives.

While doing my planting on the east side of the house, I disturbed an enormous toad, probably weighing a good kilo. I also found a dead beetle. It looks as though the three weeks here, in spite of, or perhaps thanks to, the rain, has dispelled our crisis and had meaning after all, though not without strenuous effort.

The ladder rigid in the tree.
The snake slowly
swallowing the living toad
(results in lockjaw).
The incessant rain matches the season.
A dead beetle, then, rhinoceros-like
and lovely in its shining armor.
Too much nature during a normal crisis.
But to the west of us, a landfill, we hear,
is planned and approved.

I wonder whether Uwe Johnson can be worked into the Fontane book, too. And his damaging agent-story.

Vale das Eiras, 1 November 1990
On our last day, the second Sunday (now with full moon), which apparently announces a longer run of sunny days, Ute finds a praying mantis for me, looking pale, straw-colored, and ghostly in her ladylike elegance. She manages to keep her body completely rigid while bowing her head, her two perfectly round eyes swiveling sideways.

Ute is packing. I have stowed the gardening tools in the garage. The Suhls came over today with Senhor Justo, who takes care of

their garden. The plan is for him to swing by once a week on the weekend to keep our plantings free of thistles and other weeds. He is also supposed to plant several trees: almond, olive, and pomegranate.

Ute and I are solicitous toward each other and relaxed, now that both of us have done the heavy lifting necessary to get the crisis off our backs. My discomfort in the groin (on the right). Apparently a hernia from my prostate operation three years ago. Especially when I sit for a long time and on hard Portuguese chairs I feel pressure, slight pain, and an unpleasant burning sensation inside. On Monday I am supposed to go to the doctor's in Lübeck.

I have done no writing, no drawing, no engraving, although I had five plates in my luggage, all coated. But I have made progress in thinking about "The Call of the Toad," and can anticipate an exhausting amount of work on "Handover Trust."

Took advantage of the sunshine to beat the bounds of the neighboring property and our own. Using flat fieldstones, I built a bench under the big old mimosa tree, with a view of the pond, now somewhat more full, the old house, and, with the mountains in the background, the new one, whose nakedness is gradually being filled in. Found two field mushrooms.

Fontane merely registers the castles and their condition but is not authorized to negotiate any sales.

During the GDR period Fontane was active in the Cultural Union. Since *The Stechlin* he has not written anything; he sees Johnson as picking up where he left off.

I am in a good mood, as if the crisis has been dammed up, perhaps overcome, almost as if work on drawings or on a manuscript had yielded preliminary results. Now that we are packed, one item traveling back with us will be my absolute determination to start on the actual writing of "The Call of the Toad" in November, or at the latest after the fateful date of 2 December. The only thing that could change that would be the prospect of three more weeks in Portugal; but as things stand, I will not start until late fall in Behlendorf.

Over fig brandy I thanked Ute for her forbearance; Ute thanked me for my willingness to share with her things I had been keeping to myself. We really are quite a pair!

Outside, the moon has the largest ring around it I have ever seen. How cozy the house — which we designed — feels with a fire in the fireplace.

Fontane's relationship today to England and to Hamburg and that city's aspirational Englishness; see *Jenny Treibel.*

Would Fontane have been allowed to travel abroad during his GDR period? Maybe twice to conferences. Why did he not join the Socialist Unity Party, and also not the Christian Democratic Union, but only the Cultural Union?

Fontane and his biographer Reuter.

Fontane, Dresden, and his children born out of wedlock.

At seven in the morning Germano is driving us to Faro airport. In two months we will be back here.

Behlendorf, 3 November 1990

Back to mountains of mail. Bruno with his lovable Ronja and my sister came to meet us at the airport in Fühlsbüttel. I read that Oskar L. is still betting on a victory or a partial victory (strongest party). But I feel too detached to get my hopes up. The letters to the editor reacting to the "Bargain" speech that appeared in *Die Zeit* are largely negative and in part hostile. All for the circular file.

During the past three weeks my ink extracted from inky caps has congealed; the Boskoop apples are overripe. The autumnal garden, the studio, waiting for me. If only I did not have this pain in my groin!

Am reading Peter Schneider's *German Comedy,* the most precise analysis yet of the German-German distortions, knowledgeable, based on acute observation, but in some places too glib for my taste.

Behlendorf, 4 November 1990

A year has passed. How a beginning can turn into its opposite! The usual course of revolutions, at warp speed. It is not only the GDR that is taking this intensive course in accelerated interment of hopes. At the end of this month presidential elections in Poland. If Wałęsa wins, Poland could fall behind itself yet again.

I read that the Bundeswehr is using Picasso's *Guernica* for its recruiting posters, with the caption "Enemy stereotypes are the fathers of war." Art could not be misused more cynically, history more falsified. Gathered five baskets of apples, each apple a unique miracle of ripening. A year ago in Poland, Gdańsk. Outside the covered market, next to the flower stalls, Kashubian women were selling boletes, that is how warm that fall was. After I came home, the Wall fell. (In Gdańsk my Calcutta drawings, the Bremen set, were displayed in the town hall. My futile attempt with Professor Lipski to get the Polish students we spoke to interested in social democracy.) Helene was there with me.

Has this year changed me? More than it should have. Still, I kept working on dead wood. Only the creation, the re-creation, of a nation has reduced this concept ad absurdum. I would rather be a Gypsy than a German. Or, to put it differently: if forced to choose between being a German or a Pole, my third way would be to become a Gypsy, stateless, European. I am reminded of my old teacher, Otto Pankok, whom the students used to make fun of; the only problem is that Ute would not lend herself to being a Gypsy woman. Also the dubiousness of conversion. How does one become a Gypsy? It also occurred to me that in Portugal the Gypsies are the best-looking Portuguese. If faced with another choice, Jew or Gypsy, I would prefer to be a Rom or a Sinto. Such childishly useless speculations after a year of German unity! (The would-be Gypsy has to go to the doctor's tomorrow.)

Upon my return, I find the review copies of *A Bargain . . .* in paperback (sixty pages). A meager summing-up, but that was all I had in me.

Behlendorf, 5 November 1990

The doctor in Lübeck indicated that an operation will probably be necessary. To cheer myself up, gathered five baskets of apples. Will take a small basket with me to Berlin tomorrow. Yesterday, by the way, I picked the last, overripe blackberries. Late vintage, Ute said.

Brandt is flying to Iraq and could be helpful to Oskar L., so speculators fear, or hope — if he succeeds in getting a peace plan for the Near East, including Israel, under way.

Listen again to North German Broadcasting, Channel 3: the culture business is running smoothly. The *Guernica* campaign launched by the Ministry of Defense is haunting me. I want to see the entire text. Want to write something on it. It would be suitable for the reading I am to do with de Bruyn for the federal president. Very concise, three pages. Another possible text could have the title "The Gypsies Are Here."

Would like to put my anger to work constructively. I want to look forward to Berlin. To cleanse myself, or to purge myself, I must write a poem.

Behlendorf, 14 November 1990

After the week in Berlin, during which I did not get a single word down on paper, went to the doctor's in Lübeck on Monday. The hernia operation will be in mid-December; the pain is getting worse.

Three evening rehearsals with Baby Sommer gave us a chance to rough out a possible new program based on *The Flounder.* (How fresh those texts have remained.) Baby's new instrument: a Jew's harp.

The exhibition in the stairwell of the town hall in Reinickendorf proved so stimulating that yesterday I started on a large-scale dead wood drawing in charcoal: 160 by 100 centimeters.

Today in Warsaw the treaty recognizing the Oder-Neisse border was signed at long last. Violence in Berlin. Waigel's economic policy expending money from the retirement trust fund: unity on borrowed money. The dollar falls to 1.48 deutschmarks. The danger of war in the Persian Gulf has meanwhile become part of our everyday political reality — between hopes and fears. Three weeks before the elections, the SPD is predicted to receive 36.5 percent. My own decision on how to vote is tending more and more toward the Greens/Alliance 90 (by absentee ballot). I am keeping calm by concentrating on large-scale drawing. Nonetheless, I want to write about the misuse of *Guernica*. Ute is staying close by.

After only three days of rest we are heading for Cologne tomorrow. Am looking forward to the train trip — why, I don't know.

Behlendorf, 18 November 1990

In hindsight, this three-day trip adds up to a success, insofar as public interest is concerned: Rheinbach, a Catholic town, mustered a crowd of 550 to hear me (a good 100 for the opening).

At the Jesuit church of St. Peter in Cologne, more than 1,200 crowded into the nave; and yesterday in Kiel, where I made my one election appearance, for Norbert Gansel, a factory floor was filled to the last seat with 250 listeners. But this outpouring should not blind me to the fact that these "successes" are just the flip side of the public boycott that especially influences book sales. I read aloud from the beginning of "Grimm's Forests" in *The Rat,* then the poem "I dreamt . . . ," and finally the "Obituary" from *Dead Wood.* At St. Peter's the original drawings were also on display, but because of the overflowing crowd, hardly visible. Perhaps it was being in a church that emboldened me to urge the "enlightened" Jesuits to "send the pope to hell," after I had contrasted the great expectations that had greeted the election of the Polish pope with his failures, especially vis-à-vis the Third World. The audience reacted with a partly shocked, partly relieved groan that gave way to laughter. Even if the Jesuits did not agree with me, they did not challenge me either.

In Rheinbach I saw the quite excellent rough proofs of the *Signatur* series, which Rommerskirchen had brought along. The whole thing will not be framed in plastic, which I rejected, but in simple stainless steel. I cannot warm to the Altenburg *Signatur* he gave me: the drawings are just too, too tasteful.

Neuhaus, who introduced me at the exhibition in Rheinbach and the reading in Cologne, has so much knowledge in his head that he tends to fall into breathless jabbering.

By train to Cologne and back: an opportunity to make up some of my sleep deficit. Then by car to Kiel. On the way there, we heard on the radio that Helmut Schmidt has praised Kohl and criticized Lafontaine: "He will lose the election — and deserves to do so." Schmidt measures everything by his own ego. Yet he was the one who elevated his own pragmatism to an ideology, robbed social democracy of any long-range perspective, pushed Eppler to the sidelines, and thereby contributed to the rise of the Greens.

In Berlin the Red–Green coalition is falling apart. Norbert Gansel admits that for the first time the election campaign is giving him no pleasure or even satisfaction — understandable. Unfortunately he also plans to write a book soon, without the slightest idea of what writing a book entails.

Back home, I find my large-scale drawing waiting for me. I finish it and promptly start on a new one.

Two weeks before the Bundestag elections and Kohl's expected bombastic victory, and I am still, or once more, undecided. What business is it of mine now?

After sleeping late (until noon) I managed today to shake off the three-day journey, with Ute's help. The beauty of this rainy November day. The deer out in the garden. Channel 3 as if from another planet.

In the audience in Cologne I caught sight of the rigid, motionless face of my fellow sculpture student Trude Esser, from back in 1949–52. Extreme distance and closeness. During the discussion in Kiel the danger and the possibility of an eco-dictatorship kept cropping up.

Behlendorf, 19 November 1990
Maria's birthday! This tough, unpredictable old bird, as loyal as she is sly, who has been with me all these years, from Anna to Ute, snapping away, is turning seventy-nine. At some point I should write a book about the photographer Maria, starting with *Inmarypraise*.

The second large-scale sheet (horizontal format) is done, the third (vertical format) laid out. A triptych is taking shape that cries out for a church: contemporary martyrdom.

I sleep until almost eleven to combat my exhaustion, have breakfast in bed, work uninterruptedly until just before seven P.M. By the end of the year I want to bring this dead wood topic to a close, once and for all, by means of these large-scale sheets, perhaps also the topic of soft-coal extraction (pencil).

Steidl has sent me material on the Bundeswehr's *Guernica* advertisement. The three to five pages on this subject should also be down on paper by the end of the year. Only then will I have leeway to begin "The Call of the Toad." By then the election in Poland will also have been decided; Wałęsa will probably win. In addition, food shortages are likely in Russia, especially in Moscow and Leningrad, although sufficient supplies are stored in the provinces.

The Gulf crisis is treading water, despite America's eagerness for war. Will probably vote for the SPD in Berlin and in the Federal Republic (even if only to respond to Helmut Schmidt), though with a heavy heart.

Flight from Hamburg to Berlin, 20 November 1990
Today Herr Lübcke drained the fish pond. More than fifty trout, a good twenty carp, and even more tench were caught in the net. Twenty trout that were still too small and a few ornamental tench (reddish orange) were thrown back in. None of the eels emerged from the muck. Our first share, fifteen trout, I put in the freezer. On the weekend we are having carp.

The central panel for the dead wood triptych has been composed in vertical format. I am surprised at my renewed eagerness to take up this theme again on large sheets and bring it to a conclusion.

Tomorrow Raoul and Beatrice are getting married. Today there will be a small pre-wedding party (with Anna). In the afternoon, following the wedding luncheon in the Italian restaurant on Handjerystrasse, we are flying back to Hamburg for an event at the Schwanenwik literary center.

Behlendorf, 22 November 1990
A rather meager meal the night before, at the rehearsal dinner. The guests who arrived late from England were not even served. Could it be that Raoul and Beatrice have both inherited Swiss stinginess? Apparently my children do not place much stock in bourgeois conventions.

The walls in the lobby of the Schöneberg town hall are hung with pictures of couples from the late Middle Ages, the Rococo era, and modernism (Picasso). The justice of the peace keeps the ceremony short and sweet. The wedding party a mixture of types, in the best Berlin tradition. The meal at the Italian restaurant excellent, with several courses: mushroom soup, suckling pig (cold) with asparagus, pasta with mushrooms, pike-perch with scampi. We had to leave before dessert to catch the plane to Hamburg.

Since the fall of the Wall, the proprietor does not like being in Berlin. After twenty years, though he is now a stranger in Italy, he wants to go back. "It was nicest in the sixties," he says. I barely know my daughter-in-law Beatrice. My granddaughter Rosanna, on the other hand, is blessed with charm. (A strange yet familiar feeling to be sitting next to Anna again.)

During the discussion at the Hamburg literary center, near our former apartment in Schwanenwik, I had to remind Raddatz, the newest executioner, of his time in the GDR and his revolutionary carrying-on during the '68 book fair. Schädlich speaks in well-formulated abstruse terms: there is no GDR literature and never was such a thing. Only aesthetics count. He is floating helplessly on the wave of propaganda directed against so-called ideological literature. I talked myself into a rage (which felt good). Nice that Bruno was there, paying close attention. The critic Dieckmann from East Berlin was good, if still excessively cautious. Home too late, at two in the morning; took a brief look at the drawing in progress.

Behlendorf, 25 November 1990
A week before the Bundestag elections, whose outcome the polls seem to have nailed down, the president is to be elected in Poland, and there, too, the result seems unavoidable. Although both elections will confirm my "toad calls," the prospect is not cheering.

The first central panel for the three-part altarpiece did not work: the uprooted deciduous tree came across as too powerfully alive, clashing with the two horizontal images. But my second attempt, falling, fallen, and still upright evergreens, looks promising.

Yesterday Per Øhrgaard, who stayed the night, and the Rühmkorfs came for carp, a five-pounder. Because he has been free of pain and various other ills for a year now, Peter wanted to settle down and drink brandy; Eva, on the other hand, had a terrible cold. The situation in Germany put us in a desperately cheerful mood.

A cold, sunny day. Orchard bare. Landscape receding into the mist on both sides of the poplars along the canal. Many birds pecking at the last windfalls.

Behlendorf, 30 November 1990
The fifth large-scale sheet is finished, but I will probably continue working into December on the three-part altarpiece (past the elec-

tions, that is). If it comes out well and one of Lübeck's pastors is brave enough, I will lend it to a church and, later, if the installation is guaranteed, will make a gift of it. How else to portray "crucifixions" nowadays?

My work was interrupted by an interview with B. Grimm for *Die Zeit* on the topic of dead wood, and one with a Danish journalist from *Politiken,* with whom I went over the topic of Germany yet again from start to finish. Also, in preparation for the hernia operation, which has been scheduled for the end of December, I had to have a colonoscopy, a good half of which I watched on the monitor without anesthesia, until it became too painful. I also saw the bean-sized polyp, sprouting in the shape of a mushroom, that was removed during the procedure. The interior view of one's own colon, properly cleaned out after the five liters of saline solution I had had to get down, is startlingly interesting: a delicately tinted tunnel.

Respect for Oskar, who is staying the course during the election campaign, however bitter. Maybe he will even succeed in improving the outcome by a few points and — in contrast to J. Rau's results four years ago, when we were in Calcutta — come out a little better: between 37 and 38 percent. Apparently the FDP is cutting into the CDU's lead at the moment by gaining votes for Genscher. If the FDP comes out with more than 10 percent and the Greens stay between 6 and 7 percent and the PDS gets no more than 2 or 3 percent, it is conceivable that the Social Democrats will have a stronger showing than the CDU (without the CSU), but more likely things will turn out even worse than badly, just as in Poland, where sheer senselessness carried the day. Will make my membership in the SPD contingent on whether Oskar runs for party chair after the election.

Any thought of working on a manuscript is disturbingly at a standstill. Am depending on Siberian compressed charcoal to keep me focused. Today a brilliant frosty day. The first snow fell early. Ute has bought snow tires. Raoul's wedding, which was actually rather bleak — or am I being unfair? — haunts me. I am sleeping a lot, not soundly. During the day I am able to concentrate, thanks to years of practice.

Late yesterday a telephone call from Peter Schneider, currently in America. Nothing has come of the voters' initiative we had planned with Jurek Becker. After the election we want to get together and go over everything.

At my drawing board again before we drive into the city for the reading. And before that, a glass of Spanish cognac!

Behlendorf, 1 December 1990
Stade has spruced up its Old Town, thanks to the economic boost from the nearby nuclear plant on the Elbe. My reading in the town hall auditorium, recorded by Radio Bremen, one of the small broadcasting companies whose future looks dim. Afterward the obligatory discussion, although I am sick and tired of having to explain why I position myself between the traditional idols of resignation and hope. The chronic hope-mongering blocks any recognition of the realities and stands in the way of any fundamental change.

Finally Iraq and the U.S. are starting to negotiate over the Gulf region. At least that means time can be gained, time until the next crisis.

Yesterday more women than men in the audience, as usual. The women also ask the more telling questions. The kind of questions that focus with concern on the temptation to fall silent that has plagued me since *The Rat*. Probably without women readers there would be no more literature.

And tomorrow is election night. Bruno and Malte are coming to see us through.

A few minutes ago a car with a loudspeaker mounted on its roof drove by our house, which really does lie off the beaten track. It was calling on us specifically to vote tomorrow for the NPD, the neo-Nazis who call themselves "national democrats" — a little German joke!

Feel like writing poems.

Behlendorf, 2 December 1990
On this Election Sunday, which is also the first day of Advent, Ute placed the Advent wreath with its one candle on the table. Malte and I smiled tolerantly at this special effort. In the afternoon, when Bruno gets here, we want to write down our predictions. Mine, chronically overoptimistic, will be as follows: CDU/CSU 42%, FDP 10%, Greens 6%, PDS 5.5%, SPD 36%.

Yesterday and today I began composing a longish prose poem, "Evening with Old Friends." Other titles I have in mind: "Farewell to the Cultural Supplement," "Election Sunday," "German Miscellany."

Never has my studio provided a more necessary refuge than now.

Behlendorf, 3 December 1990
In the Federal Republic and in Berlin the Social Democrats took a double beating and are now back to the one-third share of the vote they had in the fifties; the Greens' percentage was halved in the former Federal Republic, which takes them out of the Bundestag.

Even in defeat Oskar behaved like a statesman, but whether he is willing to assume leadership of the battered SPD, or is capable of doing so, is more than dubious. In any case, the CDU-state will once again take control of every corridor of power, more insistently and dangerously now that it counts the "Krauses" from the East among its supporters.

The presence of our irreverent sons made election night tolerable, but they were hit hard, too: Malte reacting cynically, Bruno at a loss.

Because in addition to the pain from the hernia my left wrist has begun to hurt — I strained it doing those large-scale drawings — sleep would not come. Strange to say, my sleeplessness focused purposefully, as if the subject were now on the docket, on bits and pieces of ideas associated with the "Handover Trust" project, which I jotted down around five in the morning in my library, while smoking:

The counterpart of the immortal Fontane could be the immortal secret agent, a continuation of Schädlich's Tallhover, who survived the fifties and made his way to the West. T. works for the West German intelligence service. He knows Fontane's file, going all the way back to the revolutionary year of 1848. He knows about Fontane's illegitimate children in Dresden and their descendants. He knows about Fontane's work as a secret agent in London. Early on, starting in the mid-sixties, he was thus able to put the squeeze on Fontane for the GDR's State Security Service. Because T. was present as a spy in the Tunnel Society, censored Fontane's poems, and knows the most intimate details of Fontane's marriage, the two men form an inseparable pair, both representative of the current situation: Christa Wolf, Stephan Hermlin, Hermann Kant, and so forth. This pair provides the arc of the entire story, with Fontane owing his position at the Handover Trust to Tallhover's intercession. I picture twelve episodes in which the Fontane-Tallhover old-boy network dominates. But in other episodes Tallhover's presence should be felt as well.

How did Fontane survive the Third Reich? As a journalist reporting from the front, especially in France? Hence the correspondences to Fontane's time in France in 1870–71, his imprisonment, his book on the Franco-Prussian War. Fontane and unification. His pertinent knowledge. The French heritage of his Huguenot family. A span of time extending from '70 to '71, from '40 to '45, that remains relatively guilt-free for Fontane, while Tallhover is otherwise engaged.

The possibility of using this journal, starting with 1 January: Fontane in Altdöbern, Cottbus: the castle, the soft-coal pits, Lusatia, the cultural centers in Hoyerswerda and Guben. Fontane in Leipzig twice: at Führer's, the round table, the SPD party convention; and at the house of the druggist Voigt on election night of 18 March 1990. Fontane in Neubrandenburg: dedication of the School of Education by M. Honecker. Fontane in Schwerin, staying at someone's house: the *Lieder* concert at the theater, the castle. Fontane in Stralsund: the scandal involving Hiddensee jewelry. Fontane in Dresden. His illegitimate children. In Radebeul he visits descendants. Baby Sommer telling stories with his drums. Tallhover's insinuations. Prenzlauer Berg and the Lichtenberg railroad station are worth considering.

Fontane and literature: his trip (as a spy) in 1968 to the Frankfurt Book Fair. Fontane on Lake Schwielow, where the boards of directors of the two writers' unions meet. Fontane discussing heliotropes with de Bruyn. Fontane at the peace discussion in East Berlin. Fontane at the readings in East Berlin between 1973 and

'76, secretly recorded by Tallhover and assessed and evaluated from a literary point of view by Fontane. Fontane on Uwe Johnson's death and on journalism.

A rather long discussion with Tallhover on the immortality of literature and censorship during a train trip from Berlin to Büchen. The dismal prospects for the future.

Fontane's work at the Handover Trust: tucked-away office. The castles. He is supposed to sort out the Academy situation, also the future of the cultural centers belonging to the Cultural Union and now part of the state-owned property on the auction block. The two Academy presidents. His period in the nineteenth century as secretary to the Prussian Academy. How Fontane finally meets Rohwedder. Fontane considers going to England (Scotland) once the Handover Trust's work is concluded: no one there knows him, and there an end to his immortality can be foreseen.

The book: Fontane's life and double life. A spy novel. Berlin: 1848, 1961, 1969 to 1990. He as the sole narrator, chatty, conversational. A book about lingering, hovering suspicions. Fontane's occasionally clipped speech, like that of the king in *Schach von Wuthenow*. Figures like Mathilde Möhring and Jenny Treibel in contemporary dress?

Shall try to get into the "Handover Trust." What choice do I have?

Behlendorf, 4 December 1990
Now, to make the defeat even more painful, Oskar L. has decided not to run for the party chairmanship. Vogel, too, no longer wants to run (in May).

Last night yielded more bits and pieces for the "Handover Trust" book.

His dawning, awakened, incarnate immortality. That is to say, Fontane is not always present. Major events and dates, however, when history is made, bring him out of the woodwork. Thus the book could begin with the building of the Wall and immediately flash to the fall of the Wall: keeping the focus on historical significance, this first chapter could lead to the Handover Trust, with *Before the Storm* furnishing the third temporal level, namely Fontane's period as a writer after 1871.

Then, in the second chapter, the story could start over with the introduction of the other "Immortal," Tallhover: Zoo Station before Fontane sets out to return to East Berlin, supplied with books he has providently purchased in the West (Heine bookstore), conversations between Fontane and Tallhover as they pace back and forth in the concourse.

Where and when Fontane lives out his immortality. He remains around sixty years old, close to retirement, although he already quotes from all the novels he will write later, up to and including *Stechlin*.

His assertion that he is immortal is at once muted and confirmed by realistic variations. Friends and colleagues (in the Cultural Union, the Academy) have always called him "our Fontane," and not only because of the similarity. The "Fontane style" to which I aspire must not become a parody, for which reason the story I have in mind cannot exceed 220 pages: forty episodes of five to six pages each.

Copenhagen, 6 December 1990
Yesterday under a cold blue sky we took the ferry from Puttgarden to Rødby. Strange to be traveling through wintry Denmark when we are usually summer guests. My eye still zeroes in on every clump

of trees. Even if the Danes do not care to admit it, the evergreens are almost done for.

According to the latest news reports, the SPD's decline continues. It is certainly true that Oskar's election platform, focused exclusively on saying no, weakened his chances for a better outcome, but it is equally true that the party unanimously chose Oskar (with his no platform) as its candidate. Brandt's slogan — "Help Oskar now!" — was ignored, especially by Schmidt and Schiller. No wonder, then, that Oskar considered the contributions of those grand old men an obstacle to electoral success and, apparently battered by so much solidarity, turned down the party chairmanship. But whether Björn Engholm has it in him to be the top dog is questionable. Not very combative, inclined to reflection, he feels more drawn to art exhibitions than to interminable meetings in Bonn.

The event at the Louisiana Museum, that splendid democratic space, was overflowing and went on and on — so many questions: two and a half hours. After that, dinner at the Boathouse. I tried again to persuade Vagn Grosen, my publisher at Gyldendal, to buy out the Hinstorff publishing house in Rostock and run it himself.

Another sleepless night, unfortunately. And the nocturnal bits and pieces for "The Handover Trust" muddled. At most it is worth noting that, along with Fontane's narrative voice, Tallhover can provide reports and spy on the immortal Fontane. Additional narrators, such as a Handover Trust staffer or a secretary at the Academy East, call him "our Fontane" and speak of a confusing likeness.

The question remains: What did Fontane do on 4 November when the artists staged their protest? Did he also make a speech? Did he want to speak but was prevented from doing so?

Broadening the narrative point of view by adding several voices is appealing, but it can make the book too long. Fontane and the revolutions of '48, '68, and '89!

Now we are going for a stroll in the Old Town.

Behlendorf, 8 December 1990

Back from Denmark yesterday over the fog-gray Baltic. The two brief days of civilized Danish ways helped me put the terrible election results in perspective. A country with no earthshaking events about to have its own elections, which will change little or nothing. The evening with Per Øhrgaard merry and rather too moist: how the Danes love to laugh at themselves.

On the way home, lunch at the Bagges'. It looks as though Ute's Vogterhus can be saved. Next year a long-term lease can be signed. Lines for water and electricity are also to be installed. We plan to turn space under the eaves into a room for Ute and me. Our current cubbyhole will become a guest room, and the pantry will probably make way for a shower.

Back to the Handover Trust (another sleepless night and more nocturnal bits and pieces): because everything comes together there in a central location, the trust has to take the blame for every failure, every bankruptcy, all responsibility; Kohl has weaseled his way out and will devote himself to making fine speeches about Europe with Mitterrand.

Fontane in reality and fiction: GDR citizen and immortal at the same time.

Why he nonetheless rejects Berlin as the capital.

Fontane plans out ex-GDR novels: Mathilde Möhring as a quintessential GDR woman. A radio broadcast with him, de Bruyn, Christa Wolf, Hermann Kant, Stephan Hermlin. Fontane offers them all mocking comfort.

Fontane's conversations in his head with his wife and daughter, who are absent.

How he disappears from the Handover Trust at the end and uses his savings to travel to England/Scotland, away from immortality. Fontane's little satirical poems. He wants to revive the pictorial narratives printed in Neuruppin.

On the ferry, while Ute is off getting coffee for us, the idea comes to me and takes root that I could publish the "Handover Trust" story under another name: Maximilian Zsarg, a source of childish pleasure.

Tomorrow to Berlin, rehearsal with Baby Sommer, the Saxon descendant of an illegitimate Fontane daughter.

Berlin, 13 December 1990

What began well, the dress rehearsal with Baby Sommer in the presence of a small audience, turned out to be more polished than the successful program we did the first time, "Once Upon a Time There Was a Country." The unanimity we two comedians surprisingly discovered in the course of working together then gave way to grumpy toil over the weekend. The shopping trip with Ingrid and Nele nerve-racking. The mail unspeakably tedious. The exhibition in Reinickendorf deserted and seemingly unnoticed. Idiotic the discussion with the audience in the half-empty hall. But maybe it is only this gastric flu that is skewing my perceptions. Nonetheless, the meal in the French restaurant yesterday was amusing because Maria finally introduced me to Hellbach, the wholesaler, who picked up the tab for all of us. Hellbach surprisingly quiet and attentive, not your typical businessman, also with an aura of loneliness; yet his new gallery still has plenty of space for his avid collecting: Buffet next to Miró.

When the house in Behlendorf was broken into — while we were in Denmark — it turns out that my tin canister containing an old passport, drafts of a will, and cash was stolen, not just the kitchen radio.

Raoul and Beatrice have flown with the baby to their island. Ute is cooking in the old kitchen on Niedstrasse. I wish I could have Nele here for supper. But she is not coming, because Ute is here. So the child gets caught in the female crossfire.

A generalized aversion — including to literature — has taken hold of me. Maybe the hernia operation, scheduled for next week, will help. Tomorrow I am flying to Stuttgart with Maria and Eva Hönisch. Engholm is supposed to speak at the exhibition opening. After he agreed to stand for election as party chairman, I wrote him a long letter. My plan of resigning from the party has been postponed for now.

On the train from Stuttgart to Frankfurt, 15 December 1990
A Swiss actor gives me his copy of the Zurich *Tages-Anzeiger,* which carries an obituary for Friedrich Dürrenmatt, and begs me to take care of myself: "Now you are all we have left!"

Yesterday's grotesque opening at the Marlies Breitling Gallery, with an excellent introduction by Björn Engholm. The painful contrast between my Calcutta images and the fancy postmodern marble architecture. Everything, including the flooring, is marked with the gallery owner's initials. My reading was perfectly chosen for the guests at the vernissage. Six or seven drawings, three sculptures, and a good two dozen etchings sold immediately. The comical yet irritating skirmishes between Maria Rama and Eva Hönisch. Engholm and I both suffering from the flu. His alert staffers. Oskar Lafontaine has vanished without a trace (in the south). The death of Dürrenmatt — seven years my senior — has sharpened my concentration. He, whom the contemporary theater and the critical mafia tried to forget while he was still living. (See the obituary in the *Frankfurter Allgemeine*.) Now I still have to endure the meeting of the Authors' Council in Frankfurt. I intend to speak frankly to the publishers.

Lübeck, University Hospital, 18 December 1990
Shaved all around my cock, across my stomach, on my upper thighs, and now all I can do is wait for the hernia operation around seven tomorrow morning. A new hospital, one façade indistinguishable from the other. The staff efficient, with a tendency to talk as if the patient were not there: "He's scheduled for tomorrow."

Yesterday de Maizière resigned from all his official positions. Tolls on the autobahn and higher telephone charges are supposed to finance unity. The election scam is becoming apparent (too late). The scam artists utterly shameless. The gurney will be here any minute now . . .

Lübeck, University Hospital, 19 December 1990
All night long, unbearable pain. Finally they gave me an injection. Then, when I was half asleep, the cannula for the drip got dislodged: a bloody mess. This hospital is really deathly boring. The nurses bustling around, coming and going without accomplishing anything. The doctors make their appearance in white, just as in the movies. I hope I can get out of here on Saturday!

Behlendorf, 23 December 1990
On Channel 3, Enzensberger, chatting casually after his latest change of heart, attacks Bloch, trivializing him and becoming

more and more arrogant. This fits in with my hospital reading, which I am continuing in my own bed in Behlendorf: *Before the Storm*. The difference is that Fontane's use of the conversational tone is chosen to promote clarity, while Enzensberger's chattiness is just one role among many. In his new "modesty in the face of projects for societal overhaul," he invokes Montaigne and Diderot while ignoring Lessing. He (like Walser) considers himself intellectually and morally free of the "absolute positions" he once subscribed to, the verbal "Off with their heads!" of the '68 generation.

I am not healing as quickly as I had hoped. Enzensberger's amusing comparison of the oligarchs in Cuba and their loss of power and possessions with that of the landed gentry east of the Elbe. (Transform the eloquent smart aleck who finds everything amusing into a Fontane-like character.)

Am still more drawn to work on the "Handover Trust" book than on "The Call of the Toad," which took shape too quickly and must now be set aside. All this while the Soviet Union and Yugoslavia are falling apart and the Gulf war seems to be a done deal.

Behlendorf, 24 December 1990
Slept in my English deck chair while Malte decorated the Christmas tree (at my feet) and Hans watched Charlie Chaplin in *Monsieur Verdoux* on television. I had to lie down because I had worked too long at my drawing board in the studio, my third large horizontal composition: the crucifixion I had laid out before the operation. I'd like to finish this drawing before the year ends.

Maria has been here since yesterday, talking exclusively about the need to sell my drawings at the highest possible price. No sooner does she see a new work of mine than she experiences a burst of enthusiasm, then estimates a price and identifies a possible buyer. She is a genius at marketing.

A year ago the occupation of Panama and the revolution in Romania overshadowed the Christmas season. This time a threat of war in the Gulf and civil war in the Soviet Union and in the Balkans.

I want to explore the area around Frankfurt on the Oder, to the west and east of the river: on the trail of *Before the Storm*.

Behlendorf, 25 December 1990
Hans, Malte, and Bruno, with their donkey's years of twenty-one, twenty-three, and twenty-five, this fraternal troika who treat one another with such rough-and-ready affection and are fond of me in a manner that ranges from gentle to petulant, and furthermore have been equipped and lovingly molded by Ute, made Christmas tolerable for me in their beguiling fashion. Late in the evening a telephone conversation with Franz, who, on account of a New Year's invitation, described Bruno, and with him his "young generation," as "not very resilient"; it makes me laugh to hear my thirty-three-year-old Franz complaining about the younger generation. How I enjoy my children.

A sleepless night, during which I did finish *Before the Storm* and, while dictating the *Guernica* piece in the dark of night, succumbed to the temptation to coin the phrase "Scammany, a Gummybear," for that is how low Heine's "Germany, a Winter's Tale" has sunk! It must have been around six in the morning that I fell asleep, exhausted, only to wake around noon, not at all rested. "Scammany" would imply thoughtless exploitation, such as the Bundeswehr's use of *Guernica* for recruiting, or the Isenheim Altar's being used to advertise aspirin or the campaign to reintroduce the death penalty. To develop this argument, the *Guernica* essay would have to be fairly long, suitable for an initial reading in the presence of the federal president.

As the year draws to a close, so does this journal. During the night, vague fears that the outbreak of war in the Gulf could trigger an Iraqi atom bomb, smuggled into New York or Tel Aviv, a bomb produced with German assistance.

Behlendorf, 27 December 1990
Today — ten days after my operation the stitches were removed — I picked up in Lübeck three packages of charcoal (previously ordered) and applied fixative to a third central panel: "Golgotha." Yesterday Björn Engholm was here with Barbara, one of his daughters, along with her boyfriend, as we had arranged in Stuttgart. Coffee and cake, fruit, brandy, then white wine from Franconia. Engholm and I sat in my studio for a good hour. I outlined for him my ideas about Germany's political future and our possible collaboration. The essential condition for any such thing would be the willingness of the SPD, and that of its future chairman, to transform the Greater Federal Republic created through simple annexation into a "Federation of German Lands," with a new constitution anchored in the Basic Law.

A prerequisite would be a constitutional convention, with intellectuals and artists also taking part, that would reinforce the federative elements, thereby enabling Germany to be shaped into a cultural nation, with cultural sovereignty residing in the individual states.

Further constitutional goals I listed were a redefinition of citizenship, discarding the principle of German blood lineage; mandatory protection of nature and the environment; gaining security through social justice, with a guaranteed right to employment and shelter, while the traditional guarantee of security by military means would be relatively less important.

I pointed out that the strengthening of culture Engholm desired could be achieved only through a continuous debate over culture. In this way a remnant of the former GDR's culture could be revived and revitalized. Some examples of priorities: theater, the Leipzig Institute of Literature, the Cultural Union, and so forth. Criticism of the SPD's previous concept of culture: the Linda Reisch circus, multimedia shows, entertainment extravaganzas.

At least Engholm listened and took notes, but promptly pointed out the resistance these concepts would encounter in the SPD (as I well know).

I remain skeptical as to whether he can muster the will to fight for such policies and remain on the offensive for any length of time. I also suggested to this future party chairman that he invite writers and intellectuals to address the SPD faction in the Bundestag and the party's governing council.

Today B.E. left for Colombo in Sri Lanka. Strange, considering that the beginning of the new year will see the start of the election campaign in Hesse.

I have mounted a new sheet for a new three-part composition. I cannot stop!

Behlendorf, 28 December 1990
After another sleepless night I sketched out the "year-end drawing" after all. At night my thoughts solidify, initially for the "Handover Trust" project. The events captured in this journal (extending back to October/November/December '89), up to the Bundestag

elections on 2 December 1990, will frame the narrated time; after that, the immortal Fontane will disappear, heading for Scotland. Tallhover will bid him farewell. *Guernica* also kept me awake. A letter from the attorney Heinrich Senfft says that he will get in touch with the Picasso family, as I had suggested. This is how the essay might look:

Description of the painting without mention of the title. Nineteen thirty-seven, the year it was painted. Spain's pavilion at the Paris World's Fair. A detailed account of the destruction of Guernica by German Legion Condor planes. Back to the picture, which is not an enemy stereotype. Only at this point bring in the Ministry of Defense advertisement in *Der Spiegel*. The timing of the two-page spread, 10 September 1990. The monstrous insensitivity that goes unmentioned, except for Hecht's protest in *art*. I'd want to engage in "ideological aesthetics." Not forgotten: the games we schoolchildren played during recess in '37. All the people who remain silent in the face of this monstrosity: artists, academies . . . The Ministry of Defense as the Augean stables. A demand that recruiting be halted until the shame has been acknowledged. Appeal to the federal president, and then back to the painting at the end.

I want to try out a new form of essay. Sharp, polished, expressive, cutting. A text that liberates Picasso's *Guernica* from the museum and brings it into the present.

Behlendorf, 29 December 1990
Slept with interruptions. Awake, lying on my side, buried in darkness, yet fixated on a white sheet of drawing paper on which the

drawing is composed in three parts, in horizontal format, then falling asleep. The hope, false from the outset, that after all the unrest and radical changes the new year would take a quieter course now appears clearly to have been a deception. Even if war does not break out in the Gulf, the tension remains explosive; social desperation, hunger, racism, and other forms of political pressure will mobilize the masses in Eastern Europe, in the southeastern Balkans, and in the Third World. The West will try (in vain) to wall itself off and lower an Iron Curtain of its own. All this will place an additional burden on the German unification process, which in any case started off on the wrong foot.

So another year around the corner that will not be easy for manuscript work. Nonetheless I intend to try.

After two hours of intensive work on the large-scale drawing on the board, we are waiting for Norbert and Lesley Gansel to arrive. An old friendship that has proved strangely durable.

Am listening to Bach, the *Magnificat*.

Behlendorf, 31 December 1990

That was a rather inane visit: this self-congratulatory Bundestag mentality that takes seriously every fart noted in the minutes. With boundless vanity, the vanity of the person under discussion (in this case, Gansel discussing Engholm) is pinpointed as his Achilles' heel. Disappointing! Yet N. Gansel is one of the few Bundestag members who consistently fight the pervasive corruption. Still, it is impossible to have a thorough conversation, let alone a bold one, with him because his wariness stifles any thought the moment it begins to take wing.

Yesterday the art dealer Gaulin came from Lübeck to have a look at my altar drawings. Two large landscape sheets with side panels, one of the central panels showing a crucifixion scene, offer alternatives; the others, all single sheets, are too powerful to come together and form a triptych. Now Gaulin wants to see what a Lübeck churchman has to say. He, too, thinks St. Mary's would be the right place.

Now that I have set aside the three-panel structure in the last horizontal-format version and, after a struggle, made up my mind to go with an undivided composition, the final sheet will not be completed until after New Year's.

Time to sum up and, as I always do on New Year's Eve, line up my work for the coming year. The texts I wrote this year, in addition to "Writing after Auschwitz," are the speech I gave in Tutzing, "Short Speech by a Rootless Cosmopolitan," then, after 18 March, "The View from Suckers Square," then, after several visits to the GDR, the "Report from Altdöbern," and finally, for 3 October, "A Bargain Called the GDR." Also the afterword for *Dead Wood:* "The Cloud as a Fist above the Forest." Then there were the captions for the pictures and a good 250 pages of this journal.

Contrary to my plans: no poems and etchings, but about fifty charcoal drawings on the theme of soft coal, and more lithos than planned.

Publications to which I committed myself in '89: *Equalizing the German Burden,* which appeared later (published by Aufbau), along with *The Plebeians Rehearse the Uprising,* in large print runs. On both sides of the border about ten thousand copies. Luchterhand's edition of *Writing after Auschwitz* sold poorly. The booksellers allegedly objected to the title; hardly a thousand copies of the paperback were sold. Steidl did a good job marketing *Germany, United Fatherland?,* the debate with R. Augstein, and, with thirteen thousand copies sold, *Dead Wood* gathered no dust in the bookstores, although Steidl had been hoping for twenty thousand.

Finally, in Denmark and in my Behlendorf studio I completed another fifty to sixty charcoal and pencil drawings, among them many large-scale ones. The portfolio for Rommerskirchen's *Signatur,* or *Letter from Altdöbern,* has gone to press.

Now to my plan for 1991:

1. A new program to perform with Baby Sommer, "Then Spake the Flounder," as an audiocassette, premiere in Kiel in March.
2. Next spring, my summer '89 reading from *The Tin Drum* in Göttingen will finally be issued on cassette by Luchterhand.
3. For the fall, the studio retrospective volume is planned, with accompanying text of approximately twenty-five pages, still to be written.
4. By March, the *Guernica* polemic, dedicated to the federal president, must be down on paper, about fifteen pages.
5. The publication of *Signatur* is guaranteed.

Plans for writing:

1. I want to finish the first, handwritten draft of "The Call of the Toad." Estimated length, if I get it done by late summer, 120 pages. Then in August (Denmark), I want to start on the typed version, and be done in December. Estimate: 180 pages. The third draft could then be finished in the spring of '92, with the book appearing in the fall of '92.
2. At some point I want to dictate this journal, which I plan to keep until 15 January, when the Gulf ultimatum

runs out, to Eva Hönisch, probably about three hundred pages.

3. Travels with Ute through Brandenburg in preparation for "Handover Trust." Will keep a travel journal (with sketches). Will start reading Fontane thoroughly, writing down my observations. Visit to the Handover Trust. Contact with Rohwedder.

4. In addition to the trip to Italy, in early May, a trip to Poland will be necessary, in July or September. In January, March, and October, to Portugal.

5. Light, small-scale pencil drawings, smudged, Portuguese, Brandenburgish. My first lithos to accompany original poems. And finally six or seven etchings on the topic of dead wood.

6. Maybe a dozen small sculptures.

That should be sufficient. Now we are driving to the Bissingers' for a foretaste of the new year with friends. Yesterday I prepared an aspic from the head of the suckling pig.

After a restless night I am drained, and, like the year '90, over and done with.

Behlendorf, 1 January 1991
In Neuland, with lots of grappa and friends — the Bissingers, the Rühmkorfs, the Flimms — drowned the old year in drink. Today came home in beautiful New Year's weather and immediately finished the last large-scale sheet for "Golgotha II" and applied fixative. Rühmkorf (his back pain has returned) tells me about diaries he has kept faithfully for twenty years. Now he wants to decipher them and copy them, possibly use them as the basis for a second autobiographical book.

Behlendorf, 2 January 1991
Among many New Year's telephone calls, a mournful conversation with Walter Höllerer. His initial expressions of pleasure gave way more and more to paranoid delusions. Now he is also afraid he may have fallen into the hands of AIDS doctors.

A good radio essay on Thomas Mann, *Reflections of an Unpolitical Man.*

Behlendorf, 4 January 1991
Shortly before our departure for Portugal, and after an alarm system has been installed in our house, in response to several break-ins.

In my luggage a blank book, to make sure nothing stands in the way of the first draft of "The Call of the Toad." Now my plan is to use a straightforward narrative after all, without the intermediary of a fictional narrator. Looking back on an agitated, politically agitating period. Facts will be asserted, a love story will take its tragicomic course, the rise and fall of the German-Polish Cemetery Association will constitute the main subject of the narrative. No shortage of apprehension, an essential part of starting a manuscript.

Vale das Eiras, 5 January 1991
During the flight to Faro — where we arrived after midnight — one hour's sleep from sheer exhaustion. Spent the night at the Hubers', in the gallery. Am captivated once more by the beauty and solitary location of our house, which Senhor Justo has taken care of in all respects: he has planted fava beans, garlic, beets, and artichokes.

Under the pines on the property next door I found several oldish and a few still edible bloody milk caps. Sautéed in butter, they made a fine appetizer. After that we had two sheep's tongues, cooked by me, also small red beans with lots of garlic and a vegetable from the Suhls called Jerusalem artichoke. All with a good Dão wine.

As soon as the sun went down, around five-fifteen, it turned cold. Now we are sitting in front of the fireplace.

Read with surprise the last fifty pages of this journal. Am wondering whether I will succeed in transforming this casual daily practice into the discipline necessary for a manuscript.

Vale das Eiras, 6 January 1991
After falling asleep, completely wiped out, I was awake much too soon, in the grip of grinding insomnia, which merged toward morning into terrifying dreams halfway between sleeping and waking: on Niedstrasse Raoul had cleared out my office, canceled the telephone service, sold my correspondence files . . .

No sooner do we get here than the sky clouds over. Toward noon a backhoe drives up, scoops dirt from the property next door, and blocks one side of our shortcut to the main road. Later we learn from Maria José that the land, including the woods and the ruin, has been bought by "foreigners": pleasant neighbors, apparently, who introduce themselves by backhoe.

I am reading Hans-Heinrich Reuter's edition of Fontane's collected *Writings on Literature*. As the dedication indicates, this volume was given to me by Reuter in March '61 in Leipzig. At the time I had been invited by Hans Mayer to be a guest at the university, and I created a minor scandal when I delivered greetings from Uwe Johnson to the packed auditorium. Bloch was in the audience. It is amusing and touching to read Reuter's introduction, with the obligatory class-struggle references scattered here and there.

In "Handover Trust" the immortal Fontane's relationship to his biographer Reuter could provide the material for a chapter. Fontane's criticism and occasional condescension directed at Storm, Keller, Schiller, and Goethe. Fontane's relationship to Scott and Alexis: interesting. Fontane's criticism of Gustav Freytag's *Debit and Credit*. How fresh these concise texts still are to read, whether they hit their target or land wide of the mark.

A key text: "The Social Position of the Writer," an essay written in 1891, which, to counteract disrespect for writers, proposes that the state serve as a patron and promoter. Fontane never suspects the danger of dependency that would become a reality during two dictatorships. Arguments for Tallhover.

We eat the last bloody milk caps from the property next door with mutton and sweet potatoes. Already have doubts again whether I can negotiate the leap into the "Call of the Toad" manuscript. This wondrous, childish fearfulness.

Vale das Eiras, 7 January 1991

Another almost sleepless night that saps my energy, leaving me with barely enough for reading Fontane in this bad weather. His last, unfinished novel, *The Likedeelers,* could bring the immortal into conflict with Barthel (KuBa) and his Störtebeker. Fontane and Lessing: his late tirades against the Enlightenment. This Berlin-Fontane reunification novel could be quite something if I can pull it off (in time for my seventieth). It might even form the second part of a trilogy, following "The Call of the Toad" and followed by another work, not yet conceived.

Without newspapers the Gulf crisis remains distant, like a nightmare from the past: the only thing we hear about (from the Suhls) is the storm that came across from England and ravaged northern Germany. I wonder whether last year's storms are going to be repeated.

Vale das Eiras, 8 January 1991
After a long sleep at last (six or seven hours) and in better weather, we went shopping for plants, including a cactus that shoots up tall and sends out long branches. Planted it among three little rosemaries.

According to yesterday's paper (the *Süddeutsche*), what is probably the decisive meeting between the Iraqi foreign minister and the American secretary of state is taking place today. Everything has begun to move, and not only in the diplomatic realm. Despite the changed world constellation, the traditional mechanisms still rule the day: the ultimatum, war, or, in the Soviet Union when things get tough, the call for a strongman. Apparently America was as much damaged and weakened by the arms race as the Soviet Union, though in a different way. It is tempting to speak of poetic justice. Is it possible that the countries that lost the Second World War, Germany and Japan, will have, if not the last laugh, at least the last smirk? A war in the Gulf would make them losers, too.

Identify Fontane characters in the former GDR; for instance, de Maizière, pastors like Eppelmann, Meckel, and even more, Führer and Magirius, but also that pastor from Schmalkalden who committed suicide after being suspected, wrongly, of being a Stasi spy. And Bärbel Bohley: might she not have been perfect as a Fontane-esque Moravian sister?

I am managing again (as Maria says) to be cheerful. Maybe the two fish (sargo) that I stuffed with sage and cooked in the skillet helped.

Vale das Eiras, 13 January 1991

Two days before the Iraq ultimatum runs out, and now that the American Congress has voted in favor of a war that seems increasingly likely, I have been engrossed for three days in the manuscript of "The Call of the Toad." The weather has also been good lately. A difficult leap from the daily realities into a fictional work that begins with the transformative events in Germany and is supposed to draw to a close late in the summer of 1991. The tone is terse and must keep the novella-like story moving. I have introduced the casual first-person narrator after all, because this figure makes it possible to present the plausibility as well as the implausibility of the underlying idea from an ironic perspective.

Today went down to the ocean for the first time. Many shells. Sun, a cool wind. Ute lay down in the dunes. I pilfered agave shoots and, on the way to the beach, several long-leafed cactus shoots.

We are still eating leftovers from the skate that I had drawn for the Suhls and then cooked when they visited two days ago. My first time drawing with wash pencils. An exciting technique that I should continue to experiment with.

Maybe it is working in the garden, or, more likely, working on the manuscript, that has been helping me get enough sleep these past three days.

And as a backdrop to this peacefulness, this longed-for solitude, the playful gardening and diving into fiction, the Gulf war, which could start any day, along with the imminent breakup of the Soviet Union (and with it the end of the Gorbachev era) and the now obvious but unacknowledged bankruptcy of the German political situation. For the next 3 October, if I have time and the desire, I should do my "told-you-so" stock-taking.

Yesterday at the Hubers'. An exhibition of English pop art in Faro. I am taking many of my drawings back to Berlin, among them early sketches of nuns and the best Calcutta pieces. To replace them, I brought Huber dead wood pieces. Afterward dinner in the gallery, at a long table with twelve people. Jules is drinking again and has regained his sense of humor. A salesman for brewery equipment describes bleak conditions in the former GDR.

Vale das Eiras, 14 January 1991
In half-overcast weather again, going to Lagoa — bank, shopping, newspapers — and further work on the manuscript, which is beginning to be headstrong, has asserted its centrality and downgraded everything else, including the possible Gulf war, to a subplot. According to the papers, anything could happen, including the opposite.

He could travel to Lübeck with her: the association of old Danzigers. Her commentary on the Malskat forgeries in St. Mary's: "The Germans want everything to be authentic always." Should the idea come to the two of them in the Hagelsberg cemetery or only later, when they are dining on mushrooms? He speaks of her idea as greater and more durable than all the major political happenings. Tomorrow Alexander and Alexandra are to be introduced to each other.

Vale das Eiras, 15 January 1991
The ominous date. All negotiations — if indeed they were serious negotiations — have failed. Absolute refusal to withdraw from Kuwait confronts the absolute demand of unconditional withdrawal. A war whose consequences (including ecological ones) cannot be foreseen is apparently now viewed by both sides as a

viable solution to the conflict. In the lee of this dangerous confrontation of weapons of destruction, the Soviets have brutally deployed tanks against demonstrators in Lithuania. Gorbachev's star is sinking.

Feeling profoundly helpless as never before, I cling to my manuscript or wear myself out gardening.

(Laughable: in Germany, or, to be more precise, in Baden-Württemberg, the so-called Cleverboy, who was not all that smart, resigns as prime minister because he let himself be wined and dined by entrepreneurs who happened to be friends of his. If such scandals were all we had to contend with!)

I massage Ute's beautiful long neck, which is hurting again around the vertebrae.

Vale das Eiras, 16 January 1991
At six P.M. central European time, the ultimatum expired; war can break out at any time. And it looks as though nothing can prevent it save the much-invoked miracle. Yet never in the history of the human race have the results of a war been calculated in advance with such accuracy, its worldwide consequences predicted. The eco-dictatorship I feared might come about twenty years hence could become a reality much sooner. The fanciful decision I made in December that next summer on Møn I would finally, with Ute's help, learn to ride a bicycle now seems much more urgent.

We are listening to the Deutsche Welle broadcasts. Gorbachev's declining credibility. Tomorrow Kohl will be reelected chancellor. In Israel no gas masks were issued to Palestinians. For the first time we are considering flying back to Germany in the event of war, if flights are still available.

Nonetheless, somewhat obstinate work in the garden and three hours of work on the manuscript. I have reached page 15 and am amazed that it is going so well.

Shortly after twelve we listen to the Deutsche Welle again. Right after the midnight news, the sports report is canceled. First bulletins, still unclear, bring word of the outbreak of war.

Vale das Eiras, 17 January 1991
After the complete failure of diplomacy, what a horrific victory for the massive Western technology of war. Almost without losses — so we hear — the Iraqi command-and-control centers, the rocket installations, and so on have been destroyed in the course of a thousand missions with equally many rockets. Hardly any counterattacks by Iraq. At least attacks on Israel with (German) poison-gas rockets have been rendered impossible. But how many casualties will the reconquest of Kuwait require, including on the American side? The military forces are already hailing their success.

In between confusing reports on German radio, Ute and I have sought relief in frantic gardening: we moved the large agaves at the entrance to the courtyard. I managed to concentrate on the manuscript (up to page 19). The weather is cold, rainy. Both fireplaces are going.

Vale das Eiras, 18 January 1991
Iraqi rockets have landed in Tel Aviv after all, though so far without Israel's having decided to strike back. But American planes have taken off from Turkey. War breaks out and the stock market goes up. Speculation on the price of gasoline. German companies, including arms manufacturers, have broken the embargo on Iraq. Vogel's speech to the Bundestag, admirable. All the talk is of the technology of war, yet the death toll in Iraq could already be in

the tens of thousands. Telephone conversation with Bruno, who is clearly frightened of the consequences of this war, including the ecological ones. The weather remains bad. Work in the garden. Work on the manuscript. The first chapter finished. How the war in the Gulf pushes German unity into the background, making it unreal or obsolete. The swearing-in of the first unified German government seems a marginal event. A Möllemann is going to be economics minister! I observe a kind of stoic quietude in myself that is disquieting.

Yesterday we ate in Lagos with the Suhls: good fish and mussels.

Vale das Eiras, 22 January 1991
Now what was to be feared from the beginning has apparently happened: the oil fields in Kuwait are ablaze, allegedly lit by the Iraqis. As yet no photos of billowing smoke have provided confirmation. After the initial euphoria of the "successful" start to the war, sobriety is setting in, including on the stock market. It is becoming clear that such wars cannot be won, despite military superiority and control of the skies. After Lithuania, Latvia is now threatened with Soviet military intervention. Constant talk of Gorbachev's being ousted and the danger of civil war. As for German unity, all that remains are the costs.

Now that the weather has improved, I am clinging to gardening and work on the manuscript. Writing an average of two pages a day, I am maintaining the desperately funny tone. Ute has made us rabbit, stewed in red wine.

Along with the pages in this blank book, my journal is coming to an end. I hope it will make way for work on the manuscript. What is happening now and taking its stupid course does not require my commentary.

Vale das Eiras, 26 January 1991

Since I have been working on the manuscript, my journal has become skimpy. Or is it the bloody farce of the Gulf war, the saber-rattling hypocrisy that leaves me speechless on these pages?

Deep down, I enjoy the regular schedule that is possible here. In the afternoon, as soon as the sun starts to set and it turns noticeably chilly, I leave off hacking holes in the rocky soil and planting to work on the manuscript, as if the two activities were connected.

America's self-confidence has vanished. The brutality of the Iraqi system finds its equivalent in the West's now only thinly veiled claim to power and assertion of economic interests, which, though more refined, is equally inhumane — or all too human. In both cases all that can be seen at work is power-hungry stupidity, for the predictable ecological disaster will make losers of us all, including the neutral parties.

I am amazed that I am apparently succeeding — now almost finished with the second of seven projected chapters — at layering the action with a tragicomic love story. The hubris of writing!

Didi, Ute's sister Undine, has been here since yesterday. A week ago, a useful pile of manure was dumped on the east side of the house. The first shoots I planted are doing well. The tilapia today was as good as ever. Have written to Helene and Nele, my beloved problem children. In the evening and at night — also when I cannot sleep — am reading Fontane: Reuter's biography. All this is certainly preparation for the next "big" book, "The Handover Trust." Starting on Monday, when I have the second chapter finished, I want to write my *Guernica* polemic, in our last days here. Nothing must, nothing should, go unsaid. Already the Berlin Week at the beginning of February, confirmed by telephone, is casting its shadow.

Vale das Eiras, 28 January 1991
Yesterday I finished the second chapter, surprised that I managed — despite all that was holding me back — to get the story
flowing. I am curious to see how I will fare back in Behlendorf
with the difficult third chapter.

And today — finally — I wrote the introduction to the *Guernica* polemic. I plan to have a first draft by the time we leave, then
dictate a second in Berlin, which I can revise in peace in Behlendorf.

All this while the Gulf war is becoming part of daily life, and
the oil slick in the Gulf is lighting up the headlines. Around here
the almond trees are blooming early. Tomorrow the Hubers are
coming. I plan to cook tripe.

Now my pleasure in gardening is beginning to wane: it's time
to plant the last rosemary plants. The cactuses are putting out real
branches. Today to Lagoa, a charming, sleepy town.

Vale das Eiras, 31 January 1991
The suitcases are packed, the last holes have been hacked in the
stony ground and filled with some extra-prickly cactuses that Didi
brought, as well as with white-and-green agave shoots from the
Suhls. The first draft of the *Guernica* polemic is written. Fiddled
in vain with the radio knob, trying to find the Deutsche Welle.
Just heard on the BBC about ground battles under way since yesterday and about the raising of the prime rate by half a percent.
And now this diary, too, must come to an end. Started here more
than a year ago, in expectation of the transformation of Germany,
which brought no real transformation, only an assertion of unity
(accompanied by social division). Nonetheless I have succeeded,
after experiencing a degree of writer's block previously unknown
to me, in getting the first and shorter of two writing projects

launched and working up enough enthusiasm to start on the expansive "Handover Trust" novel. Possibly I can finish the "Call of the Toad" story this year, but "Handover Trust" will require up to five years' worth of work before the manuscript is finished. I am writing this in full expectation of arid stretches. How would it be to have my immortal Fontane write ballads in the style of F's actual late ballads, but referring to the present, including German unity and finally the Gulf war?

The Reuter biography sugarcoats the second and third London periods. Reuter wants to salvage Fontane the leftist, the enthusiast for the revolutions of 1848. The absurd narrative situation: Fontane outlives his biographer.

For "The Call of the Toad" I must do research on burial rituals in Mexico, China, India, and elsewhere. I must work out the quotable sections of Dr. Reschke's dissertation. Also: What really happened at St. John's in February 1945? Also: the craft of gilding.

Maybe a few final possibilities will occur to me tomorrow during the flight to Hamburg.

Faro–Hamburg, 1 February 1991

We took off at three P.M. after a delay of five hours because a plane was grounded. Were invited to lunch in Faro. The view, from the sixth-floor restaurant, over the lagoon with its many arms and all the way to the dunes, shimmering white under a gray sky. Finally rain, since yesterday.

How little the Gulf war affects the Portuguese. A melancholy shake of the head, nothing more. A people who apparently put their history behind them once they lost their last colonies — a form of insight that seems impossible for the Germans. Although hesitant, and annoyed by the unexpected protests mounted by their hitherto uninterested, spoiled children, the Germans are drifting into active participation in the war, after passively tolerating arms sales to parts of the world in crisis, to preserve jobs. Now they are obliged to deliver to Israel Patriot ground-to-air missiles, intended to shoot down the same Iraqi Scud missiles whose range and technical quality were improved with German assistance.

Yesterday this war was two weeks old. I fear it will continue, spread, and have lasting consequences that will accelerate the ruin of Third World countries. This war could also become a model for the pacification of the Third World through the imposition of an American new world order.

Half asleep on the plane, I formed a picture of my Bengali rickshaw entrepreneur, Mr. Banerjee: always friendly yet slightly demonic. Not that he can walk through walls, but you get the sense he can float at will a hand's breadth above the ground. He could be a character in one of the Hindi films made in Bombay that Rushdie describes. Should I give him a devilishly drooping eyelid, like Rushdie's?

This character mustn't play a dominant role in "The Call of the Toad," but his unexpected appearances should give the story a palpable additional dimension, if only hinted at. Reschke's ride in Banerjee's bicycle rickshaw. Why Alexandra Piątkowska refuses to ride in one. "How can Poles allow themselves to be made into coolies?!"

The widower and the widow in Lübeck: Banerjee has established a branch for inner-city rickshaw transportation there. Banerjee's mild mockery of fancy cemeteries and his praise for Indian-style cremation. In one section of the Danzig shipyard he builds a factory for bicycle rickshaws. Banerjee's speculation on impending climate change: in the Vistula Delta rice will be planted under Bengali supervision. Banerjee transforms Reschke's pessimistic toad calls into cheery tunes for the future. Banerjee's lecture on the diligent Marwaris who could be helpful to the Poles, as they were to the Bengalis in Calcutta. Banerjee admits that his mother is a Marwari: pious and a skillful businesswoman. Why Banerjee refuses to get involved in the cemetery association.

To be pondered: whether the widow brings an old Kashubian woman from Danzig, almost eighty years old, into the association as a member of the board. From the Polish side, a young Pole fascinated by the remnants of German culture might become a board member: receptive to all German suggestions; for instance, for bilingual street signs in the Old Town.

But this must be the end, before we land.

Notes

I. Grass's Family

Waltraut, Grass's sister (b. 1930)

Anna Grass, ballet dancer, married Grass in 1954, separated 1972, divorced 1978. Mother of Franz and Raoul (twins, b. 1957), Laura (b. 1961), and Bruno (b. 1965)

Ute Grass, organist, married Grass in 1979. Mother of two sons, Hans (Hänschen) and Malte Grunert, from a previous marriage

Veronika Schröter, architect, Grass's partner from 1972 to 1976. Mother of Grass's daughter Helene (b. 1974) and of Katharina (Tinka) and Jette from an earlier marriage

Ingrid Krüger, book editor, mother of Grass's daughter Nele (b. 1979)

IN-LAWS AND GRANDCHILDREN:

Beatrice, wife of Raoul
Ellen, Ute's sister
Gianna (Giovanna Cappellanti), wife of Franz
Leon, child of Laura
Lucas, child of Laura
Luisa, child of Laura
Ralf, husband of Laura

Ronja, granddaughter, child of Bruno and Susan
Rosanna, child of Raoul and Beatrice
Stefano, husband of Katharina Grunert
Undine (Didi), Ute's sister

II. Persons Mentioned in Grass's Journal

Abuladze, Tengiz (1924–1994): filmmaker from Soviet Georgia, best known for the trilogy *The Plea* (1968), *The Tree of Desire* (1975), and *Repentence* (1984).

Adenauer, Konrad (1876–1967): Germany's first and longest-serving postwar chancellor, a founder of the CDU, strongly pro-West and anti-Communist.

Aichinger, Ilse (b. 1921): Austrian novelist and playwright, early participant in Group 47.

Albertz, Heinrich (1915–1993): mayor of West Berlin from 1966 to 1967, close political ally of Willy Brandt and leader of the German peace movement.

Alexis, Willibald (1798–1871): writer of realist fiction, author of the satirically titled *Keeping Quiet Is the Citizen's First Duty*. The subject of an essay by Theodor Fontane.

Augstein, Rudolf (1923–2003): founder, part owner, and editor in chief of the German newsmagazine *Der Spiegel*. Jailed for 103 days in 1962–63 for accusing the defense minister, Franz Josef Strauss, of corruption.

Aurora: Grass's lover during his trip to Italy in the early 1950s.

Bagge, Erling: teacher and local historian on the island of Møn.

Bahr, Egon (b. 1922): West German journalist and SPD politician, known as the author of the "change through rapprochement" policy toward the East bloc. Cabinet minister under Willy Brandt and Helmut Schmidt and member of the Bundestag from 1972 to 1990.

Barfoed, Niels (b. 1931): Danish writer, president of the Danish PEN Center, human rights advocate.

Baring, Arnulf (b. 1932): West German professor of history and political science, expelled by the SPD in 1983 for supporting Hans-Dietrich Genscher (FDP).

Barschel, Uwe (1944–1987): CDU prime minister in Schleswig-Holstein during the Kohl chancellorship.

Barthel, Kurt (pen name KuBa) (1914–1967): German writer who spent the

Hitler years in Czechoslovakia and England, then returned to East Germany and joined the SED in 1946.

Bebel, August (1840–1913): Marxist politician. Founder, with Wilhelm Liebknecht, of the Social Democratic Workers' Party (1869), which became the SPD (1890).

Becker, Jurek (1937–1997): Polish-born German writer, GDR dissident. Moved in 1977 to West Berlin. Author of *Jacob the Liar.*

Becker, Jürgen (b. 1932): West German poet, novelist, radio-play writer, and editor at the Suhrkamp and Rowohlt publishing houses.

Becker, Rolf (b. 1928): cultural editor of *Der Spiegel* from 1960 to 1991, author of the first *Spiegel* article on Grass.

Bichsel, Peter (b. 1935): Swiss-German fiction writer and journalist, 1967 winner of the Group 47 Literature Prize.

Biermann, Wolf (b. 1936): German singer-songwriter who moved at seventeen to the GDR. He was allowed to perform in the West but was expelled as a dissident and stripped of his citizenship in 1976.

Bissinger, Manfred (b. 1940): West German journalist, publisher, and editor associated with the magazines *konkret, Stern, Die Woche,* and *Merian.*

Blechen, Carl (1798–1840): German landscape painter.

Bloch, Ernst (1885–1977): German Marxist philosopher, exiled in the U.S., returned to the GDR in 1949. Author of the three-volume *Principle of Hope.*

Bohley, Bärbel (1945–2010): East German artist and dissident.

Böhme, Ibrahim (1949–1999): human rights advocate and cofounder of the East German SPD, which he chaired from October 1989 to March 1990. Later accused of being a Stasi collaborator.

Böhrk, Gisela (b. 1945): minister for women's affairs in the Schleswig-Holstein government under Björn Engholm. SPD member of the regional parliament from 1975 to 2005.

Bongard, Rémy: photographer in Portugal, friend of Günter and Ute Grass.

Borchert, Wolfgang (1921–1947): German writer, author of the play *The Man Outside* (1947) and of short stories depicting the suffering of postwar Germans.

Born, Nicolas (1937–1979): self-taught West German novelist and poet, protégé of Grass.

Börner, Holger (1931–2006): SPD politician, prime minister of Hesse from 1972 to 1987.

Brandt, Willy (1913–1992): leading West German SPD politician and chancellor. Mayor of Berlin from 1957 to 1966. Known for his Ostpolitik, a policy of normalizing relations with Soviet Eastern Europe.

Bucerius, Gerd (1906–1995): lawyer, politician, and journalist, one of the co-founders of *Die Zeit,* a CDU member of the Bundestag, and a benefactor to the city of Hamburg.

Bull, Hans Peter (b. 1936): SPD interior minister of Schleswig-Holstein from 1988 to 1995.

Chodowiecki, Daniel (1726–1801): Danzig-born painter and printmaker famous especially for his etchings. Director of the Berlin Academy of Art. In 1990 Grass established the Chodowiecki Prize to benefit Polish artists.

Cohn-Bendit, Daniel (b. 1945): student in Paris during the 1968 unrest, known as Danny the Red. Later a member of the German Green Party, active in a wide range of political causes.

Czechowski, Heinz (1935–2008): East German poet, dramaturge, and editor.

de Bruyn, Günter (b. 1926): East German author, president of East German PEN from 1974 to 1982.

Dedecius, Karl (b. 1921): writer and translator from the Polish and Russian. Born in Poland, imprisoned during the Stalinist period in the Soviet Union.

Delius, Friedrich Christian (b. 1943): West German author of novels, stories, and poetry, and editor at the Wagenbach and Rotbuch publishing houses.

de Maizière, Lothar (b. 1940): from April to October 1990, the first and last prime minister of the GDR, member of the CDU. Served briefly in the Kohl government, until rumors of Stasi collaboration surfaced.

Dieckmann, Friedrich (b. 1937): East German literary critic.

Dönhoff, Marion von (1909–2002): member of the East Prussian landed gentry, close to opposition circles during the Nazi period, she moved to West Germany at the end of World War II and became the editor in chief and copublisher of *Die Zeit.* Author of more than twenty books, supporter of Brandt's Ostpolitik. In 1970 she traveled with Brandt and Grass to Warsaw.

Dor, Milo (1923–2005): born in Hungary, grew up in Belgrade, and was active in the Serbian resistance during World War II. Later lived in Austria and participated in Group 47.

Dregger, Alfred (1920–2002): West German politician, leader of the CDU's conservative wing, member of the Bundestag from 1972 to 1998, staunch anti-Communist.

Ebeling, Hans-Wilhelm (b. 1934): pastor of St. Thomas's in Leipzig, which he refused to open to antigovernment demonstrators fleeing the police. Minister for economic cooperation in the de Maizière government, cofounder of the East German SPD and DSU; he resigned from the DSU in June 1990. Accused of collaboration with the Stasi.

Elias, Norbert (1897–1990): German-Jewish sociologist, student of Karl Mannheim, and professor in England and, after World War II, in Europe. Author of the two-volume *The Civilizing Process*.

Engholm, Björn (b. 1939): first SPD prime minister of Schleswig-Holstein, from 1988 to 1993, elected in the wake of the Barschel affair, in which an attempt was made to smear him with allegations of tax evasion. Chair of the SPD from 1991 to 1993.

Eppelmann, Rainer (b. 1943): GDR Lutheran pastor, cofounder of DA, cabinet member under Modrow and de Maizière, and later member of the CDU.

Eppler, Erhard (b. 1926): from 1961 to 1976 an SPD member of the Bundestag, serving as minister for economic cooperation under chancellors Kiesinger, Brandt, and, for a time, Schmidt. Later active in the Lutheran church.

Esser, Trude: classmate of Grass's at the Düsseldorf Academy of the Arts with whom he remained in contact; prominent sculptor in Düsseldorf.

Faber, Elmar (b. 1934): literary scholar, editor, and from 1983 to 1992 head of Aufbau, the leading state-sponsored publishing house in the GDR.

Fechner, Eberhard (1926–1992): German actor, director, and maker of documentary films.

Feltrinelli, Giangiacomo (1926–1972): Founder in 1954 of the Milan publishing house that bore his name. First publisher of Pasternak's *Doctor Zhivago* and Lampedusa's *The Leopard*.

Flimm, Jürgen (b. 1941): West German director of theater and opera, and professor at the University of Hamburg.

Fontane, Theodor (1819–1898): German essayist and novelist whose life is continued by Fonty, the protagonist of Grass's novel *Too Far Afield*. Fontane novels mentioned by Grass: *Cécile* (1887), *Schach von Wuthenow* (1882), *Before the Storm* (1878), *The Stechlin* (1899).

Freyer, Anne: Grass's editor at Le Seuil, French publishing house.

Freytag, Gustav (1816–1895): prolific German novelist and dramatist from Silesia. Known for the novel *Debit and Credit* (*Soll und Haben*, 1885).

Frielinghaus, Helmut (1931–2012): publisher, translator, and editor. For many years Grass's personal freelance editor, he lived in New York from 1998 to 2005. He translated works by Raymond Carver, William Faulkner, John Updike, and others. Editor of a collection of essays by Grass's translators and of *The Günter Grass Reader.* Recipient in 2008 of the German government's Medal of Honor.

Führer, Christian (b. 1943): pastor of St. Nicholas's in Leipzig and initiator and supporter of the 1989 Monday demonstrations that led to the collapse of the GDR.

Gansel, Norbert (b. 1940): SPD politician, member of the Bundestag from 1972 to 1997, later mayor of Kiel. Known for refusing campaign contributions from businesses and organizations.

Gaulin, Frank-Thomas (b. 1944): proprietor of Kunsthaus Lübeck, the gallery responsible for the sale of Günter Grass's sculptures.

Genscher, Hans-Dietrich (b. 1927): popular FDP politician who fled to West Germany in 1952. Served from 1974 to 1992 as German foreign minister and vice chancellor.

Geremek, Bronisław (1932–2008): distinguished Polish social historian, adviser to the labor union Solidarność and its leader, Lech Wałęsa.

Giebe, Hubertus (b. 1953): Dresden artist who provided etchings for a 1988 collectors' edition of Grass's *Tin Drum.*

Göschel, Eberhard (b. 1953): painter, graphic artist, and sculptor.

Greiner, Ulrich (b. 1945): culture section editor of *Die Ziet.* Author or editor of numerous books.

Grosen, Vagn (1924–2004): head of Gyldendal, Grass's Danish publishing house.

Gruner, Richard (1925–2010): longtime CEO of one of Germany's largest publishing concerns, Gruner + Jahr, publisher of *Die Zeit.*

Grunert, Bruno: first husband of Ute Grass, father of Hans and Malte.

Grüning, Uwe (b. 1942): East German teacher, poet, essayist, and short story writer. After unification, active in politics (CDU).

Gysi, Gregor (b. 1948): East German attorney, member of the SED, and a leading figure in ending communism in the GDR. Investigated and found to have been a Stasi collaborator from 1978 to 1989.

Hage, Volker (b. 1949): managing editor for literature at *Die Zeit,* later at the *Frankfurter Allgemeine Zeitung* and *Der Spiegel.*

Hager, Kurt (1912–1998): Communist who covered the Spanish Civil War and later became chief ideologist of the SED.

Harig, Günter (b. 1940): Protestant theologian and noted pastor of St. Peter's and St. Mary's in Lübeck, active in providing asylum to political refugees. Often the subject of right-wing and neo-Nazi attacks.

Havel, Václav (1936–2011): distinguished playwright and essayist who served as president of Czechoslovakia from 1989 to 1992 and of the Czech Republic from 1993 to 2003.

Hecht, Axel (b. 1944): in charge of cultural coverage for *Stern* magazine from 1973 to 1978, he then founded the magazine *art*, published by Gruner + Jahr, and served as editor in chief until 2005.

Hein, Christoph (b. 1944): East German playwright, novelist, and translator, and dramaturge of the Volksbühne in East Berlin from 1974 to 1979. He became the first president of PEN after the East and West German organizations merged.

Heindels, Jules and Mieke: friends of the Grasses in Portugal.

Heine, Heinrich (1797–1856): German poet, journalist, and essayist.

Hennecke, Adolf (1905–1975): East German miner who launched the German equivalent of the Soviet Stakhanovite movement. Member of the SED central committee.

Hermák, Josef (b. 1928): Czech literary historian and translator. Distinguished expert on Franz Kafka and a leading member of the Kafka Society, to which Grass also belongs.

Hermlin, Stephan (1915–1997): one of the most prominent and influential East German writers, with ties to Erich Honecker.

Herný, František (b. 1931): Czech radio journalist, ambassador to Germany until 2001.

Hertin, Paul (b. 1940): leading German authority on intellectual property and copyright law.

Heym, Stefan (1913–2001): German novelist exiled in the U.S. until 1953, when he returned to the GDR.

Hilsberg, Raoul (1926–2007): Austrian-born U.S. political scientist and historian of the Holocaust, author of *The Destruction of the European Jews*.

Höllerer, Walter (1922–2003): West German writer, critic, professor of literature, and founder of the Literary Colloquium in Berlin and the literary journal *Akzente*. Close friend and associate of Grass.

Honecker, Erich (1912–1994): imprisoned by the Nazis, and from 1976 to 1989 head of the GDR government and leader of the SED. Ousted three weeks before the fall of the Berlin Wall, exiled to Chile.

Hönisch, Eva: for thirty years, until 1995, Grass's secretary. Maintained his office in Berlin.

Huber, Volker and Marie: founders in 1981 of the Centro Cultural São Lourenço in Almancil, Portugal, which exhibited contemporary art, including works by Grass.

Janka, Walter (1914–1994): imprisoned by the Nazis, he escaped to Mexico. Returned to the GDR after the war.

Janssen, Horst (1929–1995): Noted Hamburg printmaker specializing in woodcuts and etchings.

Jaruzelski, Wojciech (b. 1923): Polish military officer, served as prime minister from 1981 to 1985 and as head of state from 1985 to 1990. Responsible for the 1981 imposition of martial law.

Jaspers, Karl (1884–1969): German philosopher and professor at the University of Heidelberg.

Johnson, Uwe (1934–1984): East German novelist, moved to West Berlin in 1959. Closely associated with Grass and Group 47. Became obsessed with the idea that his estranged wife had been spying on him for the Stasi. Portrayed in Grass's *Too Far Afield*.

Just, Gustav (1911–2011): East German writer and journalist. Convicted in a show trial and sentenced to four years in prison for counterrevolutionary activity.

Kafka, Vladimir (1931–1970): Czech literary critic and the translator of *The Tin Drum*.

Kant, Hermann (b. 1926): member of the SED central committee and president of the Writers' Union. Later accused of working for the Stasi.

Karasek, Hellmuth (b. 1934): West German journalist, literary critic, and novelist, appeared regularly on Marcel Reich-Ranicki's television talk show, *The Literary Quartet*.

Kästner, Erich (1899–1974): German poet, literary critic, journalist, and author.

Keller, Gottfried (1819–1890): Swiss novelist.

Kirsch, Rainer (b. 1934): East German poet, translator, and author.

Kirsch, Sarah (b. 1935): East German poet, journalist, translator, and radio commentator.

Kogon, Eugen (1903–1987): West German historian, political scientist, and sociologist, and the author of a study of the SS. He is considered one of the intellectual fathers of democratic Germany and of European integration.

Kohl, Helmut (b. 1930): the German chancellor (CDU) who presided over the unification of Germany and, in 1992, the conclusion of the Maastricht Treaty, which created the European Union.

Kohlhaase, Wolfgang (b. 1931): German film director and screenwriter whose career began in the GDR in the early 1950s and continued after unification.

Kollwitz, Käthe (1867–1945): noted German painter, printmaker, and sculptor whose work was suppressed by the Nazis.

Kosta, Tomáš (b. 1925): survivor of Theresienstadt, Auschwitz, and Buchenwald, editor and publisher in Prague until the crushing of the Prague Spring in 1968. Served as an adviser to the Czech government. Publisher-editor of Günter Grass in the Czech Republic.

Kunert, Günter (b. 1929): East German poet and writer.

Lafontaine, Oskar (b. 1943): SPD politician who became known for his opposition to the stationing of Pershing rockets in Germany.

Landsbergis, Vytautas (b. 1932): conservative Lithuanian intellectual who in 1990 became the first president of newly independent Lithuania, serving until 1992.

Lang, Jack (b. 1939): French socialist and writer, minister of culture from 1981 to 1986 and from 1988 to 1993, and later minister of education, member of the European parliament, and special envoy to Cuba and North Korea.

Leiser, Erwin (1923–1996): West German journalist, translator, and documentary filmmaker.

Lenz, Siegfried (b. 1926): West German novelist, essayist, and author of short stories and children's tales. He participated in Group 47 and joined Grass in supporting Willy Brandt's Ostpolitik.

Lessing, Gotthold Ephraim (1729–1779): German dramatist, essayist, philosopher, and critic, a leading figure in the Enlightenment.

Lipski, Jan Józef (1926–1991): Polish literary historian, critic, and socialist politician.

Magirius, Friedrich (b. 1930): West German Protestant theologian and pastor.

Malskat, Lothar (1913–1988): painter hired to restore the frescoes in Lübeck's St. Mary's, damaged during World War II, convicted for painting them himself. Grass portrays the forgery in *The Rat*.

Margull, Fritze (b. 1945): owner of a fine art printing business in West Berlin, editor and printer of Grass's graphic work for many decades.

Marquardt, Hans (1920–2004): from 1953 to 1987 director of the East German Reclam publishing company, submitted regular reports on Grass to the Stasi. Grass later came to his defense.

Marzouki, Moncef (b. 1945): Tunisian physician, human rights activist, and political figure, inspired by Gandhi.

Masur, Kurt (b. 1927): German orchestral conductor in Dresden, East Berlin, and Leipzig.

Mayer, Hans (1907–2001): Marxist literary scholar and critic.

Mazowiecki, Tadeusz (b. 1927): Polish writer, journalist, leader of Solidarity, and editor of its weekly journal. Imprisoned after the imposition of martial law in 1981. Prime minister during the presidency of Lech Wałęsa.

Meckel, Markus (b. 1952): pastor, active in the 1989 GDR demonstrations, cofounder of the East German SPD, and GDR foreign minister.

Metag, Peter (Jimi): East German jazz musician.

Meyenburg, Petra: East German interviewer and radio, television, and recording director and producer.

Michnik, Adam (b. 1946): Polish historian, essayist, political commentator, and journalist who played a major part in advocating for democracy in Poland.

Modrow, Hans (b. 1928): last Communist prime minister of the GDR, serving from November 1989 to March 1990.

Möllemann, Jürgen (1945–2003): FDP politician and member of the Kohl government, serving from 1987 to 1991 as minister of education and research.

Morgner, Irmtraud (1933–1990): East German writer known for her magical-realist style and her feminist perspective.

Mühlenhaupt, Kurt (1929–2006): a self-taught painter and sculptor who left the GDR in the 1950s and moved to West Berlin.

Müller, Heiner (1929–1995): East German poet, essayist, playwright, director, dramaturge, and producer. From 1990 to 1993 headed the Academy of Arts (East).

Müntzer, Thomas (c. 1489–1525): Reformation-era German theologian who clashed with Luther on doctrinal questions and became a leader in the Peasants' War.

Nachbar, Herbert (1930–1980): East German novelist, journalist, and editor.

Naumann, Michael (b. 1941): head of Rowohlt publishing house who, in 1995, became the head of Metropolitan Books and later of Henry Holt in New York. Active in SPD politics, he later served as German minister of culture.

Nell-Breuning, Oswald von (1890–1991): German Jesuit theologian, economist, and philosopher.

Neuhaus, Volker (b. 1943): professor at the University of Cologne whose career has been devoted to studying the works of Goethe and Günter Grass, also one of Grass's freelance editors at the Steidl publishing house.

Neuss, Wolfgang (1923–1989): German film actor, songwriter, and cabaret artist.

Nilius, Klaus: official West German SPD spokesman, later accused of being a Stasi informant.

Nölling, Willhelm (b. 1933): president of the Hamburg Landeszentralbank from 1982 to 1992 and member of the governing board of the German Federal Reserve Bank.

Novak, Helga (b. 1935): well-known poet and novelist, stripped of her GDR citizenship in 1966.

Øhrgaard, Per (b. 1944): professor of German at the University of Copenhagen and Grass's longtime Danish translator and close friend.

Olmert, Ehud (b. 1945): Israeli politician, mayor of Jerusalem, and prime minister.

Pezold, Klaus (b. 1937): literary scholar and professor of German at the University of Leipzig.

Pinkus, Theo (1909–1991): Swiss publisher, editor, and book dealer, established the Research Center for the Study of the Workers' Movement.

Raabe, Elisabeth: in 1983 purchased, together with Regina Vitali, the Arche publishing house (Zurich) and in 1987 the Luchterhand publishing house.

Raddatz, Fritz (b. 1931): editor, literary critic, writer, and publisher, moved to the Federal Republic in 1958. From 1960 to 1969 he was editor in chief of Rowohlt. From 1976 to 1985 he headed the cultural section of *Die Zeit*.

Rama, Maria (1911–1997): widow of Hans Rama, a photographer from East Prussia. A close friend of Grass and his family, she documented their lives in photos. Portrayed in fictional form in Grass's *The Box*.

Rau, Johannes (1931–2006): SPD politician and German president from 1999 to 2004.

Reich-Ranicki, Marcel (b. 1920): Polish-born literary critic who was a Communist intelligence operative in London after World War II. Participated in Group 47 and hosted the television show *Literary Quartet*.

Reuter, Hans-Heinrich (1923–1978): East German literary scholar and editor specializing in the works of Goethe and Fontane.

Richter, Hans Werner (1908–1993): guiding spirit of Group 47.

Richter, Stefan: editor and director of the Reclam publishing house, Leipzig.

Richter, Toni (1918–2004): photographer, wife of Hans Werner Richter, who documented the meetings of Group 47.

Rohwedder, Detlev (1932–1991): West German lawyer and corporate manager, member of the SPD, and head of the Treuhandanstalt, which oversaw the privatization of East German state-owned properties. He was assassinated in 1991, possibly by the Red Army Faction. Grass used elements of his biography in *Too Far Afield*.

Romberg, Walter (b. 1928): mathematician, joined the East German SPD in 1989, and served as minister without portfolio in the Modrow government and finance minister in the de Maizière government. He signed the State Treaty on behalf of the GDR in May 1990.

Rommerskirchen, Hans Theo: magazine publisher and art gallery owner who established the *Signatur* series: signed, limited editions of works by prominent writer-artists, including Grass.

Rühmkorf, Eva-Marie (b. 1937): psychologist and SPD politician.

Rühmkorf, Peter (1929–2008): noted West German poet, playwright, editor, essayist, and critic who participated in Group 47.

Rybakow, Anatoly (1911–1998): anti-Stalinist Russian writer, author of novels and stories for children.

Sager, Dirk (b. 1940): West German radio and television journalist, foreign correspondent in the GDR and in Moscow.

Schädlich, Hans Joachim (Jochen) (b. 1935): translator, essayist, and novelist. In the early 1970s in East Berlin, he participated in meetings between East and West German writers organized by Grass. Grass arranged for his writings, suppressed by the GDR government, to be published by Rowohlt. In 1977 Schädlich settled in West Germany.

Schäuble, Wolfgang (b. 1942): CDU politician, member of Helmut Kohl's cabinet from 1984 to 1991. He was shot in October 1990 after a campaign event and is confined to a wheelchair.

Schiller, Karl (1911–1994): economist and political scientist, served as federal economics minister from 1966 to 1969 under Chancellor Kiesinger and as finance minister from 1969 to 1972 under Chancellor Brandt. Godfather to Grass's son Bruno.

Schindel, Robert (b. 1944): Austrian poet, novelist, and writer for film and television.

Schneider, Peter (b. 1940): West German novelist, screenwriter, and essayist.

Schneider, Rolf (b. 1932): East German playwright, novelist, and participant in Group 47.

Schnur, Wolfgang (b. 1944): GDR lawyer and Stasi collaborator.

Schönhuber, Franz (1923–2005): right-wing West German journalist and writer.

Schorlemmer, Friedrich (b. 1944): East German theologian and pastor, active on behalf of human rights, peace, and the environment.

Schörner, Ferdinand (1892–1973): German World War II general who was imprisoned for twelve years in the USSR. He was released in 1958 to West Germany, where he served an additional sentence for ordering the execution of deserters.

Schröder, Gerhard (b. 1944): lawyer, SPD politician, member of the Bundestag, and chancellor from 1998 to 2005.

Schütte, Wolfram (b. 1939): film and book critic, head of the cultural section of the *Frankfurter Rundschau* from 1967 to 1999.

Senfft, Heinrich (b. 1928): Hamburg lawyer, noted for his defense of freedom of the press. Argued, like Grass, that the reunification of Germany was actually an annexation.

Sindermann, Horst (1915–1990): chair of the GDR council of ministers and later president of the Volkskammer. He coined the phrase "antifascist bulwark" for the Berlin Wall.

Sommer, Günter ("Baby") (b. 1943): East German percussionist, leading figure in free jazz, who has performed with Grass, Christa Wolf, and Christoph Hein.

Sommer, Maria (b. 1922): publisher and editor in chief of Gustav Kiepenheuer Bühnenvertrieb in Berlin. She met Grass at an early meeting of Group 47 and has published his works for performance ever since.

Staeck, Klaus (b. 1938): West German lawyer, graphic artist, and publisher noted for his political posters.

Steidl, Gerhard (b. 1950): owner and director of the Steidl publishing house in Göttingen, specializing in high-quality printing and design. Publisher of Grass.

Stoltenberg, Gerhard (1928–2001): CDU politician, federal minister of defense.

Storm, Theodor (1817–1888): German poet and writer.

Strauss, Botho (b. 1944): prolific West German playwright, theater critic, and writer.

Süssmuth, Rita (b. 1937): CDU politician, minister for family affairs under Helmut Kohl, and from 1988 to 1999 president of the Bundestag.

Trautwein, Wolfgang (b. 1949): director of the Literary Colloquium in West Berlin from 1983 to 1986, then a staff member at the Academy of Arts.

Ullmann, Wolfgang (1929–2004): East German theologian, scholar, pastor, and politician.

Unseld, Siegfried (1924–2002): head of Suhrkamp, the leading publisher of twentieth-century German literature.

Vaculík, Ludvík (b. 1926): Czech journalist and writer, critic of the Communist government's suppression of intellectual freedom.

Vitali, Regina (b. 1942): co-owner, with Elisabeth Raabe, of the Arche and Luchterhand publishing houses.

Vogel, Hans-Jochen (b. 1926): West German politician, leader of the SPD from 1987 to 1991.

Vollmer, Antje ((b. 1943): German pastor and Green Party member and writer.

Waigel, Theodor (b. 1939): West German politician (CSU), finance minister under Chancellor Kohl from 1989 to 1998, considered the father of the euro.

Wajda, Andrzej (b. 1926): Polish filmmaker, involved with Solidarity.

Wałęsa, Lech (b. 1943): founder of Solidarity and Poland's president from 1990 to 1995.

Walser, Martin (b. 1927): Major West German novelist.

Wästberg, Per (b. 1933): Swedish novelist, poet, essayist, biographer, and journalist, a strong advocate for human rights, and founder of the Swedish branch of Amnesty International.

Weiss, Konrad (b. 1942): East German film director, songwriter, and civil rights advocate.

Weizsäcker, Richard von (b. 1920): mayor of West Berlin from 1981 to 1984, then served two terms as president of the Federal Republic.

Wiek, Thomas: East German dramaturge at the Berliner Ensemble.

Wolf, Christa (1929–2011): East German novelist, essayist, and literary critic who joined the SED in 1949 and resigned in 1990.

Wolf, Gerhard (b. 1928): East German essayist, critic, screenwriter, and editor.

Würzbach, Peter Curt (b. 1937): CDU politician, member of the Bundestag from 1976 to 2002.

Zahrnt, Heinz (1915–2003): West German Protestant theologian.

Zeidler, Miroslav: art collector in Gdańsk.

III. Divided Germany

FRG: Federal Republic of Germany = West Germany (Bundesrepublik Deutschland, BRD). Name applied since 1990 to united Germany.

GDR: German Democratic Republic = East Germany (Deutsche Demokratische Republik, DDR). Also referred to in West Germany as the

East Zone (hence "Zonies"), the Territory under Soviet Occupation, and the Other Germany.

IV. Brief Chronology of Modern German History

1871: Germany united under Prussian leadership by Otto von Bismarck (1815–1898), who served under Kaiser Wilhelm I as the country's first chancellor.

1918: World War I ends with Germany defeated; Kaiser Wilhelm II abdicates.

1919: After major losses of territory, Germany is established as the Weimar Republic.

1923: Devastating hyperinflation.

1929: Worldwide depression brings massive unemployment to Germany.

1933: Adolf Hitler comes to power, establishing the Third Reich.

1938: Germany annexes Austria.

1939: World War II breaks out when German troops invade Poland.

1945: Germany is defeated and divided into occupation zones controlled by the United States, Great Britain, France, and the Soviet Union. Territory is lost to Poland and the Soviet Union, including Grass's birthplace, Danzig (now Gdańsk). Berlin is left a divided city in the middle of the Soviet zone.

1948–49: The Soviet Union cuts off roads and rails leading to West Berlin. From June to May, the Berlin Airlift supplies the western part of the city, eventually breaking the blockade.

1949: Germany is divided. The American, British, and French zones become the Federal Republic, with its capital in Bonn, and the Soviet zone becomes the German Democratic Republic, with its capital in East Berlin.

June 1953: Workers' uprising in East Berlin is put down by the Soviets.

1956: The Hungarian Revolution is suppressed by the Soviets.

August 1961: Construction of the Berlin Wall begins.

1968: The Prague Spring is crushed by the Soviet Union.

1981: Martial law is imposed in Poland.

May 1989: Local elections in the GDR lead to protests against irregularities and the establishment of opposition groups such as the New Forum (Neues Forum) and an East German SPD.

August–September 1989: East Germans take refuge in western embassies in Prague, Budapest, and Warsaw.

September–October 1989: Peaceful Monday demonstrations in Leipzig, centered around St. Nicholas Church, attract more and more participants and spread to other GDR cities.

11 September 1989: Hungary opens its border with Austria to East Germans seeking to flee to the West.

7 October 1989: On the fortieth anniversary of the founding of the GDR, protesters in Berlin are arrested.

9 October 1989: Seventy thousand protesters participate in a peaceful demonstration in Leipzig.

18 October 1989: Erich Honecker resigns as head of the GDR government and is replaced by Egon Krenz.

27 October 1989: Czechoslovakia opens its border to allow East Germans to enter West Germany.

8 November 1989: The GDR politburo resigns.

9 November 1989: The Berlin Wall is opened.

13 November 1989: The East German Volkskammer elects Hans Modrow as prime minister.

28 November 1989: Helmut Kohl announces a ten-point plan for unification.

18 March 1990: First (and last) democratic elections are held in the GDR, to pick members of the Volkskammer. Originally planned for May, the elections are later moved up in response to rapid developments.

12 April 1990: Lothar de Maizière elected East German prime minister.

5 May 1990: Two Plus Four negotiations begin (the U.S., Britain, France, the Soviet Union, and the two Germanys).

18 May 1990: The first State Treaty is signed, establishing the basis for economic, monetary, and social union.

1 July 1990: Implementation of the currency union, replacing the East German reichsmark with the German mark.

23 August 1990: The Volkskammer votes for the GDR to join the Federal Republic by 3 October.

31 August 1990: The second State Treaty is signed, affirming the proposed unification.

20 September 1990: Legislatures of both Germanys approve unification.

3 October 1990: Day of German Unity. The provinces of Brandenburg, Mecklenburg-Vorpommern, Saxony, Saxony-Anhalt, and Thuringia are added to the ten West German provinces.

2 December 1990: First post-unification elections for the Bundestag.

V. Principal German Political Parties

Alliance 90 (Allianz 90), formed in 1989 by several political organizations: New Forum (Neues Forum), Democracy Now (Demokratie Jetzt), and the Initiative for Peace and Human Rights (Initiative für Frieden und Menschenrechte)

CDU: Christian Democratic Party of Germany (Christlichdemokratische Union)

CSU: Christian Social Union; Bavarian branch of the CDU

DA: Democratic Awakening (Demokratischer Aufbruch)

DSU: German Social Union (Deutsche Soziale Union), founded in January 1990 in Leipzig

FDP: Free Democratic Party (Freie demokratische Partei)

Grüne: Green Party (Die Grünen)

PDS: Party of German Socialists (Partei deutscher Sozialisten)

Republicans (Republikaner)

SED: Socialist Unity Party (Sozialistische Einheitspartei Deutschlands), the Communist Party of the GDR

SPD: Social Democratic Party of Germany (Sozialdemokratische Partei Deutschlands)

VI. Postwar Chancellors of Germany

1949–63: Konrad Adenauer (1876–1967), CDU/CSU coalition with FDP

1963–66: Ludwig Erhard (1897–1977), CDU/CSU coalition with FDP
1966–69: Kurt Georg Kiesinger (1904–1988), CDU/CSU coalition with SPD ("Grand Coalition")
1969–74: Willy Brandt (1913–1992), SPD coalition with FDP
1974: Walter Scheel (b. 1919), SPD coalition with FDP
1974–82: Helmut Schmidt (b. 1918), SPD coalition with FDP
1982–98: Helmut Kohl (b. 1930), CDU/CSU coalition with FDP and DSU

VII. Newspapers and Magazines Mentioned in the Book

art, art magazine published in Hamburg

Bild-Zeitung, tabloid published daily in Hamburg

Der Spiegel, weekly published in Frankfurt, known for investigative reporting

Die Zeit, liberal weekly published in Hamburg

L'Espresso, Italian news weekly published in Rome

Frankfurter Allgemeine Zeitung, daily published in Frankfurt

Frankfurter Rundschau, daily published in Frankfurt

Süddeutsche Zeitung, daily published in Stuttgart

Tages-Anzeiger, daily published in Zurich

tageszeitung, daily published in Berlin

VIII. Grass's German-Language Publishers in 1990

Luchterhand (since 1956), Frankfurt am Main: in 1976 Grass persuaded Luchterhand to establish an Authors' Council to give writers a role in determining the house's policies and practices.

Steidl (since the mid-1980s), Göttingen: initially published Grass's graphic work. In 1993 Grass made Steidl his sole book publisher.

Gustav Kiepenheuer Bühnenvertrieb, Berlin: holder of the rights to all of Grass's nonprint works (theater, film, radio, television, and other electronic media)

Aufbau, East Berlin: in 1990 the publisher, under license from Luchterhand, of two books by Grass. After unification, Grass had no need of an East German publisher.

IX. Grass's Principal Residences

Paris, Avenue d'Italie: location of the apartment where Grass lived from 1957 to 1959 and wrote *The Tin Drum*.

Berlin-Friedenau, 13 Niedstrasse: the house Grass purchased and lived in until his marriage to Anna failed. It remained the site of his office and studio long after he had moved away; later became the home of Raoul and Beatrice.

Kirchenvogthaus: 1698 house in the village of Wewelsfleth, north of Hamburg. It was purchased and renovated by Grass with the architect Veronika Schröter, later home to him and Ute after their marriage. The house was donated to the province in 1985 to serve as the Alfred Döblin House, a retreat for writers.

Behlendorf: village near Lübeck where Grass has lived since 1985, with his studio in a converted barn. His office in Lübeck is adjacent to the Günter Grass Museum.

Vale das Eiras: village in Portugal where Grass built a house after he and Ute returned from Calcutta.

Vogterhus: historic local administrator's cottage in the locality of Ulvshale, on the Danish island of Møn, where the Grasses spend time every summer.

X. Glossary

Aktuelle Kamera (*Contemporary Lens*): the official newscast on GDR state television.

Basic Law (Grundgesetz): adopted in May 1949 with the approval of the United States, Britain, and France, the Basic Law was intentionally created as a provisional legal framework rather than as a constitution — in anticipation of eventual unification. Article 23 stipulated that territory could be added by simple majority vote of the Bundestag. Article 146, adopted in 1990, suggested the possibility of writing a new constitution, but after unification the decision was made to keep the Basic Law, with a few amendments reflecting the country's new structure.

Black Channel (*Schwarzer Kanal*): GDR weekly television program that used clips from West German television, edited to include commentary from a Communist perspective.

Black Pump collective (VEB Kombinat Schwarze Pumpe): established in 1955 in Lusatia, the vast Black Pump complex processed local soft coal and natural gas, as well as natural gas from Russia, producing the bulk of the GDR's gas, coke, and electricity.

Bundesrat: since 1949 the upper chamber of the FRG legislature. Its members represent the *Länder* (provinces).

Bundestag: since 1949 the lower chamber of the FRG legislature. Its members are elected by popular vote.

Bundeswehr: the postwar name of the West German army.

Calcutta: Günter and Ute Grass lived in Calcutta from August 1986 to January 1987.

The Call of the Toad (*Unkenrufe*, 1992): novel by Grass.

Cat and Mouse (*Katz und Maus*, 1961): novella by Grass.

Children of October: the young people who participated in the peaceful Monday demonstrations in Leipzig and elsewhere that led to the opening of the Berlin Wall.

"The Contested United Fatherland": debate between Grass and Augstein, published in 1990 by Steidl as *Deutschland, Einig Vaterland?*

Currency union: the first State Treaty leading to unification, signed on 18 May 1990, called for a single currency in East and West Germany. GDR citizens could convert a stipulated sum (depending on their age bracket) to West German marks at a 1:1 rate; remaining funds were converted at a 2:1 rate. Debts were also recalculated at a 2:1 rate. Rents, scholarships, pensions, wages, and salaries were converted at a 1:1 rate.

Dead Wood (*Totes Holz*, 1990): Grass's volume of drawings of the dying forests.

Dog Years (*Hundejahre*, 1963): novel by Grass.

The Flounder (*Der Butt*, 1977): novel by Grass.

Free German Youth: *Freie deutsche Jugend,* the East German Communist youth organization.

Group 47: an informal gathering of writers, organized by Hans Werner Richter in 1947, led to the formation of this most influential literary group in the postwar German-speaking world. The writers invited to the meetings made up the membership. They were expected to accept without protest the oral critiques that followed their readings of unpublished work. Publishers and critics soon began to attend the meetings. The group dissolved after 1967.

"The Handover Trust": working title of *Too Far Afield* (*Ein weites Feld*, 1995), Grass's novel that draws on the life of Theodor Fontane.

Hiddensee and Rügen: Baltic islands that after World War II became part of the GDR. Ute Grass comes from Rügen.

Inmarypraise (*Mariazuehren*, 1973): a book by Grass that combines graphic art and text, dedicated to Maria Rama.

Kashubians: a West Slavic people from the area around Danzig/Gdańsk. Grass is Kashubian on his mother's side.

Kennzeichen D (*D for Deutschland*): political television program launched in 1971 by Second German Television. It provided news and analysis from East and West Germany and was intended for viewing on both sides of the border.

The Likedeelers: Title of an unfinished novel by Fontane about fourteenth-century pirates who plied the Baltic coast. The most famous of the Likedeelers was Claus Störtebeker.

Literary Colloquium (Literarisches Colloquium, LCB): literary center, founded by Walter Höllerer, housed in an old villa on Berlin's Wannsee. It sponsors residencies by writers and translators and a wide variety of programs dedicated to the study and promotion of literature.

"Little Moritz": a common German reference to a folk figure drawn by the caricaturist Adolf Oberländer (1845–1923).

"Madness!" (*Wahnsinn!*): the exclamation that became the word of the day after the sudden opening of the Berlin Wall on 9 November 1989.

Martial law in Poland: massive crackdown in 1981 that remained in effect until 1983, a response to the protests spearheaded by the Solidarity movement, led by Lech Wałęsa.

Mitropa: founded in 1916, this catering company managed most of the railroad dining and sleeping cars in Europe. After World War II, its purview was limited to the GDR state railroad. When the East and West German railroads merged into the Deutsche Bahn, the Mitropa name survived.

Møn: Danish island in the Baltic where Günter and Ute Grass spend time every summer.

National Front (Nationale Front der Deutschen Demokratischen Republik): also known as the Bloc Party (Blockpartei), this alliance of political parties and mass organizations in the GDR, controlled by the Socialist Unity Party, presented one slate of candidates for elections.

National People's Army (Nationale Volksarmee): army of the GDR.

New Forum (Neues Forum): political movement that started in September 1989 in the GDR.

"Obituary" ("Nachruf"): the text accompanying the 1990 volume *Dead Wood* (*Totes Holz*).

Oder-Neisse Line: the border between Germany and Poland established by the Allies after World War II but not accepted by the FRG until 1989.

"On Rootless Cosmopolitans": published as "Short Speech by a Rootless Cosmopolitan" in *Two States — One Nation?* (1990).

Panorama: the longest-running German political television program, broadcast since 1961 by North German Broadcasting.

The Plebeians Rehearse the Uprising (*Die Plebejer proben den Aufstand,* 1966): drama by Grass that portrays a theater director in East Berlin who is more interested in the Shakespeare play he is rehearsing than in the workers' revolt taking place outside his theater; it is based on Bertolt Brecht's response to the June 1953 uprising.

Reich Railway (Deutsche Reichsbahn): the GDR rail system, its name a holdover from the Weimar Republic and the Third Reich, merged with the FRG's Deutsche Bundesbahn in 1994 to form the Deutsche Bahn.

Round table(s): following the Polish example, the Democracy Now movement in the GDR started round-table discussions in Berlin in December 1989 to bring together various stakeholders in the democratization process. The meetings continued until the March 1990 elections. Other round tables formed in Leipzig and elsewhere, meeting until the regional elections in May 1990.

St. Paul's in Frankfurt: the site of the 1848–49 national convention that drew up the first democratic constitution for Germany. The attempt to establish a constitutional democracy failed when Friedrich Wilhelm IV of Prussia refused to accept the crown, but principles worked out in Frankfurt reappeared in the 1919 Weimar constitution and the 1949 Basic Law.

Schleswig-Holstein: built in 1906, this old German warship, which had been serving as a naval training ship, was anchored in 1939 off the coast of Danzig. On 1 September it fired on the Polish garrison stationed on the Westerplatte Peninsula, an action generally seen as marking the beginning of hostilities in World War II.

Schwarzsauer: North German and Danzig culinary specialty made with pig's or goose's blood, vinegar, and herbs and spices. Other ingredients, such as onions, root vegetables, and bits of meat, may be added.

"The Secrets": colloquial reference to the Nazi Gestapo.

Seven Sleepers Day: named for the legendary Seven Sleepers of Ephesus. According to one version of an old peasant superstition, if it rains on this day (27 June), rain will continue for seven weeks.

Show Your Tongue: a published diary with drawings from Grass's stay in Calcutta.

Sorbs: a western Slavic people living predominantly in Lusatia, a region spanning territory in eastern Germany and Poland. The Sorbian languages (Wendish, Lusatian) are closely related to Polish, Kashubian, Czech, and Slovak, and are officially recognized as minority languages of Germany.

Stasi (Ministerium für Staatssicherheit): the GDR's secret police.

The Tin Drum (Die Blechtrommel, 1959): Grass's first novel.

The Trace of Stones (Spur der Steine, 1966): film directed by Frank Beyer that shows living and working conditions in the GDR in the 1960s.

Tutzing: The Lutheran Academy (Evangelische Akademie) in Tutzing, on Bavaria's Starnberg Lake, was established as a conference and study center in 1947. It hosts regular gatherings at which difficult contemporary topics are debated by philosophers, politicians, artists, and others.

Two Plus Four Treaty: signed on 12 September 1989 by the two Germanys, the Soviet Union, the United States, France, and Great Britain, paving the way for unification on 3 October. The treaty made Germany a sovereign nation, limited the size of its armed forces, banned the manufacture or possession of nuclear, biological, and chemical weapons, recognized the Oder-Neisse Line, and called for a separate treaty with Poland, to be signed in November.

Volkskammer: the unicameral legislature of the GDR from 1949 to 1990. It nominally included members of a number of parties, but all were controlled by the Socialist Unity Party. The first and only free elections to the Volkskammer took place in March 1990. On 3 October of that year the Volkskammer voted the GDR out of existence and thereby dissolved itself.

"Wandlitz Gang": reference to the top functionaries in the GDR government, who occupied an exclusive compound near Wandlitz, a town north of Berlin.

Wewelsfleth Discussion: longstanding annual gathering hosted by the SPD and Björn Engholm for discussion of pressing cultural and political topics. It takes place in the village of Wewelsfleth, in Schleswig-Holstein.

White Fleet: East German excursion line that plied the Baltic coast.

"Writing after Auschwitz": talk delivered by Grass at Frankfurt's Johann Wolfgang Goethe University under the auspices of the Frankfurt Lectures on Poetics; published in English in *Two States — One Nation?*

Zsarg, Maximilian: pseudonym Grass considers using, based on his name spelled backward. Grasz is an alternate form of Graß, the original spelling of his name.